# Industrial Development and Environmental Degradation

# Industrial Development and Environmental Degradation

A Source Book on the
Origins of Global Pollution

Se Hark Park

*Professor of Economics,*
*Yokohama National University, Japan*

Walter C. Labys

*Professor of Resource Economics,*
*West Virginia University, USA*

**Edward Elgar**
Cheltenham, UK • Northampton, MA, USA

Published by
Edward Elgar Publishing Limited
8 Lansdown Place
Cheltenham
Glos GL50 2HU
UK

Edward Elgar Publishing, Inc.
6 Market Street
Northampton
Massachusetts 01060
USA

A catalogue record for this book
is available from the British Library

**Library of Congress Cataloguing in Publication Data**

Park, Se Hark, 1935–
        Industrial development and environmental degradation: a source book on the origins of global pollution / Se Hark Park, Walter C. Labys.
        Includes bibliographical references.
        1. Industrialization—Environmental aspects. 2. Pollution.
        3. Industries—Environmental aspects.   I. Labys, Walter C., 1937–
        II. Title.
HD75.6.P375   1998
363.73'1—dc21                                                                    98–5815
                                                                                         CIP

ISBN 1 85898 883 7

Printed and bound in Great Britain by Bookcraft (Bath) Ltd.

# Contents

# List of Figures

# List of Tables

## APPENDIX

# Preface

It has become increasingly apparent that the legacy of intensive industrialization has been environmental degradation on a global scale. The degradation has not only led to short-term health and social impacts but also to long-term deterioration of the natural resource base. While these impacts are of major concern in the developed nations, much less is known about these impacts in developing countries, including technologies for pollution abatement. The purpose of this book is to provide an international data source for evaluating the environmental consequences of the growth not only of the industrial or manufacturing sector itself but also its stance in relation to other sectors of the economy. Much of what we present here is of particular importance in a developing country context.

The book is divided into six chapters. After an introduction to the problems of industrial development and environmental degradation, the second chapter deals with the depletion of water, energy and mineral resources considered as industrial inputs. The third chapter turns to air, water, and land pollutants generated as industrial outputs, including global warming, hazardous wastes and toxic chemicals. Detailed information of the pollution provided by individual industries and specific industrial processes is presented in the fourth chapter. The fifth chapter presents information on how investments in particular pollution abatement technologies can provide economic benefits. Conclusions and policy prescriptions are given in the sixth chapter.

We would like to thank the many persons who have contributed to the completion of this book. Graduate students in the Natural Resource Economics program at West Virginia University and in the Environmental and Resource Economics Seminar at the Institute for Advanced Studies in Vienna read parts of the manuscripts and offered suggestions for improvements. We are also deeply grateful to the many international organizations and the US government agencies which provided valuable data and research materials: United Nations Environmental Protection (UNEP), United Nations Industrial Development Organization (UNIDO), World Bank, Organization for Economic Cooperation and Development (OECD), and the US Environmental Protection Agency (EPA). Aref Agahei-Hervani provided competent research assistance over more than two years. Word processing assistance was given by April MacDonald and Stacia Rosenau. Gloria Nestor helped with the graphics and

Alena Smirnova with the support of the Regional Research Institute prepared the camera-ready copy. Needless to say, the views expressed in this work do not necessarily reflect those of these individuals nor of any institutions with which we have been associated during the preparation of this work.

# 1. Industry and the Environment

## 1.1 THE PROBLEM

In recent years, world-wide attention has been focused on environmental degradation as an issue of crucial importance to man's survival and a major arena for international co-operation. Despite the shared perception and heightened awareness of environmental issues, environmental degradation continues unabated as the global environment continues to have symptoms of impure air, contaminated water, oil spills, toxic wastes, acid rain, global warming, thinning of the ozone layer, desertification, deforestation and soil erosion.

Environmental issues are all-encompassing and interdisciplinary in nature and cut across all development activities. In particular, the pressing global issues of population, natural resources, environment and economic development are all closely interlinked. It seems essential, therefore, that the question of industrial pollution should be considered in the broader context of the complex interactions among these issues.

In many countries of the South, mass poverty at the pre-industrial stage of economic development is responsible for environmental degradation. From the United Nations Conference on the Human Environment held at Stockholm in 1972 to the 1992 Earth Summit in Rio de Janeiro, it has been widely accepted that abject poverty, over-population and intolerable living conditions in many regions of the South force people to resort to environmentally unsound farming, grazing and fishing, or human settlement on ecologically fragile marginal lands, giving rise to environmental disasters such as desertification, deforestation, flooding and depletion of top soils. The dumping of untreated human and other wastes into the nearest body of flowing water remains one of the most serious environmental concerns: four out of five common diseases in developing countries are caused either by contaminated water or by unsanitary living conditions. As a result, a vicious circle of poverty leads to environmental degradation which in turn further impoverishes the larger population by destroying its natural resource base.

On the other hand, economic growth via industrialization also contributes to different types of environmental degradation. For instance, certain industrial activities, apart from those of the transport sector, contribute significantly to the degradation of air quality through emission of various pollutants such as suspended particulate matter, airborne lead, sulphur dioxide, carbon dioxide and nitrogen dioxide. Many industrial activities including mining are often responsible for water pollution by discharging heavy metals and toxic chemicals into water as well as into soil and air. The industrial sources of both air and water pollution will be discussed in greater detail in the next chapter. However, it could be conceptually useful to distinguish the industrial sources of these pollutants from poverty-induced environmental degradation such as desertification, deforestation, flooding and depletion of the top soils, which are typically encountered at the pre-industrial stage of economic development (for example sub-Saharan least-developed countries with virtually no industrial base).

## 1.2   INDUSTRIAL DEVELOPMENT

In recent years, many theoretical and economic studies have been conducted to investigate the relationship between the level of economic and industrial activity and the environmental condition for many selected pollutants (see Grossman 1995; Holtz-Eakin and Selden 1992; and Grossman and Krueger 1993). For many pollutants, they found an inverted U-shape relationship on the 'environmental Kuznets curve', which shows that environmental quality deteriorates in the early stages of economic growth (as measured by per capita income) until a threshold income level is reached beyond which rising incomes are associated with reduced pollution. Of course, these threshold income levels vary markedly among the different pollutants studied. It should also be noted that for other pollutants, such as the concentrations of lead and cadmium in river basins and the concentration of suspended particles in urban air, a monotonic relationship was observed between increased per capita incomes and improved environmental conditions (Grossman 1995). In this regard, it seems reasonable to postulate that poverty-induced environmental degradation such as desertification and deforestation at the early stages of development are a monotonically decreasing function of rising per capita income, as the surplus labor in the rural sector is absorbed in the expanding manufacturing and service employment in the course of industrialization.

Environmental degradation in either form can cause irreversible changes in ecosystems and play havoc with the natural resource base upon which many countries continue to depend for industrialization and economic development. Industrialization is a means to fight poverty, and its primacy as an element of development strategy can hardly be called into question. But uncontrolled industrial development can bring about damage to the environment and can deplete related natural and environmental resources. Against the backdrop of deepening environmental crisis, environmentally sound industrialization seems to be of paramount importance. Above all, environmentally sound development calls, *inter alia*, for the rational management of natural resources and the adoption of low-waste or environmentally clean technologies. More importantly, in recent years there has been mounting evidence that growth and environment do not necessarily conflict with each other and can evolve in a complementary fashion. Many new clean or low-waste technologies not only reduce pollutants substantially, but can also economize on the use of energy and raw materials to such an extent that the resultant material and energy cost savings more than offset initial higher investment costs, thus reducing the unit production cost. Many examples will be given later in the book. In short, the new clean or low-waste technologies are economically profitable in their own right in many cases.

As discussed earlier, environmental issues cut across all sectors of the economy and national boundaries. While industry is only one of many sources of environmental pollution in the economy, it is a very important one. Agriculture, mining, energy, transport, services and households all contribute in varying degrees to the total of environmental degradation. The relative extent to which industry is responsible for this degradation is little known in developing countries. In fact, the relative importance of industry in environmental degradation may vary considerably according to different types of pollutants and to the wide variety of natural resources used in industrial processes. In assessing the impact of industrialization on the environment, it is important to recognize that rapid structural change in the world industrial landscape fueled by dynamic technological developments may bring about far-reaching environmental changes in different regions of the world. This is simply because changing world patterns of industrial production can shift the distribution of environmental pressures created by different industrial activities, and because new technologies may open new avenues for reducing industrial pollution and for economizing on the use of natural resources.

In this regard, it seems important to note a marked redeployment in the last decade from the North to the South of traditional industries such as textiles, leather, iron and steel, industrial chemicals and petrochemicals. At the same time, the North has forged ahead with the growth of new technology-based industries such as microelectronics, information-processing and biotechnology. For instance, the manufacturing value added (MVA) of 15 manufacturing industries in developing countries grew at least twice as fast as their counterparts in the North during the period 1980–85; included were tobacco, petroleum refineries, textiles, other non-mineral products, food products, beverages, footwear, wearing apparel, wood products, glass and glass products, pottery and china, iron and steel, industrial chemicals, petroleum and coal products, and non-ferrous metals (UNIDO 1990, p. 106). The developing countries as a whole have yet to penetrate significantly into the domain of high-technology and skill-intensive industries such as microelectronics and information-processing equipment.

This overall trend toward rapid growth of traditional industries in developing countries seems likely to accelerate in the late 1990s, and many of those traditional manufacturing industries are known to be heavy polluters. As a result, such structural changes could lead to increased environmental pressures in the South, unless clean and efficient technologies are adopted on a large scale. In the North, environmental burdens could be mitigated, particularly as a result of the combined effects of improved energy efficiency in industry and structural shifts away from energy and material-intensive industries.

However, the growing technology-based industries (such as microelectronics) can create new types of pollution problems, since some toxic materials are used in their production processes and hence can produce more complex toxic pollutants instead of traditional pollutants. These include heavy metals, toxic air and water pollutants and hazardous wastes. Worse yet, the environmental impacts of some high-technology industries are not widely known, particularly in such areas as biotechnology or engineering materials. The problem of industrial pollution from high-technology industries will be examined later in greater detail.

## 1.3   ENVIRONMENTAL DEGRADATION

Industry plays a critical role in economic development and in enhancing the economic welfare of the society. Industry produces a wide range of consumer goods and, more importantly, a whole range of intermediate and capital goods for other sectors and branches of the economy (such as agriculture, services, mining, construction and utilities) as well as those required for diverse manufacturing industries. Industry also generates substantial employment in producing a variety of consumer and investment goods and is the most dynamic sector of the economy in generating and disseminating technological change.

Despite the obvious benefits of industrial development, it frequently results in damage to the environment and human health. Industry contributes to environmental degradation on both the input and the output sides of its activities. As summarized in Figure 1.1, the production of manufactured goods involves the extraction and exploitation of natural resources as inputs to manufacturing processes. On the input side, industry is a major consumer of energy, and power generation is to a significant extent responsible for air pollution and environmental damage such as acid rain and global warming. Industrial production requires the use of a wide variety of natural resources such as minerals, forest products and other raw materials whose rapid depletion may

*Figure 1.1   Industrial production and environmental impacts*

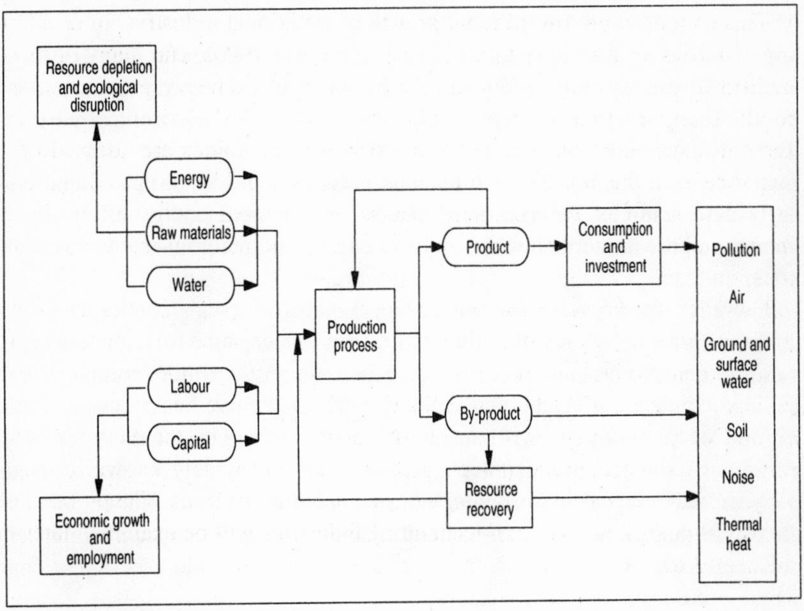

Source:   UNEP (1988)

contribute to serious ecological disequilibrium and environmental damage. Many industrial processes rely heavily on the use of water, which may create water scarcity and bring about ecological disruption, although agriculture production absorbs much more water. In particular, the wasteful use and depletion of scarce natural resources may pose serious long-term danger to the sustainability of industrialization and even to man's survival on earth.

On the output side, manufacturing processes generate myriad forms of waste that may pose serious environmental hazards. Gaseous by-products pollute air; liquid wastes pollute the soil as well as underground and surface water; and hazardous solid wastes lead to soil contamination and the pollution of surface and underground water, and above all create public health hazards. In a similar vein, the use of final products produced by industry for consumption and investment also creates a similar negative environmental impact on air, water and land, as exemplified by pesticides, detergents, plastics and the combustion engines of motor vehicles. In addition, industry creates a major problem of industrial safety, including risk of accident, risk of exposure to dangerous chemicals, and risk in the workplace.

## 1.4   PLAN OF THE BOOK

The major focus of this book is to identify and to quantify the origins of industrial sources of environmental degradations given the extent of data availability, and to provide a basis for drawing some environmental implications of pursuing a given strategy of industrial development in developing countries. The consequence of this focus is to develop a broad perspective of where the industrial sector stands *vis-à-vis* other sectors of the economy in the depletion of broad categories of natural resources. These include the use of water, energy and raw materials on the input side, and the generation of selected air, water and land pollutants comprising hazardous wastes on the output side. We follow this sectoral overview of environmental pollution with a more detailed analysis of industry-specific pollutants within the manufacturing sector, and of some selected process-specific industrial pollutants within particular manufacturing industries. The book concludes with a review of the economic implications of promoting environmentally sound industrial development, and particularly the question of the conflict or complementarity which may exist between environmental goods and industrial production. It should be noted at the outset that the terms 'industry' and 'manufacturing' are used interchangeably, referring to the manufacturing sector proper and excluding mining and public utilities, unless otherwise specified.

# 2. Industry and Natural Resources

## 2.1 THE PROBLEM

Industrialization at almost all stages of economic development involves the extraction, processing, fabrication and utilization of all natural resources, whether from water, land or air. Industrial production transforms fuel and non-fuel mineral resources as well as agricultural raw materials, including timber, into intermediate and final products. The transformation process additionally requires water and energy. The consequences of industrialization are not only the depletion of non-renewable natural resources but also the degradation of those resources which can be renewed. In this chapter, we address the impacts of industrial development on water consumption, energy consumption and mineral resource consumption.

## 2.2 INDUSTRIAL WATER CONSUMPTION

Unlike other natural resources such as minerals and timber, the total amount of water on earth is constant, estimated at 1,400 million km.$^3$ However, the vast majority of this (about 97 percent) is sea water, while the remaining 3 percent is fresh water. Regarding sources of the latter, slightly over 20 percent is ground water and the rest is ice. Even such a very small share of freshwater in the total volume of water available on earth is believed to be sufficient to meet the crisis of growing water demands. We are referring, therefore, to the extremely uneven distribution of the supply of freshwater (UNEP 1988). The key issue is not so much the scarcity of freshwater as the rising cost of delivering usable water to wherever it is needed. The supply costs of water are rising partly because of the necessity to carry it over longer distances using costly, energy-using distribution systems to meet increasing competing demands, and partly because of the additional water treatment costs where lower-quality sources are tapped.

More importantly, the problem of rising supply costs and scarcity of water stems to a large extent from the inappropriate pricing and the consequent inefficient and suboptimal allocation of water resources. This problem applies equally to the industrial and agricultural demands for water. In particular, the

7

absence of a market pricing mechanism or, put differently, a market failure, arises from the existing institutional arrangement of water distribution, namely a queuing allocation, where water-use priorities begin with those who have the rights of original endowment use at zero marginal cost, and successively pass through the subsequent rights holders with zero marginal revenues (Easter 1986). Of course, the absence of appropriate pricing (for example marginal cost pricing) and incentive schemes, and particularly subsidized water, encourages the wasteful use of water and discourages water conservation, thus contributing to water scarcity and the higher delivery costs. For instance, irrigation water changes in Morocco amount to less than 10 percent of the long-run marginal cost of supplying water to agriculture. Water tariffs in the industrial and urban sectors in the same country are estimated to be less than the one-half of the marginal cost of water delivery (Golding and Roland-Holst 1995, p. 178). It is apparent, therefore, that appropriate market pricing and incentive policies are essential to enhance the conservation and efficiency of water use in the industrial sector, and hence increase overall output and income.

The agricultural sector consumes the most freshwater, about 73 percent of the total supply, used mainly for irrigation; industry uses much less, about 21 percent; and domestic use is 6 percent globally, according to UNEP estimates (UNEP 1988). According to the above water use study in Morocco, irrigation claims 92 percent of total water demand, urban households 5 percent, and industry only 3 percent. However, the industrial demand for water is expected to increase by approximately 5 percent per year, as the Moroccan growth rate increases. .

Although industry's share is much smaller than that of agriculture, industry pollutes water much more. Although more than 80 percent of the water used for cooling and cleaning is returned, this water is often contaminated by industrial effluents and thermal pollution. The share of industrial water in total water demand, however, varies substantially among nations, since shares of industrial water demand depend on a number of factors, such as the stage of industrialization, the resource endowments, the structure of the economy, the composition of manufactured output, geographic and climatic conditions, the prevailing process technologies, population density, the extent of urbanization and other socio-economic factors.

Figure 2.1 provides a comparison of total per capita water withdrawals and its share distribution between different uses in selected developing countries. The figure reveals wide variations in the per capita water withdrawal and the industry share. The US consumes more than four or five times the rest of the countries shown in the figure in terms of per capita withdrawal. In general, the industry share is relatively small except in Finland. The relatively low share of

*Figure 2.1 Sectoral water consumption in selected countries, 1993*[a]

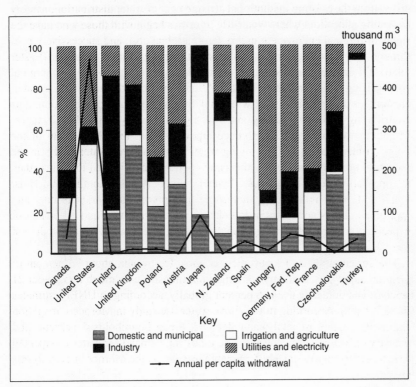

*Note:* a. Percentage share for early 1990s.

*Source:* OECD (1995)

industry water withdrawals, despite its advanced stage of industrialization, both in the US and Japan, may reflect the use of water-efficient technologies.

Table 2.1 summarizes freshwater withdrawals and their share distribution between agriculture (mainly irrigation) and industry uses in selected developing countries for various years. It seems quite clear from the table that the greater share of freshwater is used for agricultural purposes and a smaller share for industry (particularly at early stages of industrialization). The industry share, however, is expected to rise sharply as developing countries accelerate their industrialization process.

There are obviously wide variations in industrial water use among different manufacturing branches. According to the 1976 survey of industrial water uses in Canada, total water withdrawals for manufacturing were 8,693 billion liters per year (see Table 2.2). Of this total, the paper and allied industries accounted for most (36 percent), followed by primary metals (24 percent), chemical and chemical products (17 percent) and petroleum and coal products (7 percent) (Tates and Reynold 1981). It is worth noting that heavy industries

*Table 2.1    Freshwater withdrawal in developing countries, 1970–92 (billion cubic meters)*

| Country | Year of data | Total | % used by public & industry | % used by agriculture |
|---|---|---|---|---|
| Algeria | 1980 | 3.00 | 26 | 74 |
| Argentina | 1976 | 27.60 | 27 | 73 |
| Botswana | 1980 | 0.09 | 15 | 85 |
| Cape Verde | 1972 | 0.04 | 11 | 89 |
| China | 1980 | 460.00 | 13 | 87 |
| Colombia | 1987 | 5.34 | 57 | 43 |
| Costa Rica | 1970 | 1.35 | 11 | 89 |
| Cuba | 1975 | 8.10 | 11 | 89 |
| Cyprus | 1985 | 0.54 | 9 | 91 |
| Egypt | 1992 | 56.40 | 12 | 88 |
| El Salvador | 1975 | 1.00 | 11 | 89 |
| Ghana | 1970 | 0.30 | 48 | 52 |
| Guatemala | 1970 | 0.73 | 26 | 74 |
| Honduras | 1992 | 1.52 | 9 | 91 |
| India | 1975 | 380.00 | 7 | 93 |
| Iran | 1975 | 54.40 | 13 | 87 |
| Iraq | 1970 | 42.80 | 8 | 92 |
| Israel | 1989 | 1.85 | 21 | 79 |
| Jordan | 1975 | 0.45 | 25 | 65 |
| Madagascar | 1984 | 16.30 | 1 | 99 |
| Mauritania | 1978 | 0.73 | 16 | 84 |
| Mexico | 1975 | 54.20 | 14 | 86 |
| Morocco | 1992 | 10.85 | 9 | 92 |
| Oman | 1975 | 0.48 | 6 | 94 |
| Peru | 1987 | 6.10 | 28 | 72 |
| Saudi Arabia | 1975 | 3.60 | 53 | 47 |
| South Africa | 1990 | 14.67 | 48 | 52 |
| Sri Lanka | 1970 | 6.30 | 4 | 96 |
| Sudan | 1977 | 18.60 | 1 | 99 |
| Syrian Arab Republic | 1976 | 3.34 | 17 | 83 |
| Tunisia | 1985 | 2.30 | 20 | 80 |
| Turkey | 1989 | 23.75 | 43 | 57 |
| Yemen | 1987 | 3.40 | 7 | 93 |

*Source:    World Resources* (1987; 1995)

*Table 2.2*   *Water use in the Canadian manufacturing industry,*
*by major industrial groups, 1976*

| Industry | Number of establish- ments | Water withdrawal (million liters per year) | | |
|---|---|---|---|---|
| | | Total | Fresh | Brackish |
| Food and beverages | 2,123 | 358,811 (4.14) | 307,373 | 51,438 |
| Rubber and plastic products | 359 | 59,471 (0.69) | 58,507 | 964 |
| Leather | 1 | 214 (—) | 214 | — |
| Textile | 414 | 138,717 (1.60) | 138,717 | — |
| Wood | 1,079 | 331,040 (3.82) | 271,324 | 59,716 |
| Furniture and fixture | 2 | 14 (—) | 14 | — |
| Paper and allied industries | 461 | 3,132,171 (36.12) | 121,361 | 10,810 |
| Printing, publishing and allied industries | 6 | 164 (—) | 164 | — |
| Primary metals | 238 | 2,094,329 (24.15) | 1,988,626 | 95,702 |
| Fabricated metal products | 22 | 8,406 (0.09) | 8,406 | — |
| Non-electrical machinery | 5 | 246 (—) | 246 | — |
| Transport equipment | 476 | 375,709 (4.33) | 375,677 | 32 |
| Electrical products | 3 | 255 (—) | 255 | — |
| Non-metallic minerals | 641 | 94,711 (1.09) | 93,175 | 1,536 |
| Petroleum and coal products | 8 | 615,750 (7.10) | 535,603 | 62,148 |
| Chemicals and chemical products | 656 | 1,462,730 (16.86) | 1,395,927 | 66,804 |
| Total | 6,571 | 8,672,718 (100.00) | 8,323,571 | 349,146 |

*Note:*   Figures in brackets are percentages.

*Source:*   Tates and Reynold (1981)

producing basic industrial materials such as primary metals, chemicals, petroleum products and paper products, and some of the resource-based light industries such as food and beverages, textiles and leather, tend to consume a large volume of water; most of the light industries (for example, metal fabrication, machinery and electrical machinery with the exception of transport equipment) are likely to consume relatively less water.

Table 2.3 reveals that a large proportion of industrial water supplies is used for cooling. For example, almost 77 percent of total industrial water use in Belgium is for cooling, while about 13 percent is for processing. Heavy industry usually requires a larger volume of water than light industry for cooling purposes. In the Belgian case, industries which absorbed more than 80 percent of the total intake for cooling were chemicals, rubber, coke manufacturing, steam power plants, iron and steel, petroleum, fabricated metal products and

*Table 2.3    Magnitudes of basic water use in major industries in Belgium, 1965*

| Industry | Gross intake (million cubic meters) | Percentage distribution | | |
|---|---|---|---|---|
| | | Process water | Cooling water | Other uses |
| Mines | 149 | 10 | 80 | 10 |
| Quarries | 48 | 46 | — | 54 |
| Chemicals | 404 | 11 | 86.5 | 2.5 |
| Rubber | 7 | 8.6 | 85.7 | 5.7 |
| Paper | 95 | 75.8 | 21 | 3.2 |
| Leather | 5 | 80 | 14 | 6 |
| Textiles | 58 | 55 | 35 | 10 |
| Coke manufacturing | 79 | 11.4 | 84.8 | 3.8 |
| Steam power plants | 3,298 | 0.1 | 99.2 | 0.4 |
| Glass | 21 | 38 | 47.7 | 14.3 |
| Terracotta | 2 | 60 | 30 | 10 |
| Ceramics | 1 | 60 | 20 | 20 |
| Iron and steel | 1,010 | 7.6 | 84.6 | 7.8 |
| Foods | 107 | 16.6 | 66.4 | 16.8 |
| Non-ferrous metals | 191 | 1 | 59 | 40 |
| Cement | 14 | 36 | 57 | 7 |
| Wood products | 2 | 30 | 20 | 50 |
| Petroleum | 201 | 1 | 98.75 | 0.25 |
| Fabricated metal products | 134 | 11 | 80 | 9 |
| Total, excluding steam power plants | 2,528 | 13.0 | 76.8 | 10.2 |
| Total | 5,826 | 5.9 | 89.5 | 4.6 |

*Source:*   Government of Belgium (1966)

mining. In the case of processing industries which used a high proportion of water intake, the major consumers were paper (76 percent), leather (80 percent), textiles (55 percent), terracotta (60 percent) and ceramics (60 percent).

A more meaningful measure of industrial water requirements may be the water-use intensity coefficient, which measures the amount of water required per unit of output. Such water-use coefficients are greatly influenced by industrial products, process-specific technologies and the kind of raw materials used in production. Statistics on industrial water-use coefficients are very difficult to find. One available study notes a dramatic improvement in water-use efficiency across industries in the Netherlands between 1967 and 1976, except for rubber, plastic products, and primary metals (Muelschlegel 1979). As shown in Figure 2.2, the water-use coefficient for the manufacturing sector as

*Figure 2.2* *Water use intensity in Netherlands industry,*
*1967, 1972 and 1976*

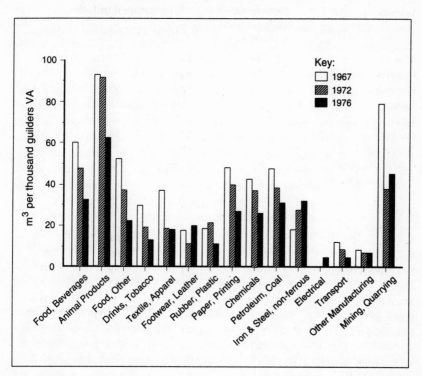

*Source:* Muelschlegel (1979)

a whole declined by one-half, from 30.4 to 18.1, between 1967 and 1976. Remarkable gains in water-use efficiency were noted in this period in food processing, textiles and apparel, paper and publishing, and industrial equipment. Based on the 1976 coefficients, the heavy water users (excluding mining and quarrying) are, in descending order, animal products processing (63.5), primary metals (32.8), petroleum products (31.8), paper products (30.6), industrial chemicals (25.8) and rubber and plastic products (21.4) (UN 1976). The enforcement of water-pollution control programs may account for a large part of the notable improvement in industrial water-use efficiency.

Once again, basic industrial materials industries (for example, primary metals, chemicals, petroleum and coal products, pulp and paper) are shown to be the most water-intensive not only in terms of total amount used, as shown earlier, but also in terms of water use per unit of output. By contrast, fabricating and assembly industries such as electrical machinery (5.5), transport equipment (5.4), and other manufacturing (5.8) seem to use much less water than basic industrial materials industries.

At the process level, apart from different climatic conditions, the amount of water required is predominantly determined by the type of process technology employed. Given a wide range of available technologies for the production of a given product, industrial water requirements diverge sharply even among firms producing the same products, let alone across different products and different countries. Statistics on process-specific water requirements are relatively scarce and fragmentary. In 1976, the United Nations used questionnaires to assemble process-specific data on industrial water requirements for a large number of industries in various countries (ibid.). Some examples selected from the United Nations data are given in appendix Table A-1 to illustrate vast inter-industry and inter-country variations in industrial water requirements at the process level. In general, paper and pulp products and chemicals including synthetic rubbers tend to use more water per ton of output than any other product groups. It is worth noting that water requirements per ton of iron and steel products vary remarkably, depending on the process technology used, as shown in the cases of France and the United States. Also the same product may require vastly different amounts of water, depending on whether or not water recycling technology is used, as shown in the case of the Netherlands where the particular finished and semi-finished steel process requires 61,000 liters of water per ton of steel without recycling, but only 27,000 liters of water with recycling technology. Equally noteworthy are considerable inter-country variations in the industrial water requirements per ton of the same goods produced, such as sugar-beets, beer, cheese, milk, ammonia, caustic soda and soap.

Process-level data thus seem to suggest that the inter-industry comparison and generalization of industrial water-use become more difficult at the process level, because of the extremely wide range of the process technologies used in different industries and in different countries. The data also provide the valuable lesson that increasing industrial output need not necessarily be accompanied by increasing industrial water requirements. New water-saving technology designed to increase recirculation and water reuse can reduce industrial water requirements as well as their pollution loads. However, proper economic incentives and appropriate market pricing, as discussed earlier, are needed to induce industry to adopt water-saving technology. The same holds for energy conservation.

## 2.3   INDUSTRIAL ENERGY CONSUMPTION

Energy consumption is vital to all spheres of economic activity, and industry is only one of these spheres. There are many different forms of energy: oil, gas, coal, nuclear, hydropower and several renewable sources. Energy-sector behavior encompasses all phases of activity ranging from the extraction, conversion, transport and consumption of energy to the disposal of energy wastes. These activities, in turn, have many significant impacts on both the economy and the environment.

It is well known that energy scarcity leads to various economic problems such as price inflation, rising input costs, foreign exchange squeezes, increasing developing-country debt and even production disruptions. The environmental impacts of energy-sector activity are equally serious. Environmental problems such as acid rain, the greenhouse effect, thermal pollution and the general degradation of the quality of air, water and land are exacerbated by excessive energy use. It is beyond the scope of this study to describe fully the major environmental consequences of energy-sector activities. However, some of the consequences for different parts of the environment (air, water, land and soils, and wild life) are summarized in appendix Table A-2. Given the energy–environment link, the determination of the relative importance of the industry share in total energy consumption and the identification of the energy intensity of various manufacturing branches within the industrial sector could help to assess how the industrial sector as a whole as well as individual manufacturing industries create environmental problems through industrial energy consumption. At the same time it may suggest ways of alleviating environmental burdens, for instance, through the promotion of industrial energy efficiency and conservation. Below we provide a cross-country comparison of energy consumption across the industries mentioned.

Among the OECD countries, the industrial production sector employed more energy than any other sector during the period 1970–91, ranging from a share of 40 percent in 1970 to 33 percent in 1991 (see Table 2.4 and Figure 2.3). Energy consumption in the transport sector increased from 24 percent in 1970 to 30 percent in 1991, while energy consumption in residential, commercial and public establishments averaged around 32 percent over the whole period. However, the sectoral distribution of energy consumption in non-OECD countries differed markedly from those of the OECD. Among Eastern European countries, industry accounted for 52 percent of total energy consumption on average in 1983, although the same share in the then USSR in 1987 was only 33 percent. Variations in the industrial share of energy consumption among developing countries were more pronounced than in any other country groups; the shares reported for different years in Table 2.4 are Brazil 45 percent, China 63 percent, India 22 percent, Indonesia 44 percent, Latin America 38 percent, West Africa 20 percent, and the Republic of Korea 41 percent. India's relatively low intensity is due to the inclusion in total consumption of sizeable non-commercial energy. The share of transport among developing countries varied widely, from 8 percent in China to 44 percent in West Africa. Despite considerable inter-country variations and regardless of

Table 2.4  Sectoral energy consumption of selected regions, countries and economic groupings (petajoules)[a]

| Sector | OECD[b] 1985 | Former USSR 1987 | Eastern Europe[c] 1983 | China 1980 | India 1984 | West Africa[d] 1984 | Latin America[d] 1984 | Brazil 1983 | Indonesia 1984 | Republic of Korea 1985 |
|---|---|---|---|---|---|---|---|---|---|---|
| Agriculture[f] | 1,748 (1.63) | 934 (2.01) | —[g] — | 1,237 (7.00) | 251 (3.34) | — — | —[g] — | 274 (5.36) | — — | — — |
| Industry[f] | 37,878 (35.40) | 15,295 (32.89) | 5,920 (52.38) | 11,130 (63.10) | 1,667 (22.18) | 172 (19.93) | 2,066 (37.82) | 2,309 (45.12) | 516 (43.77) | 801 (41.00) |
| Transportation[f] | 32,750 (30.62) | 6,045 (13.00) | 870 (7.70) | 1,413 (8.00) | 746 (9.92) | 381 (44.15) | 2,071 (37.92) | 1,067 (20.85) | 328 (27.82) | 281 (14.38) |
| Residential/commercial/ public[f] | 33,260 (31.10) | 6,729 (14.47) | — — | 3,887 (22.00) | 489 (6.51) | 109 (12.63) | —[g] — | 1,467 (28.67) | 335 (28.41) | 787 (40.28) |
| Other[f] | 1,336 (1.25) | — — | 4,511[h] (39.92) | — — | 4,364[i] (58.05) | 201[j] (23.29) | 1,325[k] (24.26) | — — | — — | — (4.35) |
| Total[l] | 106,972 (100) | 46,509[m] (100)[n] | 11,301 (100) | 17,667 (100) | 7,517 (100) | 863 (100) | 5,462 (100) | 5,117 (100) | 1,179 (100) | 1,954 (100) |

16

*Notes*

a. Conversion factors: 1 petajoule = $10^{15}$ joules; 1 megaton of oil equivalent (mton) = 41.87 petajoules; 1 megaton of coal equivalent (mton) = 29.31 petajoules.

b. Australia, Austria, Belgium, Canada, Denmark, Finland, France, Germany, Federal Republic of, Greece, Iceland, Italy, Japan, Luxembourg, Netherlands, New Zealand, Norway, Portugal, Spain, Sweden, Switzerland, Turkey, the United Kingdom, the United States and Yugoslavia.

c. Bulgaria, Czechoslovakia, German Democratic Republic, Hungary, Poland and Romania.

d. Senegal, Morocco, Nigeria and Côte d'Ivoire.

e. Argentina, Mexico, Paraguay and Venezuela.

f. Data are not from sources, but are a summation of individual fuel consumption from sources.

g. Data for agriculture and residential/commercial/public sectors are included in the "other" sector.

h. Combination of the residential, agricultural, trade and other sectors.

i. Estimated 1984 consumption of non-commercial energy: fuelwood, agricultural waste and animal dung.

j. Undefined use: balance of total consumption unaccounted for in sectoral data.

k. Combination of agriculture, commercial, residential and public sectors.

l. Data are not from sources, but are a summation of sectoral energy consumption.

m. Primary electricity and heat are included in total energy consumption, but are not presented on a sectoral basis.

n. Rounded figure.

Figures in parentheses are sectoral percentage shares.

*Source: World Resources* (1989)

*Figure 2.3    Total final consumption of energy, by sector, in the OECD, 1970–91*

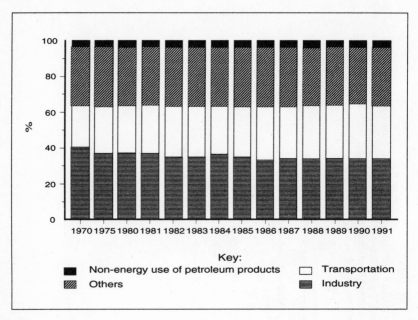

*Source:*   OECD (1993)

the stage of industrialization, it seems quite clear that industry is likely to be the largest source of energy consumption in both developed and developing countries, except perhaps for the West African countries.

The pattern of the industrial use of energy is less clear. According to one United States study in 1973, about 37 percent of industrial energy was used for process steam, 24 percent for direct heat, 22 percent for electric drive, 13 percent for feedstocks, 3 percent for electrolytic process and 1 percent for other electric processes (Ehrlich *et al.* 1977, p. 396).

The sources of the energy used also vary widely (see Figure 2.4). In the OECD countries, industrial energy use has been more or less equally distributed among four sources: oil (30 percent), coal (25 percent), natural gas (25 percent) and electricity (20 percent). In the former USSR and Eastern Europe, industry relies heavily on both coal and natural gas. Coal is the dominant source of energy for industry in China (67 percent) and India (72 percent). Brazilian industry depends on hydroelectricity (41 percent) and non-coal solid fuels (35 percent) such as fuel wood and biomass. Oil is also important for Indonesia (50 percent) and West Africa (73 percent), but Indonesia's industry also uses natural gas (40 percent).

*Figure 2.4    Industrial energy consumption by sources of energy
for selected countries and regions*

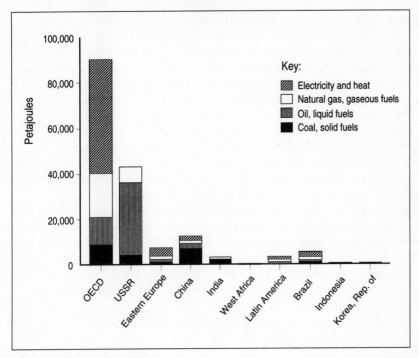

*Source:    World Resources* (1989)

The importance of coal in the energy consumed should be noted. Since OPEC first disrupted the world oil market equilibrium by artificially increasing oil prices in 1973–74, coal consumption has risen sharply. In the 1980s, world consumption rose over 31 percent even after oil prices dropped by more than 50 percent in 1986. Coal consumption increased sharply in China (53 percent), Turkey (400 percent), the Republic of Korea (170 percent) and Canada (180 percent) during the period 1978–88, while consumption in the former Soviet Union and Britain was down by 10 percent and 7 percent respectively. Electricity generation dominated coal consumption; between 70 percent and 90 percent of the total quantity of coal consumed in centrally planned economies has been utilized for electricity generation. Among OECD countries, the percentage of electricity generated from oil dropped sharply from 41 percent to 25 percent in 1983. Globally, the coal share ranges from 55 percent in the United States, 70 percent in the United Kingdom and 64 percent in the former Federal Republic of Germany to 13 percent in Japan. Other countries with rich water resources are highly dependent on hydroelectricity, particularly Norway (99 percent), Canada (65 percent), and Sweden (58 percent) (OECD 1985a, p. 209).

Given the large known coal reserves world-wide (over 600 billion tons of hard coal and brown coal), the increasing utilization of coal may represent a viable energy alternative if oil reserves ever begin to decline. However, major environmental concerns about increased coal utilization have been raised, since coal combustion produces sulphur dioxide, radioactive materials and other pollutants contributing to acid deposition, with effects on human health and other natural ecosystems. More specifically, coal combustion generates a considerable number of gaseous and liquid effluents as well as solid wastes. The effluents from a coal-fired power plant generating 1,000 megawatts of electricity per year are listed in Table 2.5. Many of the effluents are known to be environmentally damaging. For instance, apart from the relatively well-known environmental significance of sulphur dioxides, nitrogen oxides and carbon monoxide, also emitted are the hydrocarbons (PAHs). Many PAH compounds such as benzo(a)pyrene are carcinogenic and could be potentially dangerous in spite of their low concentrations in emissions (Chadwick 1987, p. 91). The bulk of the benzo(a)pyrene emissions to the atmosphere world-wide originates from coal sources: coal heating and power generation (47 percent), industrial coke production (20 percent), and open-burning of coal refuse (14 percent), as shown in Table 2.6. It seems clear that as developing countries

*Table 2.5    Annual effluent production from a 1,000-megawatt coal-fired power plant*

| Effluents | Production (tons) |
|---|---|
| Airborne emissions | |
| Particulates | 3,000.0 |
| Sulphur dioxides | 110,000.0 |
| Nitrogen oxides | 27,000.0 |
| Carbon monoxide | 2,000.0 |
| Hydrocarbons | 400.0 |
| Liquid effluents | |
| Organic material | 66.2 |
| Sulphuric acid | 82.5 |
| Chloride | 26.3 |
| Phosphate | 41.7 |
| Boron | 331.0 |
| Suspended solids | 497.0 |
| Solid wastes | |
| Bottom ash and recovered fly ash | 360,000.0 |

*Source:*    Chadwick (1987)

*Table 2.6   Estimated benzo(a)pyrene emissions to the atmosphere (tons per year)*

| Emission sources | United States | World-wide excluding United States | World-wide |
|---|---|---|---|
| Heating and power generation | | | |
| Coal | 431(34.0) | 1,945(52.0) | 2,376(47.0) |
| Oil | 2 (0.2) | 3 (0.1) | 5 (0.1) |
| Gas | 2 (0.2) | 1 (0.1) | 3 (0.1) |
| Wood | 40 (3.0) | 180 (5.0) | 220 (4.0) |
| Total | 475(37.0) | 2,129(57.0) | 2,604(52.0) |
| Industrial processes | | | |
| Coke production | 192(15.0) | 841(22.0) | 1,033(20.0) |
| Catalytic cracking | 6 (0.5) | 6 (0.1) | 12 (0.2) |
| Total | 198(15.0) | 847(23.0) | 1,045(21.0) |
| Refuse and open burning | | | |
| Enclosed incineration | | | |
| Commerce and industry | 23 (1.8) | 46 (1.0) | 69 (1.4) |
| Other | 11 (0.1) | 22 (0.6) | 33 (0.7) |
| Open burning | | | |
| Coal refuse | 340(27.0) | 340 (9.0) | 680(13.5) |
| Forest and agriculture | 140(11.0) | 280 (7.5) | 420 (8.0) |
| Other | 74 (6.0) | 74 (2.0) | 148 (3.0) |
| Total | 588(46.0) | 762(20.0) | 1,350(27.0) |
| Vehicles | | | |
| Trucks and buses | 12 (1.0) | 17 (0.5) | 29 (0.6) |
| Automobiles | 12 (0.8) | 6 (0.2) | 16 (0.3) |
| Total | 22 (1.7) | 23 (0.6) | 45 (0.9) |
| Total | 1,283 | 3,761 | 5,044 |

*Note:*   Figures in parentheses are percentage shares.

*Source:*   Chadwick (1987, p. 219)

depend increasingly on coal as an alternative source of energy to facilitate rapid industrialization, the environmental problems of coal combustion such as acid rain and thermal pollution will not only become serious but will also pose a formidable challenge to any sustainable development strategies, unless more environmentally sound coal-combustion technologies are developed and adopted.

It is more difficult to decipher the pattern of energy use among industries. According to one United States study, in 1973 about 37 percent of industrial energy was used for process steam, 24 percent for direct heat, 22 percent for electric drive, 13 percent for feedstocks, 3 percent for electrolytic processes, and 1 percent for other electric processes (Ehrlich *et al.* 1977, p. 396).

These shares can be further examined at the disaggregated manufacturing industry level. The annual Energy Review of United States manufacturing energy consumption by the US Department of Energy (EIA 1994a) reports energy-use coefficients at the two-digit United States industrial classification levels for the period 1980–91, where the energy-use coefficient is measured by the ratio of energy consumption to the constant dollar value of shipments. A decrease in the coefficient shows an improvement in energy efficiency. As shown in Table 2.7, United States manufacturing industries as a whole improved their energy-use efficiency considerably in the years following the second oil market disruption of 1979–80, largely prompted by escalating energy prices and the misunderstanding of the then ample energy supplies, particularly that of imported oil. In 1985, the United States manufacturing sector consumed 9.7 quadrillion ($9.7 \times 10^{15}$) Btu of energy as compared with 11.9 quadrillion ($11.9 \times 10^{15}$) Btu in 1980, while manufacturing output at the 1980 constant prices rose 8 percent. As a result, the energy use coefficient of all United States manufacturing industries improved by 24 percent, given the drop in the use coefficient from 5.8 to 4.4 between 1980 and 1985. Meanwhile, the drop in energy intensity moderated for all manufacturing industries to about 4 percent in the period of 1988 to 1991, a result perhaps of increasing energy prices.

Among the individual industry groups included in Table 2.7, the largest energy users in 1985 are listed in Table 2.8. As major producers of basic industrial materials, the four industry groups mentioned in the table accounted for 71.7 percent of all manufacturing energy consumption in 1991. The same four energy-intensive industry groups increased their energy consumption by almost 36 percent from 11,052 thousand billion Btu to 15,027 thousand billion Btu between 1985 and 1991. This contrasts sharply with a 12 percent increase in the energy consumption of those industries between 1981 and 1985. However, output grew much faster than energy consumption in the energy-intensive industries. In other industries, the opposite picture emerged, with energy consumption rising faster than output. For instance, energy consumption in apparel and other textile products increased by almost 13 percent per year, compared with an annual MVA growth rate of 5 percent; energy consumption grew by 8 percent per year, while the output of tobacco products declined by almost 9 percent annually; energy consumption in professional instruments increased by 12 percent per year, compared with an annual increase of 9 percent in MVA; an increase of 8 percent per year in energy consumption in furniture and fixtures was coupled with an annual MVA growth rate of less than 1 percent; and energy consumption increased by 6.19 percent in printing and publishing, as compared with annual MVA

*Table 2.7 Energy-use coefficients and changes in energy intensity by United States manufacturing industries, 1980–91*

| US SIC code | Industry | Energy intensity[a] ('000 Btu per $ of shipment value) | | | | Energy intensity change (%) | | | |
|---|---|---|---|---|---|---|---|---|---|
| | | 1980 | 1985 | 1988 | 1991 | 1980–85 | 1985–88 | 1988–91 | 1985–91 |
| 20 | Food and kindred products | 3.50 | 3.64 | 3.96 | 3.71 | –4.00 | –8.79 | 6.31 | –2.20 |
| 21 | Tobacco manufactures | n.a. | n.a. | n.a. | n.a. | n.a. | n.a. | n.a. | n.a. |
| 22 | Textile mill products | 5.70 | 7.75 | 7.92 | 8.21 | –35.96 | –2.19 | –3.66 | –5.94 |
| 23 | Apparel and other textile products | n.a. | n.a. | n.a. | n.a. | n.a. | n.a. | n.a. | n.a. |
| 24 | Lumber and wood products | n.a. | n.a. | n.a. | n.a. | n.a. | n.a. | n.a. | n.a. |
| 25 | Furniture and fixture | 1.90 | 2.56 | 2.82 | 3.08 | –34.74 | –10.16 | –9.22 | –20.31 |
| 26 | Paper and allied products | 16.00 | 23.53 | 21.85 | 26.01 | –47.06 | 7.14 | –19.04 | –10.54 |
| 27 | Printing and publishing | 1.10 | n.a. | n.a. | n.a. | n.a. | –18.20 | n.a. | n.a. |
| 28 | Chemicals and allied products | 15.10 | 17.72 | 16.27 | 16.99 | –17.35 | 8.18 | –4.43 | 4.12 |
| 29 | Petroleum and coal products | 5.40 | 22.16 | 24.43 | 23.43 | –310.37 | –10.24 | 4.09 | –5.73 |
| 30 | Rubber and miscellaneous plastic products | 4.30 | 5.64 | 5.70 | 5.26 | –31.16 | –1.06 | 7.72 | 6.74 |
| 31 | Leather and leather products | n.a. | n.a. | n.a. | n.a. | n.a. | n.a. | n.a. | n.a. |
| 32 | Stone, clay and glass products | 21.60 | 19.59 | 20.35 | 21.90 | 9.31 | –3.88 | –7.62 | –11.79 |
| 33 | Primary metal industries | 16.40 | 30.43 | 28.15 | 28.37 | –85.55 | 7.49 | –0.78 | 6.77 |
| 34 | Fabricated metal products | 2.80 | 3.58 | 3.79 | 3.76 | –27.86 | –5.87 | 0.79 | –5.03 |
| 35 | Machinery, except electrical equipment | 1.70 | 2.19 | 2.01 | 1.80 | –28.82 | 8.22 | 6.97 | 14.61 |
| 36 | Electrical and electronic machinery | 1.70 | 2.35 | 2.44 | 2.16 | –38.24 | –3.83 | 11.48 | 8.09 |
| 37 | Transport equipment | 1.50 | 1.77 | 1.68 | 1.80 | –18.00 | 5.08 | –7.14 | –1.69 |
| 38 | Instruments and related products | 1.70 | 1.84 | 1.73 | 1.68 | –8.24 | 5.98 | 2.89 | 8.70 |
| 39 | Miscellaneous manufacturing industries | 1.80 | 2.28 | 2.19 | 2.01 | –26.67 | 3.95 | 8.22 | 11.84 |
| | All manufacturing | 5.80 | 8.05 | 7.82 | 8.13 | –38.79 | 2.86 | –3.96 | –0.99 |

*Notes*

n.a. = not available.

a. Positive percentage change indicates a decrease in energy intensity and an increase in energy efficiency. Negative percentage change indicates an increase in energy intensity and a decrease in energy efficiency.

*Source:* EIA (1994a)

*Table 2.8    Largest energy users in the United States manufacturing
sectors, 1985–91*

| Industry | Energy consumption ($10^{15}$ Btu) | | | | | |
|---|---|---|---|---|---|---|
| | 1981 | | 1985 | | 1991 | |
| | Quantity | % of all manufac- turing | Quantity | % of all manufac- turing | Quantity | % of all manufac- turing |
| Chemicals and allied products | 2.2 | 22.7 | 2.568 | 23.2 | 2.472 | 16.4 |
| Primary metals | 1.5 | 15.5 | 1.773 | 16.0 | 3.040 | 20.2 |
| Paper and allied products | 1.3 | 13.4 | 1.409 | 12.7 | 2.987 | 19.8 |
| Petroleum and coal products | 0.9 | 9.3 | 1.070 | 9.7 | 2.292 | 15.3 |
| All other manufacturing industries | 0.9 | 39.1 | 4.232 | 38.3 | 4.236 | 28.3 |
| Total | 6.8 | 100.0 | 11.052 | 100.0 | 15.027 | 100.0 |

*Source:*   EIA (1994a)

growth of 2 percent. Other industries covered in Table 2.7 account for a very small fraction of total manufacturing energy consumption; exceptions are machinery, fabricated metals, rubber products and textile mill products, of which the rate of output growth was considerably faster than the rate of energy consumption. But these industries have consumed a far larger quantity of energy than tobacco, printing and publishing, textile and apparel, furniture, and professional instruments, though total amounts are far less than the energy-intensive industries.

An analysis of United States data for the period since the collapse of oil prices in 1985 shows that the sensitivity of manufacturing energy consumption to a substantial drop in energy prices (that is price elasticities) depends on the relative importance of energy costs as a percentage of total production costs in different industries. In energy-intensive industries, where energy costs are a significant part of production costs, energy consumption has been stimulated in response to lower energy prices, but energy has been used efficiently so as to improve energy intensity as part of cost-cutting measures. By contrast, some light industries (such as textile and apparel, tobacco, and furniture), where energy constitutes a small fraction of total costs, appear to have paid little attention to energy efficiency and to have increased their energy consumption disproportionately greater than their output. Their high annual growth rates of energy consumption are also partly due to their small base figures.[1]

An analysis of recent United States data also shows that lower energy prices tend to stimulate industrial energy consumption, but do not necessarily promote inefficient energy use and increased industrial energy intensity. In fact, the United States data show a general improvement, although it may have been somewhat slow. This phenomenon may be explained in part by the positive impact of low energy prices on economic growth, which in turn stimulates capital investment in different industries. New equipment and machinery are likely to embody technological improvements in the form of the more efficient use of raw materials including energy. Moreover, extensive industrial restructing in developed countries since the 1982 global recession has led some manufacturing industries, particularly the 'smokestack' industries, to phase out their old plants permanently. As a result, old capacity is no longer available to be reactivated in new periods of economic growth.

The recent United States experience is likely to be repeated at least in other highly industrialized countries, where industrial energy consumption since 1985 would have been much higher in the absence of technological change. The question of how much energy is saved by improvements in energy intensity through technological change will be covered later.

The heavy energy users in 1985, based on the energy consumption to shipment ratios (thousand Btu per constant 1980 dollar of value of shipments and receipts), in descending order were: stone, clay and glass products (16.6); primary metals (14.6); paper and allied products (13.9); chemicals and allied products (12.4); textile mill products (4.8); and petroleum and coal products (4.4). Once again, the energy-intensive industries measured in terms of the energy-use coefficient are those producing basic industrial materials, except textiles.

Data on total energy consumption by disaggregated manufacturing groups in other countries are scarce. However, data on the industrial consumption of electricity can be used for comparative purposes. Table 2.9 provides such an inter-country comparison of the intensity of industrial electricity use as measured by kilowatts per dollar of value added. Needless to say, electrical energy intensity varies substantially among countries and industries, given the wide range of manufacturing technologies and the different energy sources used to generate electricity. The table further suggests that, for manufacturing industry as a whole, Japan and the former Federal Republic of Germany are the most efficient in the use of electricity, while India uses almost five times the amount of electricity per dollar value added in those two countries. It is also surprising to find industry in the Republic of Korea using electricity more efficiently than in Canada or the Netherlands, perhaps because electricity costs are much higher in the Republic of Korea because of its limited energy sources.

Table 2.9 also reports that the manufacture of basic industrial materials such as chemicals, iron and steel, non-ferrous metals, and paper and pulp tends to be far more energy-intensive than the manufacture of capital goods such as

Table 2.9  Coefficients of electrical energy use in manufacturing industry in selected countries, 1983 (kW per $ of value added)

| ISIC code | Industry | Canada | | Netherlands, The | | Germany, Federal Republic of | | Japan | | Mexico | | India | | Korea, Republic of | |
|---|---|---|---|---|---|---|---|---|---|---|---|---|---|---|---|
| | | Coefficient | Rank | Coefficient | Rank | Coefficient | Rank | Coefficient | Rank | Coefficient | Rank | Coefficient | Rank | Coefficient | Rank |
| 311/312 | Food products | 0.55 | 14 | | | 0.13 | 20 | 0.34 | 13 | 0.19 | 15 | 2.33 | 10 | 0.77 | 9 |
| 31 | Beverages | 0.31 | 21 | 0.76[a] | 9 | 0.24 | 15 | 0.22 | 16 | 0.30 | 14 | 1.22 | 16 | 0.27 | 20 |
| 314 | Tobacco | 0.24 | 23 | | | 0.03 | 22 | — | | 0.06 | 21 | 1.12 | 26 | 0.04 | 24 |
| 321 | Textiles | 0.93 | 10 | 0.92 | 8 | 0.68 | 7 | 0.56 | 9 | 0.36 | 12 | 3.45 | 7 | 1.85 | 5 |
| 322 | Wearing apparel | 0.15 | 26 | 0.15 | 12 | 0.09 | 21 | 0.08 | 23 | — | — | 0.60 | 22 | 0.16 | 22 |
| 323 | Leather and products | 0.41 | 17 | | | 0.21 | 16 | 0.11 | 21 | — | — | 1.00 | 17 | 0.45 | 13 |
| 324 | Footwear | 0.22 | 24 | 0.30[a] | 11 | 0.14 | 19 | 0.08 | 29 | — | — | 0.56 | 24 | 0.27 | 19 |
| 331 | Wood products | 1.62 | 7 | | | 0.40 | | 0.22 | 16 | 0.12 | 19 | 1.37 | 13 | 0.00 | 25 |
| 332 | Furniture, fixtures | 0.33 | 19 | 0.43 | 10 | 2.00 | 12 | 0.14 | 19 | — | | 1.35 | 14 | 0.26 | 21 |
| 341 | Paper and products | 6.67 | 1 | 2.44 | 5 | 0.31 | 3 | 2.50 | 4 | 2.17 | 4 | 10.00 | 1 | 2.63 | 3 |
| 342 | Printing, publishing | 0.19 | 25 | 0.32 | 11 | 2.44 | 14 | 0.10 | 22 | — | | 0.58 | 23 | 0.18 | 22 |
| 351 | Industrial chemicals | 5.26 | 2 | 5.00 | 4 | — | 1 | 2.63 | 3 | 0.63 | 10 | 9.09 | 2 | 2.63 | 3 |
| 352 | Other chemical products | 0.27 | 22 | — | | — | | 0.24 | 15 | 0.18 | 16 | 1.30 | 15 | 0.48 | 12 |

26

| Code | Industry | | | | | | | | | | | | | |
|---|---|---|---|---|---|---|---|---|---|---|---|---|---|---|
| 353 | Petroleum refining | 1.64 | 6 | 1.82 | 6 | 0.46ᵃ | | 1.14 | 7 | — | — | 5.56 | 3 | 0.22 | 21 |
| 354 | Petroleum, coal products | 0.70 | 12 | 1.32 | 7 | | 10 | 1.56 | 5 | 1.15 | 6 | 9.09 | 2 | 0.31 | 18 |
| 366 | Rubber products | 0.83 | 11 | 7.69 | 3 | 0.55 | 9 | 0.58 | 9 | 0.32 | 13 | 2.17 | 12 | 0.76 | 10 |
| 356 | Plastic products, n.e.c. | 0.97 | 9 | — | | 0.71 | 6 | 0.56 | 10 | — | | 2.38 | 9 | 0.89 | 7 |
| 361 | Pottery, china, etc. | 0.68 | 13 | | | 0.41 | 11 | 0.53 | 11 | — | | 2.27 | 11 | 0.87 | 8 |
| 362 | Glass products | 1.19 | 8 | | | 1.08 | 4 | 0.65 | 8 | 1.37 | 5 | 4.00 | 6 | 1.09 | 6 |
| 369 | Non-metal products n.e.c. | 2.22 | 4 | 1.32ᵃ | 7 | 1.03 | 5 | 1.16 | 6 | 2.50 | 3 | 5.00 | 5 | 3.03 | 2 |
| 371 | Iron and steel | 1.96 | 5 | 8.33 | 2 | 2.13 | 2 | 13.00 | 1 | 3.70 | 1 | 5.26 | 4 | 2.22 | 4 |
| 372 | Non-ferrous metals | 4.35 | 3 | 11.11 | 1 | 0.58 | 8 | 2.70 | 2 | 2.63 | 2 | 2.94 | 8 | 4.35 | 1 |
| 381 | Metal products | 0.42 | 16 | | | 0.32 | 13 | 0.21 | 17 | 0.09 | 20 | 1.00 | 17 | 0.71 | 11 |
| 382 | Machinery n.e.c. | 0.32 | 20 | 0.76ᵃ | 9 | 0.19 | 17 | 0.21 | 17 | 0.04 | 22 | 0.71 | 21 | 0.39 | 16 |
| 383 | Electrical machinery | 0.35 | 18 | — | | 0.19 | 17 | 0.26 | 14 | 0.13 | 18 | 0.75 | 20 | 0.42 | 15 |
| 384 | Transport equipment | 0.43 | 15 | — | | 0.15 | 18 | 0.38 | 12 | 0.17 | 17 | 0.96 | 18 | 0.44 | 14 |
| 385 | Professional goods | 0.22 | 24 | | | 0.15 | 18 | 0.19 | 18 | — | | 0.42 | 25 | 0.30 | 19 |
| 390 | Other industries | 0.24 | 26 | 0.15 | 12 | 0.15 | 18 | 0.12 | 20 | — | | 0.80 | 19 | 0.36 | 17 |
| 3 | Manufacturing | 1.39 | | 1.24 | | 0.66 | | 0.68 | | — | | 3.16 | — | 1.01 | |

*Notes:* a. Weighted industry average.

*Source:* UNIDO (1987, pp. 75, 202, 258, 309, 323, 394 and 405)

general machinery, electrical machinery, transport equipment and professional goods. The energy intensity of the former group tends to be several times higher than that of the latter group, and this is the case for all seven countries listed in the table.

Finally, the list of heavy users of electrical energy is likely to be the same everywhere, regardless of the stage of industrialization reached and the industrial technologies used. The five major energy-intensive industries given in Table 2.10 are ranked among the top five energy consumers for each country, although the ranking order and their energy intensity differ from country to country. They are the basic material-producing industries, namely paper and paper products, industrial chemicals, iron and steel, non-ferrous metals, glass, rubber products, and petroleum and coal products.

Most of the industrial energy efficiency and conservation measures taken in developed countries came in the aftermath of the oil price rises of 1973 and 1979. It seems reasonable to assume that energy intensity is sensitive to energy prices. This is particularly true in energy-intensive industries but less likely in other manufacturing industries where energy costs account for a relatively small fraction of total production costs. On the other hand, as energy prices decrease the decline in energy intensity is also expected to become slower or may even reverse itself. During the period of the collapse in oil prices between 1986 and the invasion of Kuwait in August 1990,[2] there was much speculation about the impact of falling energy prices on manufacturing energy consumption and energy intensity. Evidence which shows now manufacturing energy efficiency has changed since 1985 in various countries is very limited. It would be useful to ascertain whether the decoupling of energy and output that has occurred in industrialized countries since the first oil crisis of 1973 is a temporary phenomenon, or whether it is a permanent shift that will continue to hold even in a period of falling, or more recently stable, energy prices.

Survey data on United States manufacturing energy consumption in 1985 and preliminary data for 1988 may shed light on recent trends in manufacturing energy consumption in highly industrialized countries. Manufacturing energy consumption for two-digit industry groups and selected four-digit energy-intensive industries in the United States in 1985 and 1988 is summarized in Table 2.11. Comparable MVA data for 1985 and 1988 are also provided. In Table 2.8, the United States data for 1980 and 1985 cover consumption only for off-site energy purchased by various industries, whereas the data for 1985 and 1988 presented in Table 2.11 are for total energy inputs by manufacturing industries, including energy produced on-site. Bearing this discrepancy in mind, the relationships between energy and output during the periods 1980–85 and 1985–88 may now be assessed and compared. Total manufacturing energy consumption declined by around 20 percent, while industrial output increased by 8 percent between 1980 and 1985. In contrast, total manufacturing energy

*Table 2.10    Top five electrical energy-intensive industries
(kW per $ of value added)*

| Rank | Industry | Coef-ficient | Industry | Coef-ficient |
|------|----------|--------------|----------|--------------|
| | *Canada* | | | |
| 1 | Paper and products | 6.67 | | |
| 2 | Industrial chemicals | 5.00 | | |
| 3 | Non-metal products n.e.c. | 2.22 | | |
| 4 | Iron and steel | 1.96 | | |
| | Manufacturing average | 1.39 | | |
| | *Federal Rep. of Germany* | | *The Netherlands* | |
| 1 | Industrial chemicals | 2.44 | Non-ferrous metals | 11.11 |
| 2 | Iron and steel | 2.13 | Iron and steel | 8.33 |
| 3 | Paper and products | 2.00 | Rubber products | 7.69 |
| 4 | Glass products | 1.08 | Industrial chemicals | 5.00 |
| 5 | Non-metal products | 1.03 | Paper and products | 2.44 |
| | Manufacturing average | 0.66 | Manufacturing average | 1.24 |
| | *Mexico* | | *Japan* | |
| 1 | Iron and steel | 3.70 | Iron and steel | 3.13 |
| 2 | Non-ferrous metals | 2.63 | Non-ferrous metals | 2.70 |
| 3 | Non-metal products, n.e.c. | 2.50 | Industrial chemicals | 2.63 |
| 4 | Paper and products | 2.17 | Papers and products | 2.50 |
| 5 | Glass products | 1.37 | Petroleum, coal products | 1.56 |
| | Manufacturing average | 2.11 | Manufacturing average | 0.68 |
| | *Republic of Korea* | | *India* | |
| 1 | Non-ferrous metals | 4.35 | Paper and products | 10.00 |
| 2 | Non-metal products, n.e.c. | 3.03 | Petroleum, coal products | 9.09 |
| 3 | Industrial chemicals | 2.63 | Industrial chemicals | 9.09 |
| 4 | Paper and products | 2.63 | Petroleum refining | 5.56 |
| 5 | Iron and steel | 2.22 | Iron and steel | 5.26 |
| | Manufacturing average | 1.01 | Manufacturing average | 3.16 |

*Source:*    UNIDO (1987, pp. 75, 202, 258, 309, 323, 394 and 405)

consumption increased by approximately 6 percent (an annual growth rate of 2 percent) from 13,600 billion Btu to 14,400 billion Btu between 1985 and 1988, while output (in 1982 constant dollars) increased by approximately 20 percent (an annual rate of 6 percent) from $780 billion to almost $930 billion in the same period. In short, increased industrial output was achieved with decreased energy consumption between 1980 and 1985, showing a clear decoupling of

*Table 2.11    Total inputs of energy for heat, power and electricity in
selected industries in the United States, 1985 and 1988*[a]

| SIC[b] codes | Industry | Energy consumption ('000 billion Btu) | | MVA ($ billion 1982) | | Average annual growth rates 1985–88 (%) | |
|---|---|---|---|---|---|---|---|
| | | 1985 | 1988 | 1985 | 1988 | Energy consump-tion | MVA |
| 20 | Food and kindred products | 946 | 1,005 | 64.8 | 67.8 | 2.04 | 1.52 |
| 21 | Tobacco manufacturers | 19 | 24 | 6.2 | 4.7 | 8.10 | −8.82 |
| 22 | Textile mill products | 248 | 260 | 15.6 | 16.8 | 1.59 | 2.50 |
| 23 | Apparel and other textile products | 30 | 43 | 20.1 | 23.2 | 12.75 | 4.90 |
| 24 | Lumber and wood products | 333 | 365 | 19.8 | 25.7 | 3.11 | 9.08 |
| 25 | Furniture and fixtures | 48 | 61 | 12.1 | 12.3 | 8.32 | 0.55 |
| 26 | Paper and allied products | 2,198 | 2,268 | 30.2 | 34.9 | 1.05 | 4.94 |
| 2621 | Paper mills, except building paper | 996 | 1,091 | — | — | 3.08 | — |
| 2631 | Paperboard mills | 758 | 804 | — | — | 1.98 | — |
| 27 | Printing and publishing | 76 | 91 | 42.5 | 45.5 | 6.19 | 2.30 |
| 28 | Chemicals and allied products | 2,407 | 2,694 | 59.1 | 74.2 | 3.83 | 7.88 |
| 2819 | Industrial organic chemicals | 797 | 1,036 | — | — | −6.65 | — |
| 2821 | Plastics materials and resins | 277 | 298 | — | — | 2.47 | — |
| 2869 | Industrial organic chemicals | 797 | 1,036 | — | — | 9.14 | — |
| 2873 | Nitrogen fertilizers | 213 | 181 | — | — | −5.28 | — |
| 29 | Petroleum and coal products | 2,631 | 2,897 | 39.4 | 44.6 | 3.26 | 4.22 |
| 2911 | Petroleum refining | 257 | 2,833 | — | — | 3.30 | — |
| 30 | Rubber and miscellaneous plastic products | 212 | 232 | 26.6 | 29.8 | 3.05 | 3.86 |
| 31 | Leather and leather products | 13 | 12 | 3.2 | 2.9 | −2.63 | −3.23 |
| 32 | Stone, clay and glass products | 896 | 995 | 22.2 | 25.2 | 3.56 | 4.32 |
| 3241 | Cement, hydraulic | 328 | 338 | — | — | 1.01 | — |
| 33 | Primary metal industries | 2,391 | 2,282 | 32.7 | 37.9 | −1.54 | 5.04 |
| 3312 | Blast furnaces and steel mills | 1,677 | 1,590 | — | — | −1.76 | — |
| 3334 | Primary aluminum | 234 | 209 | — | — | −3.70 | — |
| 34 | Fabricated metal products | 298 | 300 | 26.2 | 63.2 | 0.22 | 3.99 |
| 35 | Machinery, except electrical | 239 | 242 | 124.2 | 170.5 | 0.42 | 11.14 |
| 36 | Electric and electronic equipment | 209 | 189 | 74.3 | 88.1 | −3.30 | 5.84 |
| 37 | Transport equipment | 317 | 343 | 92.8 | 112.6 | 2.66 | 6.66 |

*Table 2.11    Continued*

| SIC[b] codes | Industry | Energy consumption ('000 billion Btu) | | MVA ($ billion 1982) | | Average annual growth rates 1985–88 (%) | |
|---|---|---|---|---|---|---|---|
| | | 1985 | 1988 | 1985 | 1988 | Energy consump- tion | MVA |
| 38 | Instruments and related products | 73 | 103 | 24.2 | 31.5 | 12.16 | 9.19 |
| 39 | Miscellaneous manufactur- ing industries | 13 | 35 | 13.0 | 16.1 | 4.13 | 7.39 |
| | Total | 13,615 | 14,441 | 779.2 | 927.5 | 1.98 | 5.98 |

*Notes*
a.   US Standard Industrial Classification.
b.   MVA growth rates are measured in 1982 constant dollars.

*Sources:*   US Department of Commerce (1991, Table 6); for 1985 energy figures, EIA (1985); for 1988 figures, EIA (1988)

energy and output. Although apparently associated with an increase in energy consumption between 1985 and 1988, output grew three times faster, thus reducing the aggregate energy intensity of the manufacturing sector.

An important implication for developing countries can be derived from the preceding cross-country assessment of manufacturing energy consumption. A large number of developing countries, particularly those at early stages of industrialization, are about to initiate or have already begun a process of structural change involving a shift away from traditional labor-intensive light manufacturing to a more energy- and materials-intensive phase of industrialization based on the processing of industrial raw materials. A small number of industries processing industrial raw materials, in particular iron and steel, non-ferrous metals, non-metallic minerals, chemicals, and paper and pulp, have consistently accounted for the bulk of total manufacturing energy consumption, while producing a relatively small share of manufacturing output, and hence these industries will have a disproportionate impact on aggregate manufacturing energy consumption. On the other hand, particularly in highly industrialized OECD countries, energy consumption in these basic industries, markedly declined despite increasing output and energy prices during the 1970s and early 1980s. When energy prices started to fall in the mid-1980s, energy consumption rose, but at a far slower pace than output. In both cases, energy intensity in these industries continued to fall. The key to energy-efficient industrialization in the developing countries is to adopt the many energy-efficient manufacturing technologies available from the developed countries.

Another important conclusion is that any industrial energy efficiency and conservation strategy for developing countries should target a small number of strategic energy-intensive industries, given their decisive impact on aggregate manufacturing consumption.

The energy and environmental implications of the patterns of energy consumption among different manufacturing industries in developing countries seem quite significant. Those heavy energy-consuming industries, mainly the basic materials producers at the early stages of the manufacturing hierarchy of processing and fabrication, are the growth industries in the South, and their growth is expected to accelerate in the late 1990s. However, the importance of these industries in the North is markedly declining as the structure of the economy in the North shifts rapidly towards service-oriented and high-technology industries.

Three major implications may be drawn from the above facts. First, the problem of energy scarcity may grow more severe if most developing countries undergo the energy-intensive phase of industrialization with emphasis on the production of basic industrial materials. Second, the environmental pressures of this trend toward energy-intensive industrialization are likely to increase sharply, since both the manufacturing processes of basic industrial materials and the heavy power generation that those processes require are significant sources of environmental pollution. In this regard, industrial energy efficiency takes on added importance, since it plays the dual role of simultaneously alleviating energy scarcity and mitigating the environmental burden. Third, energy requirements associated with the manufacture of specific products, which could be estimated from particular process technologies, are undoubtedly more useful and revealing than aggregate information. There are literally thousands of case-studies on product-specific energy requirements, but it is outside the scope of the present study to search and compile such product- and process-level data.

## 2.4   INDUSTRIAL MINERAL RESOURCE CONSUMPTION

Industry uses a wide variety of raw materials in manufacturing processes (see appendix Table A-3 for a list of selected raw materials used by different industries). These industrial raw materials can be divided into two groups: renewable and non-renewable raw materials. Generally speaking, food processing and light industries such as textiles, wearing apparel, leather goods and wood products use largely renewable agricultural and forest resources, whereas heavy industries producing basic industrial raw materials (for example, iron and steel, chemicals, glass products, non-ferrous metals and metal products) rely heavily on non-renewable mineral resources, as shown in appendix Table A-3. Our intent is to focus mainly on the industrial use of non-renewable mineral resources, excluding fossil fuels which were discussed earlier.

The industrial use of mineral resources raises two fundamental problems: first, the extraction and depletion of finite, limited resources; and second, the environmental impacts of that extraction. The theoretical controversies surrounding the depletion of exhaustible resources have been extensively debated and widely published.[3] More recently, considerable evidence now exists that the overly pessimistic predictions of the 'limits-to-growth' approach to resource exhaustibility in the 1970s are not true. The central issue is the role of technology and relative prices in determining the availability of exhaustible resources. Technology launched a two-pronged assault on the resource problem: a steady reduction of the extraction costs of raw materials through greater recovery and a remarkable improvement in the efficiency of the industrial use of raw materials. Moreover, as a natural resource becomes scarcer, its relative price should rise to induce conservation and greater investment to develop substitutes. As a result, an increase in total demand for raw materials is likely to be less than proportionate to the increase in output. At the same time, the total supply of raw materials may expand in response to lower extraction costs and higher relative prices.

The implausibility of the depletion of natural resources, at least in the coming several decades, seems to be corroborated by the expanding world reserves of four major minerals: copper, lead, zinc and aluminum, as shown in Table 2.12. These reserves are shown to have steadily increased up to the end of the 1970s, although they declined slightly in the first half of the 1980s

*Table 2.12   Growth of world reserves of selected minerals (million tons near end of relevant decade)*

| Year | Copper | Lead | Zinc | Aluminum |
|------|--------|------|------|----------|
| 1940s | 91 | 31–45 | 54–70 | 1,605 |
| 1950s | 124 | 45–54 | 77–86 | 3,224 |
| 1960s | 280 | 86 | 106 | 11,600 |
| 1970s | 543 | 157 | 240 | 22,700 |
| 1980s | 500 | 135 | 300 | 22,335 |
| 1990s | 352 | 70 | 147 | 23,200 |
| Annual growth, 1950s–1960s (%) | 7.5 | 5.00–5.75 | 4.75–5.25 | 9.75 |
| Annual production, 1960s–1970s (%) | 3.75 | 1.75 | 2.75 | 7.00 |
| Annual growth, 1970s–1990s (%) | –2.14 | –3.96 | –2.42 | 0.11 |

*Source: Minerals Handbook* (1990)

owing to a drop in metal prices relative to their extraction costs. Most importantly, reserves of those minerals grew considerably faster than their production. This pattern of reserve growth is likely to be true for many other minerals, where minimum estimated reserves grew as fast as production until the 1980s. In essence, there seems to be no cause for concern about supply exhaustion within the foreseeable future, although political disruptions could lead to temporary shortages. The more important long-run view, that of Labys and Waddell (1989), explains that different minerals eventually reach the end of their life cycles, and consequently are replaced by other minerals. Table 2.13, for example, suggests the strong role that many minerals still play in the United States economy despite their recent decline relative to other industrial sectors.

Concerning the environmental problems that the production and industrial use of mineral raw materials pose, the environmental pollution from mining takes many different forms, and some of the more well-known pollutants are the following: mine gases, dust, radiation and mine drainage.

There are many other types of damage to the environment and human health resulting from mining operations. They include excessive heat and humidity, and noise pollution that can lead to possible loss of hearing. The technical literature on this subject is abundant and should be consulted for further detailed information (for example, see Ripley *et al.* 1996).

Table 2.12 provides rankings of various minerals in world trade excluding energy resources. The top five most important non-oil minerals in world trade in 1991 as measured by value of exports in descending order are: iron ore, nickel, copper, sulphur, phosphate and tin. It is well known that many developing regions account for a sizeable share of the world reserves. For instance, South America and Asia together hold about 30 percent of world reserves of iron ore; South America and Africa together about 40 percent of world reserves of copper; all developing countries 22 percent of world lead deposits, 45 percent of total zinc reserves, and 70 percent of all bauxite reserves.

The environmental implications of the presence of substantial mineral reserves and increasing mining activities in developing countries could be quite significant. The majority of mineral-producing developing countries depend on mineral export revenues to reduce problems of foreign exchange deficits, debt-servicing and development finance. The extent of world trade in various minerals is given in Table 2.14. For example, copper accounts for 70 percent of exports in Chile and 80 percent in Bolivia. It seems plausible to expect, therefore, that mineral production in developing countries will continue to rise to meet the import requirements of high-consuming developed countries as well as their own ever-increasing domestic demand resulting from accelerated industrialization. Unless environmentally sound mining technologies are soon adopted on a massive scale in developing countries, the pollution

*Table 2.13*   *Mineral production value in the United States,*
*1990 and 1995 ($ million)*[a]

| Mineral | 1990 | 1995 |
|---|---|---|
| **Mineral production, total** | **150,530** | **27,025** |
| **Mineral fuels, total** | **117,066** | **97,025** |
| Coal | 31,336 | 28,926 |
| Natural gas | 31,789 | 36,179 |
| Petroleum (crude) | 53,8101 | 31,920 |
| **Industrial minerals, total** | **21,022** | **20,100** |
| Asphalt, related bitumens (native) | 3,480 | n.a. |
| Boron mineral, sold/used by producers | 436 | 370 |
| Bromine, sold/used by producers | 173 | 157 |
| Cements: | | |
| Portland | 3,683 | 4,155 |
| Masonry | 225 | 264 |
| Clays | 1,620 | 1,597 |
| Diatomite | 138 | 162 |
| Feldspar | 28 | 30 |
| Gemstones (estimate) | 53 | 52 |
| Gypsum crude | 100 | 118 |
| Lime, sold/used by producers | 902 | 996 |
| Phosphate rock (marketable) | 1,075 | 902 |
| Potash ($K_2O$ equivalent) | 303 | 274 |
| Salt (common), sold/used by producers | 827 | 906 |
| Sands and gravel, sold/used by producers | 3,686 | 4,293 |
| Construction | 3,249 | 3,835 |
| Industrial | 436 | 458 |
| Sodium carbonate (natural) (soda ash) | 836 | 650 |
| Stone | 5,822 | 6,731 |
| Crushed and broken | 5,591 | 6,731 |
| Dimension | 231 | n.a. |
| Sulfur: Frasch mines (shipments) | 335 | 135 |
| Industrial minerals, undistributed | 504 | 136 |
| **Metals total** | **12,442** | **n.a.** |
| Copper (recoverable content) | 4,331 | 4,382 |
| Gold (recoverable content) | 3,650 | 3,843 |
| Iron ore (gross weight) | 1,741 | 1,700 |
| Lead (recoverable content) | 491 | 286 |
| Magnesium | 433 | n.a. |
| Molybdenum (concentrate) | 348 | 215 |
| Palladium metal | 22 | 25 |

*Table 2.13    Continued*

| Mineral | 1990 | 1995 |
|---|---|---|
| Platinum metal | 27 | 21 |
| Silver (recoverable content) | 329 | 192 |
| Zinc mine production | 847 | 549 |
| Metal, undistributed | 242 | 113 |

*Note:*    a.    Some values represent estimates rather than complete counts.

*Source:*    US Bureau of the Census (1996)

*Table 2.14    Ranking of minerals in world trade, 1980–91 ($ million)*

| Commodity | Value of exports 1980 | Rank | Value of exports 1991 | Rank |
|---|---|---|---|---|
| Aluminum | 1,082.5 | 8 | 942.4 | 9 |
| Copper | 2,479.0 | 4 | 1,789.9 | 4 |
| Iron | 7,071.3 | 2 | 8,550.7 | 2 |
| Lead | 1,802.6 | 6 | 952.4 | 8 |
| Nickel | 2,677.6 | 3 | 3,893.4 | 3 |
| Phosphate | 2,178.1 | 5 | 1,285.1 | 6 |
| Sulphur | 1,433.8 | 7 | 1,322.1 | 5 |
| Tin | 458.0 | 9 | 1,000.6 | 7 |
| Crude petroleum | 336,746.3 | 1 | 174,303.0 | 1 |

*Source:*    UNCTAD (1993)

problems stemming from mining activities will further deteriorate and add to present intolerable levels of environmental pollution from other major sources such as industry, agriculture, energy use and households.

To analyze such environmental problems more fully, it is important to identify those manufacturing industries which use mineral resources most intensively. The problem in identifying the principal users of a particular resource is that the intermediate producers of a good are the largest users of a particular mineral resource; for instance, the aluminum fabrication industry is a major user of aluminum. It is therefore essential to observe the path of inputs through successive processes to reach product outputs. This can be done in two ways. First, a complete microeconomic analysis of material flows can be conducted, involving an integrated set of technical activities such as the exploration, extraction, refinement, conversion, transport and fabrication of material resources into the final products. This method is often referred to as the reference materials systems (RMS) approach, an example of which will be given shortly. Second, a sufficiently disaggregated input–output table can be used to trace resource flows through different industries until they are transformed into end-products. Various United States input–output tables have been used to derive a sample of end uses for selected minerals, as shown in Table 2.15.

The table suggests that a small number of industries are the most notable users of mineral resources. For instance, the construction and motor vehicle industries together consume 50 percent of steel, about 40 percent of lead and 38 percent of copper and aluminum. It is important to remember that the notion of resource depletion and zero growth seems irrelevant when the problem of resource depletion is examined at more detailed product levels. As Pearce and Rose (1975, p. 159) correctly stipulated: 'when we know that lead mostly goes into car batteries, we realize that if we want to conserve lead it is a good deal easier and more effective to design a car that does not need a lead-acid accumulator than to halt economic growth.'

As in the case of energy and water, the wide variations in the patterns of use of raw materials by both country and industry suggest that the process-specific approach mentioned above is more useful. In particular, the RMS approach could be highly useful not only for assessing the industrial use of raw materials, but also for determining energy requirements, labor and capital needs and environmental effects. The RMS approach provides a network representation of the flow of materials. It is not difficult to see that the technical coefficients and material substitution for input–output tables can also be estimated from the information given in the RMS. In particular, the RMS method may make it possible to identify promising areas for substituting non-renewables by renewables, recycling used material, conserving scarce raw materials, improving energy efficiency and reducing industrial pollutants.

*Table 2.15   Principal uses of resources in the United States, 1987*

| | $ million | % | | $ million | % |
|---|---|---|---|---|---|
| *Crude petroleum and natural gas* | | | *Agricultural fertilizers and chemicals* | | |
| Maintenance and repair constriction | 1,844 | 7 | Maintenance and repair constriction | 55 | 1 |
| Industrial and other chemicals | 837 | 3 | Industrial and other chemicals | 1,371 | 18 |
| Industrial machinery | 157 | 1 | Industrial machinery | 16 | 0 |
| Air transportation | 86 | 0 | Air transportation | 15 | 0 |
| Engines and turbines | 22 | 0 | Food and kindred products | 92 | 1 |
| Stone and clay products | 265 | 1 | Railroads and related services | 281 | 4 |
| Electric services (utilities) | 1,292 | 5 | Rubber and miscellaneous plastics products | 115 | 2 |

*Table 2.15    Continued*

| | $ million | % | | $ million | % |
|---|---|---|---|---|---|
| Communication equipment | 120 | 0 | Communication equipment | 39 | 1 |
| Wholesale and retail trade | 529 | 2 | Wholesale and retail trade | 750 | 10 |
| Water transportation | 103 | 0 | Water transportation | 40 | 1 |
| Total of these | | 19 | Total of these | | 38 |
| *Stone and clay products* | | | *Primary iron and steel manufacturing* | | |
| Maintenance and repair construction | 328 | 2 | Maintenance and repair constriction | 1,294 | 4 |
| Industrial and other chemicals | 1,269 | 7 | Industrial and other chemicals | 1,723 | 5 |
| General industrial machinery | 32 | 0 | Industrial machinery | 868 | 3 |
| Air transportation | 61 | 0 | Air transportation | 78 | 0 |
| Food and kindred products | 25 | 0 | Electric services (utilities) | 2,813 | 9 |
| Ordinance and accessories | 57 | 0 | Advertising | 2,010 | 6 |
| Railroads and related services | 644 | 4 | Railroads and related services | 1,149 | 4 |
| Communication equipment | 295 | 2 | Communication equipment | 150 | 0 |
| Wholesale and retail trade | 1,297 | 7 | Wholesale and retail trade | 4,497 | 14 |
| Water transportation | 154 | 1 | Water transportation | 319 | 1 |
| Total of these | | 23 | Total of these | | 46 |
| *Lumber wood products* | | | *Primary non-ferrous metals manufacturing* | | |
| Maintenance and repair construction | 423 | 2 | Maintenance and repair construction | 273 | 1 |
| Industrial and other chemicals | 848 | 3 | Industrial and other chemicals | 715 | 3 |
| General industrial machinery | 113 | 0 | Industrial machinery | 556 | 2 |
| Air transportation | 81 | 0 | Air transportation | 102 | 0 |
| Forestry and fishery products | 5,874 | 23 | Advertising | 537 | 2 |
| Ordinance and accessories | 423 | 2 | Rubber and miscellaneous plastics products | 647 | 3 |
| Advertising | 987 | 4 | Railroads and related services | 336 | 1 |
| Electric services (utilities) | 1,044 | 4 | Communication equipment | 111 | 0 |
| Wholesale and retail trade | 3,879 | 15 | Wholesale and retail trade | 3,444 | 14 |
| Water transportation | 111 | 0 | Water transportation | 57 | 0 |
| Total of these | | 53 | Total of these | | 26 |

*Source:*    US Department of Commerce (1994)

An example of the flow of materials and the pollutants generated is provided in Figure 2.5. Material and energy requirements are shown as well as the pollutive output from de-inked newsprint processing.

Apart from the apparent advantage of adopting low-waste technology, industry could minimize the environmental impact associated with the industrial use of raw materials in two principal ways: by substituting high-pollution-content materials with low-pollution-content materials; and by recycling as secondary industrial raw materials. In principle, recycling can considerably reduce the new materials needed in industrial production. But apart from some inevitable loss due to irretrievable dispersal of materials in the production process, there are also engineering and economic limitations on the amount of

*Figure 2.5    Raw material and energy requirements, and effluent characteristics for de-inked newsprint process (new mill basis)*[a]

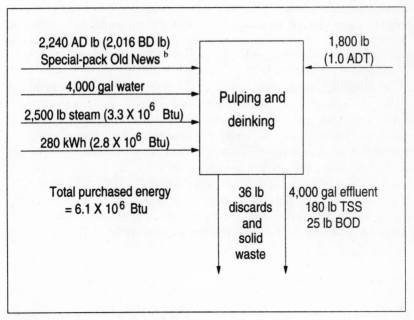

*Notes*
a.   Basis: 1.0 ADT (1,800 BD lb) slush pulp
b.   Since some old news is purchased wet, average moisture content is 10 percent.
Definition of parameters:
AD = air-dried                    ADT = air-dried total
BD = blow-dried                 BOD = biological oxygen demand
TSS = total suspended solids

*Source:*   Mann (1977)

recycling possible, given the difficulties of obtaining a product from recycled materials at a quality level comparable to and at a price competitive with original materials. Obviously, as the price of the latter rises, more sophisticated technologies for recycling become economically profitable. In addition, there are a number of institutional barriers to recycling. These include freight rates, tax policies, regulations, existing capital equipment or tradition-bound practices; all of these have deterred the increased use of recycled materials in the United States (Smith 1972).

Substitution of one material for another has been widespread practice in manufacturing for a long time and for many reasons. For instance, the rapid growth of the use of aluminum and plastics as substitutes for wood or steel can be explained by the superior properties of those materials, not by the scarcity or high prices of iron or wood. By and large, however, the material substitutions have been dominated by economic considerations and have taken on greater urgency since the sharp escalation of oil prices in the 1970s. Environmental considerations have seldom in the past been a major factor in decisions about substitution, although to the extent that material substitution is motivated by energy saving, such substitution may also have a favorable effect on the environment. Further research is thus needed to develop a rational approach to industrial material substitution which carefully balances economic benefits against environmental costs.

The actual data for the recycling of some key materials and some examples of the use of substitute materials are summarized in Table 2.16. A more detailed analysis, particularly of non-ferrous metal recycling, appears in Henstock (1996). It must be noted that only the technical possibilities for substitution are listed, but the economic and environmental costs of substitution for those minerals are not given. In short, the choice of mineral resources in manufacturing depends on the quantity and quality of their long-term supply potential, the costs of exploration, extraction and refinement, the energy requirements for converting them into useful materials, the environmental impacts, and many other social and institutional factors.

## 2.5   CONCLUSIONS

Let us now draw some conclusions concerning the impact of industrial development on natural resources.

### Industrial Water Consumption

Industry uses much less water than agriculture, but it pollutes the water more. Although over 80 percent of the water used for cooling and cleaning is

*Table 2.16    Recycling percentages, usage patterns and substitutes for
selected metals*

| Metal | Percent-age recycled | Uses with good recovery | Uses with poor recovery | Uses | Substitutes |
|-------|----------------------|-------------------------|-------------------------|------|-------------|
| Copper | 37.7 | Brass alloys Coinage Electrical | Chemicals Fungicides Fertilizers | Electrical Construction | Aluminum Sodium alloys Stainless steel |
| Gold | 16.0 | Alloys | Jewelry Electronics Bullion | Plumbing Jewelry Electronical Dental | Plastics Platinum Palladium Silver Aluminum Plastics |
| Lead | 53.3 | Storage batteries Lead- and copper-base | Gasoline additives Solder Pigments | Storage cells | Cadmium Mercury Nickel Silver Zinc |
| Mercury | 32.0 | Mercury cells in chloride plants Electrical Amalgams | Fungicides Germicides Paints | Gasoline additives Pigments Cable cover Plumbing Mercury cells | Nickel (catalytic reforming) Tin Zinc Plastics Other processes |
| Silver | 47.2 | Stampings Bimetal scrap Batteries | Photographic solutions | Medical Germicides Protective paint Photographic Reflectors Coinage | Sulphur Organics Plastics Copper paint Selenium Aluminum Rhodium Copper-nickel alloys |
| Zinc | 28.3 | News scrap (75 percent) Brass Bronze alloys Batteries | Galvanized products Pigments | Diecasting Anti-corrosion agent Reducing agent | Aluminum Magnesium Plastics Aluminum sheet Stannum Ceramics |

*Sources:*    Mann (1977); Henstock (1996, pp. 58, 181 and 263)

returned, the returned water is often contaminated by industrial effluents and
thermal pollution. In general, heavy industries producing basic industrial
materials (primary metals, chemicals, petroleum products, paper products, and
so on) and resource-based light industries (food and beverages, textiles and
leather, and so on) tend to consume a large volume of water. A large

proportion of the industrial water supplies is used for cooling, particularly in heavy industries, and less for processing.

At the process levels, there exist vast inter-industry and inter-country variations in industrial water requirements. In general, paper and pulp products, chemicals and primary metals tend to use more water per ton of output than any other product groups. The wide variations in industrial water use reflect wide differences in the process technologies used in different countries. The process-level information suggests that increasing industrial output need not necessarily be accompanied by increasing industrial water requirements. New water-saving technology designed to increase recirculation and water reuse can reduce industrial water requirements and at the same time lower their pollution load.

## Industrial Energy Consumption

Among the OECD countries, industry used more energy than any other sector during the period 1970–87, ranging between 40 percent in 1970 to 33 percent in 1987. The industrial share of energy consumption in developing countries varied widely from country to country, ranging from 63 percent in China to 20 percent in West Africa. Despite considerable inter-country variations and regardless of the stages of industrialization, it seems quite clear that industry is likely to be the largest source of energy consumption in both developed and developing countries, except perhaps for West African countries.

Industry depends on different sources of energy, and this varies among countries. The industrial energy used in OECD countries is more or less equally distributed among four mineral sources: namely oil, coal, natural gas and electricity. In the former USSR and Eastern Europe, industry relies heavily on both coal and natural gas. Coal is the dominant source of energy for industry in China (67 percent) and India (72 percent). Since OPEC first disrupted the world petroleum market in 1973–74, coal consumption has risen sharply. In the 1980s, world consumption rose over 31 percent even after oil prices dropped more than 50 percent in 1986. More recently, European energy consumption has shifted towards natural gas. Given the world-wide known coal reserves, over 600 billion tons of hard coal and brown coal, the increasing utilization of coal may represent a viable alternative source of energy in face of the diminishing oil reserves. As developing countries depend increasingly on coal as an alternative source of energy for rapid industrialization, the environmental problems of coal combustion such as acid deposits and other gaseous and liquid pollution could pose a formidable challenge to sustainable industrial development, unless clean technologies are developed and adopted on a massive scale.

Subsequent to the second shock to the oil markets in 1979–80, the manufacturing sectors in developed countries have experienced considerable improvements in energy efficiency, largely prompted by rising energy prices and the uncertainty of energy supplies, particularly of imported oil. For instance, the energy efficiency of the United States manufacturing sector improved by 25 percent between 1980 and 1985.

According to the last energy consumption survey of United States manufacturing industries by the Energy Information Administration (EIA 1994a), the heavy energy users in terms of total consumption are again major producers of basic industrial materials, namely: chemicals, primary metals, paper and allied products, petroleum and coal products, stone, clay and glass products. The five industry groups accounted for 70 percent of all manufacturing energy consumption in 1985. Statistics on total energy consumption by disaggregated manufacturing groups in different countries are scarce, but some data on industrial consumption of electricity are available for international comparison. An international comparison of the intensity of industrial electricity use in 1983 as measured in kilowatts per dollar of value added shows, among other things, that across countries and irrespective of the stage of industrialization and the technologies used, the most electrical-energy-intensive tend to be producers of basic industrial materials, namely paper and paper products, industrial chemicals, iron and steel, non-ferrous metals, glass, rubber products, and petroleum and coal products.

The past trends of industrial energy consumption have important implications for developing countries. First, the problem of energy scarcity may grow more severe if most developing countries undergo an energy-intensive phase of industrialization with emphasis on the production of basic industrial materials on a massive scale. Second, the environmental pressures of this trend toward energy-intensive industrialization are likely to increase sharply, since both the manufacturing processes of basic industrial materials and the power generation which those processes require are significant sources of environmental pollution. In this regard, industrial energy efficiency takes on added importance; it plays the dual role of simultaneously alleviating energy scarcity and mitigating environmental burdens.

## Industrial Mineral Resources Consumption

There seems to be no cause for concern about the exhaustion of the supply of mineral resources within the foreseeable future, although political disruption might lead to temporary shortages. A more important issue relating to mineral resources concerns the environmental problems posed by their production and industrial use. The environmental pollution by mining takes many different forms, such as mine gases, dust, radiation and mine drainage effluents, and some of these pollutants are known to be quite harmful.

The environmental implications of substantial mineral reserves and increasing mining activities in developing countries could be quite significant. The majority of mineral-producing developing countries depend on mineral export revenues to escape problems of foreign exchange deficits, debt servicing and development finance. Unless environmentally sound mining technologies are soon adopted extensively all across developing countries, the pollution problems stemming from mining activities will further deteriorate and add to already intolerable levels of environmental pollution from other major sources such as industry, agriculture, energy use and households.

Obviously, the principal users of mineral resources are intermediate producers of goods; for instance, the aluminum fabrication industry, which is a major user of aluminum. Excluding all such intermediate goods producers, a small number of industries are found to be the most notable users of mineral resources. For instance, the construction and motor vehicle industries together consumed 50 percent of steel, about 40 percent of lead and 38 percent of copper and aluminum in the United States in 1970. In addition, industrial chemicals, industrial machinery, food manufacture, aircraft and other transport equipment were identified as principal users of mineral resources.

Apart from the apparent advantage of adopting low-waste technology, industries around the world could minimize the environmental impacts associated with the industrial use of raw materials in two principal ways: by substituting for high-pollution-content materials with low-pollution-content materials; and by recycling and re-use of waste as secondary industrial raw materials (see Table 2.16). Material substitution is even more urgent since the sharp escalation of oil prices in the 1970s. However, environmental considerations have seldom been a major factor in decisions about substitution in the past. To the extent that material substitution is motivated by energy saving, such substitution may also have a favorable effect on the environment. Further research is needed to develop a rational approach to industrial material substitution that carefully balances economic benefits with environmental costs.

## CHAPTER NOTES

1. For instance, a United Kingdom Study estimated typical industrial energy costs as a percentage of total production costs in United Kingdom industries in 1976 as follows: iron and steel, 30 percent; chemicals, 20 percent; building materials, 20 percent; textiles, 10 percent; food, 5 percent; paper, 5 percent; and other industries, 5 percent. The above figures represent only direct costs, excluding indirect energy costs embodied in various inputs. Energy costs are a significant proportion of total costs in energy-intensive industries such as the first three mentioned above, while for the last four industries, which accounted for 80 percent of total

industrial production, the share of energy costs is small. For further details, see Walter Murgatroyd, 'Industrial energy consumption and potential for conservation,' in *World Energy Issues and Policies*, Robert Mabro (ed.) Oxford: Oxford University Press, 1980, pp. 113–26.

2. The prices of crude oil and gas in the United States declined sharply from $27 per barrel (current dollars) in 1985 to $14 in 1988. See Energy Information Administration, 'Landed cost of imports,' *Monthly Energy Review*, August 1989.

3. For instance, see Barnett and Morse (1963); Dasgupta and Heal (1974); Kneese and Sweeny (1985); Koopmans (1973); Pearce *et al.* (1989); Smith (1979); Stiglitz (1974).

# 3.  Industrial Pollution

## 3.1  THE PROBLEM

The manufacturing sector contributes to environmental degradation through the use of inputs and the production of outputs. On the input side, it uses natural resources; in particular, energy, water and raw materials. This aspect of the environmental impact of manufacturing has already been discussed. On the output side, manufacturing industries also directly generate both traditional and newly emerging pollutants in three major forms, namely air, water and solid wastes, including hazardous wastes. These output pollutants are examined in this chapter. The relative importance of industry as opposed to other sectors of the economy in generating major pollutants is assessed, and the major polluters among manufacturing industries are identified.

At the outset, it will be useful to present an overview of the major pollutants generated by various industries in the process of their manufacturing activities. The known major water pollutants generated by 27 selected industries are listed in appendix Table A-4. Such information may prove useful not only in identifying the sources of specific pollutants, but also in providing a check-list for identifying environmental problems in planning and designing industrial plants.

Another useful approach to the present analysis is to characterize manufacturing industries by the potential environmental stress that they can create. A Canadian government study has classified manufacturing industries by three stress types: high, medium and low. The high stressor group is associated with processes that extract raw materials from the environment and transform them into early-stage industrial materials, such as pulp and paper, metal smelting and refining, industrial chemicals, mining and thermal power generation. The medium stressor group is characterized by the further processing of materials into specialized products required for the next and final stage of manufacturing, although some final products are included in this category because of special environmental considerations (for example, processed foods and pharmaceuticals). The low stressor group captures the remaining industries, which are composed mainly of a large proportion of the industries producing final goods. Such an industrial classification by stressor type is given in appendix Table A-5. The environmental stress of industrial plants is determined by a multitude of factors such as the scale of operations, the process technology employed, the type of pollution abatement equipment used, ecological characteristics of the surrounding area and meteorological conditions. The classification in the table should be considered, therefore, as a first approximation to a more thorough stress evaluation of the different manufacturing processes.

## 3.2  INDUSTRIAL AIR POLLUTION

The major air pollutants most commonly found are particulates, sulphur dioxide, carbon monoxide, nitrogen dioxide and hydrocarbons. Their principal characteristics, emission sources, health and other effects, control techniques and United States ambient standards are summarized in appendix Table A-6. It is evident that natural events such as forest fires and volcanic eruptions are in great measure responsible for the emission of these pollutants. As far as anthropogenic emissions are concerned, air pollution is generated by six major sources: transport, domestic heating, electric power generation, refuse burning, agricultural fires, and industrial fuel burning and process emissions. In general, manufacturing is not responsible for the emissions of most pollutants. Each major pollutant has its own major sources. Most importantly, electricity generation accounts for the major bulk of anthropogenic emissions of sulphur dioxide, transport activities for nitrogen oxides and carbon monoxide, and motor vehicles for hydrocarbons and lead. Industry, however, is a major source of particulate emissions in different countries, as shown in Table 3.1. Some estimates suggest that industrial sources contribute about 20 percent of total air pollution, but this may be an understatement. Many manufacturing industries consume a large amount of electricity, as described earlier, and power generation is a major source of pollution, particularly of sulphur dioxide. The manufacturing sector should be held responsible for some of the air pollution problems caused by electricity generation.

A major question is: How much does industry contribute to the emissions of major air pollutants? Unfortunately, statistics on pollutants by major sources are scarce. United States data given in Table 3.2 provide a rough estimate of the industry contribution to particulate emissions into air during the period 1982–91. Industrial process and fuel combustion were mainly responsible for industrial particulates emitted during this period, each accounting for 30–40 percent of total emissions. It is important to note, however, that industrial activities are in varying degrees related to the activities of other sectors, and hence any industry's real contribution to air pollution would be far greater than is indicated by its direct emissions. For instance, industry is a major consumer of commercial energy: about 33 percent of total energy consumption in

*Table 3.1  Anthropogenic emissions of air pollutants in selected countries, 1970–91*

| Year | Australia | Canada | France | Former Republic of Germany | Former Czecho-slovakia | Hungary | Ireland | Japan | United Kingdom | United States |
|---|---|---|---|---|---|---|---|---|---|---|
| **Sulphur dioxide** | | | | | | | | | | |
| *Total emissions* | | | | | | | | | | |
| 1970 | | 6,677 | 2,966 | 7,517 | | | | 4,973 | 6,424 | 28,410 |
| 1980 | 1,479 | 4,643 | 3,348 | 7,785 | 3,100 | 1,633 | 220 | 1,263 | 4,898 | 23,722 |
| 1985 | | 3,692 | 1,451 | 5,697 | 3,150 | 1,404 | 135 | | 3,742 | 21,634 |
| 1990 | | 3,323 | 1,200 | | | 1,085 | 187 | | 3,780 | 21,010 |
| 1991 | | 3,306 | 1,314 | | | | | | 3,565 | 20,720 |
| *Industrial Process* | | | | | | | | | | |
| *Total emissions* | | | | | | | | | | |
| 1970 | | 5,044 | 505 | 90,118 | | | | | 40 | 6,471 |
| 1980 | | 3,127 | 302 | 103 | | | | | 35 | 3,704 |
| 1985 | | 2,573 | 194 | 90 | | | | 706 | 26 | 3,106 |
| 1990 | | 2,626 | 183 | | | | | 525 | 19 | 3,042 |
| 1991 | | 2,274 | 183 | | | | | | 18 | 3,132 |
| *Power Generation* | | | | | | | | | | |
| *Total emissions* | | | | | | | | | | |
| 1970 | | 502 | 770 | 1,704 | | | | | 2,913 | 15,768 |
| 1980 | | 768 | 1,222 | 1,879 | | | | | 3,007 | 15,811 |
| 1985 | | 736 | 408 | 1,500 | | | | | 2,627 | 14,723 |
| 1990 | | 677 | 313 | 322 | | | | | 2,722 | 14,358 |
| 1991 | | 641 | 403 | | | | | | 2,534 | 14,119 |
| **Nitrogen dioxide** | | | | | | | | | | |
| *Total emissions* | | | | | | | | | | |
| 1970 | | 1,364 | 1,322 | 2,345 | | | | 1,651 | 2,293 | 18,907 |
| 1980 | 242 | 1,959 | 1,646 | 2,994 | 1,204 | 1,633 | | 1,400 | 2,365 | 23,506 |
| 1985 | | 1,958 | 1,400 | 2,928 | 1,120 | 1,404 | | | 2,392 | 19,324 |

| | | | | | | | | | | | |
|---|---|---|---|---|---|---|---|---|---|---|---|
| | 1990 | | 1,923 | 1,487 | 2,605 | | 1,085 | | | 2,779 | 19,311 |
| | 1991 | | | 1,507 | | | | | | 2,747 | 18,742 |
| *Transport sector (mobile sector)* | | | | | | | | | | | |
| Total emissions | 1970 | | 818 | 537 | | | | | | 828 | 8,411 |
| | 1980 | 59 | 1,297 | 660 | 1,876 | | 111 | | 805 | 975 | 12,420 |
| | 1985 | | 1,525 | 910 | 1,975 | 5 | 111 | | | 1,136 | 9,104 |
| | 1990 | | 1,121 | 1,060 | 2,181 | | | | | 1,559 | 7,835 |
| | 1991 | | | 1,088 | | | | | | 1,579 | 7,223 |
| **Particulates** | | | | | | | | | | | |
| Total emissions | 1970 | | 1,850 | 1,324 | 692 | | | | | 1,028 | 18,917 |
| | 1980 | 271 | 1,907 | 427 | 574 | | 576 | | | 560 | 9,011 |
| | 1985 | | 1,709 | 303 | 450 | 1,370 | 492 | | | 545 | 7,808 |
| | 1990 | | | 276 | | | | | | 473 | 7,413 |
| | 1991 | | | 287 | | | | | | 498 | 7,452 |
| *Stationary sources (industry)* | | | | | | | | | | | |
| Total emissions | 1970 | | 1,781 | 1,240 | | | | | | 920 | 17,812 |
| | 1980 | | | 373 | 628 | | 557 | | | 437 | 7,724 |
| | 1985 | | 1,598 | 238 | 504 | | 481 | | | 400 | 6,423 |
| | 1990 | | | 188 | 374 | | | | | 262 | 5,811 |
| | 1991 | | | 194 | | | | | | 286 | 5,806 |
| **Carbon monoxide** | | | | | | | | | | | |
| Total emissions | 1970 | | 10,057 | | 14,540 | | | | | 4,627 | 123,617 |
| | 1980 | 2,416 | 10,273 | 9,316 | 12,006 | | 1,730 | 497 | | 5,034 | 99,907 |
| | 1985 | | 10,781 | 8,399 | 8,894 | 899 | 1,800 | 456 | | 5,554 | 83,114 |
| | 1990 | | | 7,580 | 8,177 | 888 | | 454 | | 6,701 | 67,725 |
| | 1991 | | | 7,338 | | | | | | 6,735 | 62,132 |

*Source:* OECD (1993)

*Table 3.2    Total industrial particulate emissions into air, estimated for the United States, 1982–91 (kg billions)*

| Source category | 1982 | 1985 | 1988 | 1989 | 1990 | 1991 |
|---|---|---|---|---|---|---|
| Transportation | 1.30 | 1.38 | 1.48 | 1.52 | 1.54 | 1.57 |
| Fuel combustion | 2.75 | 2.47 | 2.40 | 2.41 | 1.87 | 1.94 |
| Industrial processes | 2.57 | 2.70 | 2.48 | 2.46 | 2.53 | 2.55 |
| Solid waste disposal | 0.31 | 0.29 | 0.28 | 0.27 | 0.28 | 0.34 |
| Miscellaneous | 0.75 | 1.01 | 1.30 | 0.92 | 1.19 | 1.01 |
| Total | 7.67 | 7.85 | 7.94 | 7.57 | 7.40 | 7.41 |

*Source:*   EPA (1992)

OECD countries in 1983 (OECD 1984); all transport equipment is produced by industry; and industrial waste accounted for about 12 percent of the 8 billion tons of all waste generated in OECD countries in 1980; and municipal waste accounted for 350 million tons, part of which was also from industrial sources (OECD 1985a, p. 159).

Data on air pollutant emissions by disaggregated industry sources are not easy to come by. Not surprisingly, the fragmentary data available point to the dominant share of total air pollution accounted for by the industries producing basic industrial materials. The top ten heavily polluting industries in the United States in terms of the total quantity of emissions per year are listed in Table 3.3. These industries roughly correspond to the list of industries earlier classified as high stressors.

More revealing are direct pollution coefficients for all industries, namely the quantity of emissions per unit value of output. Usually an input–output table has been linked to a pollutant matrix to derive the direct and indirect pollution coefficients for different sectors. Coefficients can be estimated for individual pollutants or for a composite weighted emission index of any number of pollutants combined. These coefficients tend to vary substantially across countries and studies, mainly owing to differences in industrial classifications as well as coefficient measurement problems. Moreover, the ranking of industries by the size of its direct coefficients often varies from one study to another.

Direct composite emission indicators of 15 major air pollutants for 60 industries in the Netherlands in 1973 are given in descending order in appendix Table A-8. The total direct coefficients are broken down by process emissions, combustion emissions and transport emissions. Except for transport and other services, the highest coefficients are again found among producers of basic industrial materials such as fertilizers, chemicals, building materials and primary metals. However, like any country, these coefficient estimates reflect

*Table 3.3    Industrial air pollutant emissions in the United States, 1970*

| Type of industry | Annual emission levels (kg billions) | Types of emissions |
|---|---|---|
| Petroleum refining | 3.8 | Particulates, sulfur oxides, hydrocarbons, CO |
| Smelters for Al, Cu, Pb, Zn | 3.7 | Particulates, sulfur oxides |
| Iron foundries | 3.4 | Particulates, CO |
| Kraft pulp and paper mills | 3.0 | Particulates, CO, sulfur oxides |
| Coal cleaning and refuse | 2.1 | Particulates, CO |
| Coke (for steel manufacturing) | 2.0 | Particulates, CO, sulfur oxides |
| Iron and steel mills | 1.6 | Particulates, CO |
| Grain mills and grain handling | 1.0 | Particulates |
| Cement manufacturing | 0.8 | Particulates |
| Phosphate fertilizer plants | 0.3 | Particulates, fluorides |

*Source:*   EPA (1992)

primarily the Netherlands experience, and may be less relevant to other countries.

## 3.3   INDUSTRIAL WATER POLLUTION

Water pollution require that industries precondition water before its use and treat waste water afterwards. Pre-treatment of the water is required to avoid many problems such as: alkalinity and hardness which cause scaling, particularly in boilers; staining of iron and manganese; and micro-organisms which form coatings in pipes, produce stains, tastes and odor, and decompose organic substances.

Although the pre-treatment problem is important in its own right, we focus primarily on the problems of industrial waste waters. In contrast to the general uniformity of substances found in domestic waste waters, industrial waste waters show remarkable variations in the type of contaminants found in them; some are shown in Table 3.4.

The type of contaminants found depends on the type of industry and the manufacturing processes in question. These contaminants can be classified into three broad categories: floating materials such as oils and greases; suspended matter such as mineral tailings; and dissolved impurities such as acids, alkalis, heavy metals and insecticides.

There is also the problem of thermal pollution, the raising of the temperature of a waterway by heat discharged from the cooling system or effluent

*Table 3.4    Selected examples of industrial water wastes*

| Industry | Process or waste | Result |
|---|---|---|
| Brewery and distillery | Malt and fermented liquors | Organic lead |
| Chemicals | Various | Stable organics, phenols, inks |
| Dairy | Milk-processing, bottling, butter- and cheese-making | Acid |
| Dyeing | Spent dye, sizings, bleach | Color, acid or alkaline |
| Food-processing | Canning and freezing | Organic load |
| Laundry | Washing | Alkaline |
| Leather-tanning | Leather-cleaning and -tanning | Organic load, acid and alkaline |
| Meat-packing | Slaughter, preparation | Organic load |
| Paper | Pulp and paper manufacturing | Organic load, waste wood fibers |
| Steel | Pickling, plating, etc. | Acid |
| Textile manufacture | Wood-scouring, dyeing | Organic load, alkaline |

*Source:*   UNIDO (1990)

wastes of an industrial establishment. Thermal pollution disturbs the ecological balance of a waterway and poses a threat to the aquatic environment. Power stations are responsible for most thermal pollution.

Industry discharges in waste water account for a fairly large share of traditional water pollutants. In addition, contributions to water pollution come from domestic sources, agricultural run-off and many others, such as precipitation of air pollutants, soil pollution caused by the application of fertilizers and pesticides, intensive animal husbandry, land-fill disposals and urban run-off. Moreover, in most countries, industry also discharges into municipal waste-water systems. These factors make it extremely difficult to estimate the industry share of total waste-water generated.

Conventional water pollution is usually determined by the amount of biological oxygen and chemical oxygen demands, total suspended solids, fecal coliform bacteria, the level of acidity, the amount of phosphorus, and the oil and grease content. Industry-level and process-level data on some of these conventional water pollutants are available in some countries. Some of the available data are presented below for illustrative purposes. While almost all industrial activities generate some pollution, a relatively small number of industrial processes are responsible for the bulk of the industrial water, air and solid waste loads generated in a given area. Careful identification of the main heavy-polluting industries can thus help to simplify the pollution assessment, while still presenting most of the polluting loads originating from industry. For example, Table 3.5 reflects the dominance of a small number of industries in industrial waste-water discharges. Chemicals, primary metals, paper, and petroleum and coal accounted for about 85 percent of the total volume of waste waters in the United States manufacturing sector in 1983. It is worth noting that over 55 percent of the total water used in the manufacturing sector was discharged untreated and the percentage of untreated discharged water was much higher for many individual industries. Moreover, according to a United States Environmental Protection Agency survey of toxic chemical release inventories in 1987, five industries accounted for over 90 percent of total industry releases of toxic chemicals to surface water in 1987, estimated at 4,355 billion kg. These top five industries are chemicals (2,648 billion kg), paper products (990 billion kg), petroleum refining (166 billion kg), textile mill products (82.6 billion kg) and primary metals (48.1 billion kg) (see appendix Table A-11). It should be noted that in terms of the measurements of strength and volume usually quoted, wastes of manufacturing establishments are about 2.5 times as great as those of the United States sewage establishments.

The character of the effluents from different industries is remarkably varied, and hence the complexity of the effects of industrial waste and the measures needed to control them also vary greatly. Data on more detailed characteristics of discharged water wastes are needed for a more meaningful assessment of industrial water pollution. Data for India given in Table 3.6 provide detailed information on industrial waste-water discharges. The volume of waste-water and various pollutants per unit of output are given for different processes. The characteristics, volume of wastes and pollutants vary, depending on the nature of the product, raw materials and processes used and the by-products recovered.

A recent case-study of industrial water pollution in the metropolitan area of Alexandria, Egypt (Hamza and Gallup 1982, pp. 56–61), provides useful insights into the nature and magnitude of industrial water-pollution problems in developing countries. The study showed that 57 industries out of about 1,243 industrial plants and production units located in the metropolitan area in 1980 were found to be major sources of water pollution. Waste loads from different industries in the metropolitan area are summarized in Table 3.7, and the average concentration of trace metals appears in Table 3.8. The paper, textile and food industries are the major contributors to the organic load. The concentration of trace metals is extremely high in tannery wastes, which are discharged without treatment into the sea. High levels of some trace metals are also found in paper conversion, foundry, copper and electronic effluents.

One useful approach to the assessment of pollutant loads generated by different industrial processes is to analyze industrial waste-load factors. Waste-load factors are the normalized waste volume, or the waste volume per unit of product or raw materials. The waste-load factors are usually derived from different industrial processes. There is at present no comprehensive compilation of waste-load factors for several industrial processes, although a

Table 3.5  *Water use in manufacturing by year, 1968–83, and by industry group, 1983[a]*

| Industry or year | Reporting establishments[b] | Water (billion liters) | | | | Percentage untreated | ($ million) | |
|---|---|---|---|---|---|---|---|---|
| | | Total | Intake | Recycled | Discharged | | Capital expenditure | Operating cost |
| 1968 | 9,402 | 135,664 | 58,775 | —[d] | 54,249 | 69.5 | — | — |
| 1973 | 10,668 | 164,970 | 57,091 | | 53,747 | 56.5 | 511 | 866 |
| 1978 | 9,605 | 179,326 | 49,370 | 129,956 | 44,392 | 59.7 | 1,249 | 2,119 |
| 1983 | 10,262 | 128,573 | 38,148 | 90,425 | 33,873 | 54.9 | 819 | 3,259 |
| Food and allied products | 2,656 | 6,346 | 2,462 | 2,884 | 2,098 | 64.5 | 105 | 187 |
| Tobacco products | 20 | 129 | 19 | 110 | 15 | —[e] | —[e] | 5 |
| Textile mill products | 761 | 1,265 | 505 | 760 | 441 | 52.6 | —[e] | 25 |
| Lumber and wood products | 223 | 829 | 327 | 502 | 270 | 63.4 | 4 | 23 |
| Furniture and fixtures | 66 | 22 | 11 | 11 | 11 | 100.0 | 2 | 4 |
| Paper and allied products | 600 | 28,257 | 7,216 | 21,041 | 6,718 | 27.1 | 66 | 438 |
| Chemicals and allied products | 1,315 | 36,594 | 12,924 | 23,670 | 11,324 | 67.0 | 187 | 1,013 |
| Petroleum and coal products | 260 | 23,476 | 3,108 | 20,364 | 2,656 | 46.2 | 165 | 543 |

| | | | | | | | | |
|---|---|---|---|---|---|---|---|---|
| Rubber, miscellaneous plastic products | 375 | 1,227 | 289 | 938 | 239 | 63.5 | 4 | 37 |
| Leather and leather products | 69 | 27 | 23 | 4 | 23 | —e | —f | 6 |
| Stone, clay and glass products | 602 | 1,281 | 589 | 692 | 505 | 75.2 | 10 | 38 |
| Primary metal products | 776 | 22,266 | 8,879 | 13,387 | 8,026 | 58.1 | 100 | 421 |
| Fabricated metal products | 724 | 980 | 247 | 733 | 232 | 49.2 | 33 | 100 |
| Non-electrical machinery | 523 | 1,163 | 456 | 707 | 399 | 67.6 | 19 | 76 |
| Electrical and electronic equipment | 678 | 1,273 | 281 | 992 | 266 | 61.4 | 45 | 108 |
| Transport equipment | 380 | 3,845 | 581 | 3,264 | 528 | 67.6 | 55 | 171 |
| Instruments and related products | 154 | 426 | 114 | 312 | 106 | 50.0 | 10 | 45 |
| Miscellaneous manufacturing | 80 | 57 | 15 | 42 | 15 | —e | 2 | 7 |

*Notes*

a. Based on establishments reporting water intake of 76 million liters. This represented 95 percent and 96 percent of the total water use estimated for mining and manufacturing industries. Water intake refers to that which is used or consumed in the production and processing operations and for sanitary services.

b. Establishments reporting water intake of 76 million liters or more. These counts do not apply to water pollutant abatement columns for manufacturing in 1983.

c. Refers to water recirculated and water used.

d. Data estimated; not strictly comparable to other years.

e. Withheld to avoid disclosing individual company data.

f. Figure does not meet publication standards.

*Source:* US Bureau of the Census (1989)

Table 3.6  *Characteristics of waste-waters from different industries in India, 1970*

| Industry | Volume of waste water (gallons) | pH value | Suspended solids | Biological oxygen demand | Chemical oxygen demand | Miscellaneous constituents | Pollutional aspects |
|---|---|---|---|---|---|---|---|
| Pulp and paper (kraft) | 50,000–100,000 per ton of paper | 6.9–9.8 | 600–2,300 | 150–420 | 700–1,000 | Mercaptans | Large volume, high pH and SS, color and toxity |
| Strawboard | 20,000 per ton of board | 7.5–12.9 | 3,000 | 2,000 | 5,000 | — | High pH, SS and BOD |
| Cotton, textiles | 30,000–93,000 per 1,000 yards of cloth | 8.0–11.0 | 30–50 | 200–600 | — | Detergents, chromium (3 mg/1) | Alkalis, BOD, dyes and varying chemical quality |
| Tannery | 340 per 100 lb of processed hide | 9.5 | 3,200 | 7,000 | — | Chromium (15–20mg/1) | High BOD, SS, chromium and color |
| Slaughter-house | — | 6.8 | 2,000 | 600–2,500 | 3,000–6,800 | — | High BOD and SS |
| Milk-bottling | 4–6 per gallon of milk handled | 8.1 | 1,800 | 3,100 | 4,500 | Fat (1,400 mg/1) | High BOD, SS and grease and ready putrescibility |
| Distillery | 600 per 1,000 lb of molasses | 4.3 | 4,000 | 29,000 | 65,000 | High sulphate | High BOD, SS and putrescibility and low pH |

| | | | | | | | |
|---|---|---|---|---|---|---|---|
| Synthetic drugs, alkaline waste | 33,000 per ton | 9.3 | — | 15,300 | 28,500 | Ammonia and several organics | Alkaline, highly toxic organics and ammonia |
| Acid waste | 29,000 per ton | 1.0 | — | 9,400 | 13,700 | Sulphanilic acid (1 percent) | Highly acidic |
| Steel mill, coke ovens | 125–155 per ton of steel | — | — | 630 | — | Grease and oil (1,000 mg/1), $NH_4$-N (460 mg/1), phenols (1,300 mg/1) | Highly toxic phenols, cyanides and ammonia |
| Steel (finished) | 530–650 per ton | — | 310 | 280 | — | Phenols (97.5 mg/1), $NH_4$-N (440 mg/1), cyanide (12 mg/1), CNS (180 mg/1), sulphides | Highly toxic phenols, cyanides and ammonia |
| Refining | 350–400 per ton of oil processed | — | — | 200 | — | Oil (30 mg/1), phenols (30 mg/1) | Mineral oils and phenols |
| Fertilizers, ammonia, urea | 2,000 per ton of $NH_3$; 1,500 per ton of urea | 8.0 | 3,700 | 30 | 330 | $NH_4$-N (510 mg/1); arsenic | Toxic ammonia and arsenic, promotes eutrophication |

*Notes:*   BOD = biological oxygen demand; pH = acidity; SS = suspended solids; 1 gallon = 4.554 liters; 1 lb = 0.45 kg

*Source:*   Mohanrao and Subrahmanyam (1970)

57

*Table 3.7  Estimated waste loads of pollution-contributing industries in Alexandria Metropolitan Area, Egypt, 1982*

| Industry | No. of plants | Discharge | Flow (million liters per day) | Biological oxygen demand | Chemical oxygen demand | Oil and gas | Suspended residues | Volatile residues | Phenols | Aqueous ammonia |
|---|---|---|---|---|---|---|---|---|---|---|
| | | | | | | (kg/day) | | | | |
| Pulp and paper | 2 | Sea | 93.0 | 83,462 | 103,356 | 1,817 | 56,059 | 80,635 | 302.0 | 210.0 |
| Paper conversion | 3 | Lake, sea, drain | 5.0 | 3,679 | 7,379 | 1,996 | 7,543 | 7,454 | 43.0 | 12.5 |
| Textiles | 13 | Lake, sea, drain | 37.0 | 19,895 | 37,877 | 3,114 | 29,949 | 41,312 | 116.0 | 123.0 |
| Dyes | 1 | Sea | 4.0 | 983 | 580 | 48 | 366 | 447 | 3.1 | 2.5 |
| Fertilizers | 1 | Sea | 30.0 | 252 | 1,392 | 276 | 558 | 1,032 | | |
| Steel | 1 | Sewer | 13.0 | 520 | 1,430 | 170 | 585 | 890 | 8.6 | |
| Oil and soap | 8 | Sewer, canal | 32.5 | 30,935 | 61,943 | 9,800 | 44,685 | 51,202 | 6.7 | 4.3 |
| Tyres | 1 | Sewer | 4.3 | 504 | 1,260 | 286 | 940 | 1,092 | 5.4 | 4.3 |
| Refineries | 2 | Sea, lake | 230.0 | 12,615 | 4,875 | 10,740 | 24,370 | 44,770 | 36.6 | 37.5 |
| Chemical (inorganic) | 1 | Sea | 35.0 | 10,850 | 22,035 | 3,215 | 39,050 | 35,600 | 74.1 | 195.0 |
| Tanneries | 6 | Sea | 1.6 | 2,688 | 4,109 | 405 | 13,600 | 11,424 | 43.1 | 24.3 |
| Power | 2 | Canal | 324.0 | 7,662 | 12,022 | 11,248 | 15,606 | 12,987 | 135.0 | 128.0 |
| Match | 2 | Lake | 1.1 | 496 | 862 | 98 | 1,085 | 1,452 | 8.2 | 28.6 |
| Electronics | 1 | Drain | 0.5 | 138 | 269 | 59 | 320 | 356 | | 2.1 |
| Refractories | 1 | Drain | 0.5 | 147 | 297 | 171 | 806 | 716 | | |
| Plastics | 1 | Drain | 2.5 | 788 | 725 | 395 | 713 | 905 | 11.3 | 19.4 |
| Bottling | 2 | Sewer | 1.9 | 484 | 693 | 89 | 256 | 432 | 6.0 | 9.3 |
| Canning | 2 | Drain | 4.0 | 3,000 | 4,264 | 177 | 1,137 | 2,258 | 5.4 | 3.1 |
| Dairy | 1 | Drain | 0.8 | 1,240 | 3,660 | 950 | 2,982 | 6,055 | 2.5 | 3.0 |
| Yeast and starch | 3 | Sewer, lake | 3.2 | 2,440 | 3,360 | 106 | 1,950 | 2,130 | 8.6 | 5.1 |

| | | | | | | | | | |
|---|---|---|---|---|---|---|---|---|---|
| Brewery | 1 | Sewer | 1.2 | 386 | 184 | 41 | 160 | 192 | 1.6 | 0.6 |
| Poultry | 1 | Drain | 0.5 | 429 | 583 | 51 | 681 | 693 | 2.5 | 3.1 |
| Pharmaceuticals | 1 | Sewer | 0.9 | 576 | 936 | 39 | 108 | 475 | 4.5 | 0.7 |

*Source:* Easter (1986)

*Table 3.8 Average analysis of trace metals in selected industrial effluents in Alexandria Metropolitan Area, Egypt, 1980 (mg/l/day)*

| Industry source | Zinc | Copper | Nickel | Chromium | Cadmium | Iron | Manganese | Lead |
|---|---|---|---|---|---|---|---|---|
| Copperworks | 594 | 450 | 388 | —[a] | —[a] | 1,392 | 144 | 209 |
| Canning | 1,800 | 30 | 5 | 20 | 0.5 | 2,200 | 340 | 30 |
| Dairy | 1,144 | 185 | 234 | 210 | 0.5 | 3,275 | 355 | 255 |
| Tyres | 6,285 | 400 | —[a] | 150 | 0.5 | 2,550 | 205 | 45 |
| Textiles | 101 | 107 | 198 | —[a] | 2 | 320 | 119 | 102 |
| Paper conversion | 11.3[b] | 220 | 20 | 360 | 3 | 4,050 | 480 | 410 |
| Electronics | 6,250 | 70 | —[a] | 50 | 8 | 1,525 | 373 | 255 |
| Oil and soap | 5,550 | 95 | 60 | 30 | 0.5 | 3,625 | 445 | 285 |
| Tanneries | 2,133 | 603 | 545 | 127[b] | 715 | 14[b] | 979 | 1,238 |
| Chemicals (inorganic) | 381 | 355 | 475 | —[a] | 29 | 1,776 | 216 | 527 |
| Foundry | 8,400 | 290 | 30 | 460 | 3 | 21,800 | 630 | 260 |

*Notes*
a. Not detected.
b. Concentrations in milligrams per liter.

*Source:* As for Table 3.7

limited list can be found, and its results are applicable to several developing countries and yield a reasonable initial assessment of industrial waste-water loads (Economopoulos 1982). These factors are still preliminary, however, and as more data and factor survey results become available they should be periodically reviewed and adjusted and the coverage of the list expanded.

## 3.4   INDUSTRIAL SOLID WASTES

Solid waste generation is largely determined by the patterns of consumption and production in the economy. Municipal waste and industrial waste are particularly important, but a considerable amount of waste also results from air and water pollution abatement. As before, we will only review the nature and sources of industrial solid waste, but not the problems of waste management such as the transport and disposal of industrial solid waste. Furthermore, hazardous industrial waste will be treated separately in the following section, because of its crucial importance to the environment and human health.

It must be noted at the outset that the problem of solid waste is closely interrelated with that of air and water pollution. For instance, an open dump can contribute to air, water and land pollution. Likewise, solid wastes dumped into the sea can pollute the marine environment. Moreover, waste generated by air and water pollution abatement can create a solid waste disposal problem.

The generation of industrial solid waste is also significantly influenced by the rising prices of raw materials and of energy on world markets in recent years. Particularly, higher prices of energy and raw materials coupled with higher waste-disposal costs have prompted the development of low-waste and clean technologies in developed countries which reduce and recycle industrial waste within a production cycle. The environmental and economic implications of low-waste and clean technologies will be examined in greater detail later.

Table 3.9 shows total amounts of waste generated by different sources in different OECD countries. Although a cross-country comparison of waste generation using this table may not be entirely correct because of the different definitions used by the various member countries for each category of waste, the table nevertheless makes it possible to gauge the relative quantitative importance of industrial wastes compared with that from other sources. For instance, solid waste production in the United States in 1985 was almost 4 billion tons per year, and agriculture and mining accounted for the bulk of this total, about 38 percent and 35 percent, respectively. The industry share of total waste production was less, at about 17 percent. Likewise, in France agricultural waste claimed a lion's share of about 70 percent of total waste generation, equaling 600 million tons in 1985, followed by 17 percent by the mining sector, compared with an industry share of about 9 percent. In contrast, agriculture and mining generated only 17 and 5 percent, respectively, of slightly over 0.5 billion tons of the total wastes generated in 1985 in Japan, while agriculture and mining are more important in the United States and France.

Agricultural wastes are principally organic, such as crop wastes, and a large part is either ploughed back into the soil or composted. On the other hand, municipal and industrial wastes are relatively heterogeneous in nature, consisting of both organic and inorganic materials, and pose special problems of disposal with varying degrees of toxicity and hazardous contents. In general, industry generates a far large quantity of waste than municipal sources, for instance 3.8 times more in Canada, 3.5 times in the United States, 3.3 times in France and 7.5 times in Japan. In all cases, industrial waste generation is much greater than municipal sources, even considering significant inter-country variations.

Appendix Table A-9 provides information on selected groups of industrial wastes generated in OECD countries. Data do not represent all industrial wastes nor their potential toxicity, but reveal the relative importance of different types in different countries, such as waste oil, concentrated acids, and waste from metal finishing and plastics and rubber.

Data on solid wastes generated by various industries is very scarce, and average data, even if available, tend to be less useful because of wide variations in process technologies, production efficiencies and waste recycling among different industries. However, the types of wastes that are expected to be generated by various industries are known, and they have been identified in appendix Table A-10.

## 3.5   HAZARDOUS INDUSTRIAL WASTES

The question of what constitutes hazardous waste is highly contentious from both conceptual and practical viewpoints. Some rough estimates of the contribution of hazardous wastes in selected countries is given in Table 3.10. Tremendous differences exist between countries in both the methods used for defining wastes and the type of wastes included, owing to variations in the legal, institutional, and environmental conditions in different countries. Thus, what is considered hazardous in one country may not be so in another. This makes it extremely difficult to make an international comparison of hazardous waste generation. Different countries, including Belgium, Denmark, France, former Federal Republic of Germany, Netherlands, Sweden, United Kingdom and United States, have developed their own comprehensive list of hazardous wastes for regulatory purposes. The merits and demerits of the listing

Table 3.9 *Amounts of waste generated by source in selected countries, 1980–94 (billion tons)*

| Country | Year | Municipal | Industrial | Energy production | Agriculture | Mining | Demolition wastes | Dredge spoils | Sewage sludge | Other |
|---|---|---|---|---|---|---|---|---|---|---|
| Austria | 1983 | 1,727 | 13,258 | 707 | | 466 | 390 | 2,100 | 1,350 | |
| | 1990 | 4,783 | 31,801 | 1,150 | 880 | 21 | 18,309 | 111 | 365 | |
| Australia | 1980 | 10,000 | 20,000 | 2,760 | | | | | | |
| | 1990 | | | | | | | | | |
| Belgium | 1980 | 3,082 | 8,000 | | 53,000 | 7,069 | | | 18 | |
| | 1990 | 3,410 | 27,000 | 1,069 | | | 680 | 4,805 | 687 | 2,830 |
| Canada | 1985 | 16,000 | 61,000 | 12,400 | 48,000 | 910,213 | 1,540 | 26,000 | 500 | 38,500 |
| | 1990 | 16,000 | | 12,400 | 14,000 | 1,052,990 | 9,000 | 7,540 | 500 | |
| Denmark | 1985 | 2,161 | 1,317 | 1,173 | | | 1,200 | | 82 | |
| | 1990 | 2,430 | 2,304 | 1,532 | | | 1,747 | | 1,263 | |
| Finland | 1985 | 2,000 | 15,000 | 700 | 41,000 | 17,700 | 2,000 | 1,500 | 137 | |
| | 1990 | 3,100 | 10,160 | 950 | 23,000 | 21,650 | 7,000 | 3,000 | 1,000 | 150 |
| France | 1985 | 15,000 | 50,000 | | 399,400 | 100,000 | | | 600 | 2,800 |
| | 1990 | 20,320 | 50,000 | | 400,000 | 100,000 | | | 600 | 9,800 |
| Germany, Federal Republic of | 1984 | 19,387 | 55,932 | 10,605 | | 3,454 | 12,428 | | 1,591 | |
| | 1990 | 21,172 | 68,829 | 12,677 | | 15,230 | 120,394 | | 1,750 | |
| Greece | 1985 | 2,500 | 3,904 | 1,280 | | 3,900 | | | | |
| | 1990 | 3,000 | 4,304 | 7,680 | 90 | 3,900 | | | | |
| Ireland | 1984 | 1,100 | 1,580 | 130 | 22,000 | 1,930 | 240 | | 570 | 860 |
| | 1990 | 1,100 | 1,580 | 130 | 22,000 | 1,930 | 240 | | 570 | 860 |

| Country | Year | | | | | | | | | |
|---|---|---|---|---|---|---|---|---|---|---|
| Italy | 1984 | 15,000 | 35,000 | | | | | | | |
| | 1991 | 20,033 | 34,710 | | 29,830 | 57,000 | | 34,374 | 3,428 | |
| Japan | 1985 | 41,530 | 312,000 | 7,595 | 90,544 | 26,017 | 48,948 | | 2,003 | |
| | 1985 | 50,441 | 132,304 | 27,748 | 62,690 | 26,017 | 57,886 | | 2,001 | 63,492 |
| Luxembourg | 1985 | 131 | 135 | | | | | | 11 | |
| | 1990 | 170 | 1,300 | | | | | 5,240 | 15 | |
| Netherlands | 1985 | 6,510 | 3,942 | 876 | 40,000 | 99 | 7,700 | | 250 | |
| | 1990 | 7,430 | 7,665 | 1,553 | 19,210 | 391 | 12,390 | 17,500 | 320 | 544 |
| New Zealand | 1982 | 2,106 | 300 | | | | | | 45 | 594 |
| | 1990 | | | | | | | | | |
| Norway | 1985 | | 2,186 | 260 | 18,547 | 9,000 | | | 70 | |
| | 1990 | 2,000 | 2,000 | | 18,000 | 9,000 | 2,000 | | 100 | |
| Portugal | 1985 | 2,246 | 11,200 | | | 3,900 | | | | |
| | 1990 | 2,538 | 662 | 165 | | 202 | | | | 15 |
| Spain | 1986 | 10,568 | 5,108 | | 45,000 | 180,000 | | | 10,000 | |
| | 1990 | 12,546 | 13,800 | | 112,102 | 70,000 | 22,000 | | 10,000 | |
| Switzerland | 1985 | 2,500 | | | | | 3,000 | | 372 | |
| | 1990 | 3,000 | 1,000 | | | | 2,000 | | 260 | |
| Sweden | 1985 | 2,630 | 2,630 | 4,000 | 550 | 17,000 | 1,200 | | 255 | |
| | 1990 | 3,200 | 13,000 | 625 | 21,000 | 28,000 | 3,000 | | 220 | 3,850 |
| United Kingdom | 1984 | 16,668 | 16,668 | 50,000 | 12,000 | 250,000 | | | | |
| | 1990 | 20,000 | 56,000 | 13,000 | 80,000 | 107,000 | 32,000 | 21,000 | 1,000 | |
| United States | 1985 | 178,000 | 178,000 | 628,000 | 72,000 | 1,400,000 | 97,960 | | 8,400 | |
| | 1990 | 177,500 | 7,080,000 | 1,093,039 | 165,821 | 1,541,850 | 34,692 | | 11,454 | 15,400 |

*Source:* OECD (1993)

63

*Table 3.10  Total waste generation in selected countries, 1975–90*

| Country or area | Average annual municipal waste generation | | | | | | Year of estimate | Industrial waste generation | | | Year of estimate | Hazardous and special waste generation | |
|---|---|---|---|---|---|---|---|---|---|---|---|---|---|
| | Total | | | | Per capita (kg) | Per unit area (tons/ km²/yr) | | Total ('000 tons/yr) | Per million dollars industrial GDP | Per unit area (tons/ km²/yr) | | Total ('000 tons/yr) | Per unit area (tons/ km²/yr) |
| | 1975 | 1980 | 1985 | 1990 | | | | | | | | | |
| *America* | | | | | | | | | | | | | |
| Canada | | 12,600 | | 16,000 | 642 | 1.7 | 1980 | 61,000 | 730 | 6.6 | 1990 | 6,080 | 0.4 |
| Costa Rica | | | | 534 | 211 | 10.5 | 1986 | 192 | 3 | 0.1 | | | |
| Mexico | 140,000 | 160,000 | | 177,500 | 744 | 19.4 | 1990 | 7,080,000 | 501 | 66.9 | 1989 | 180,000 | 27.3 |
| *Asia* | | | | | | | | | | | | | |
| Cyprus | | | | | | | 1985 | 132,304 | | | | | |
| Israel | | | 1,400 | | 330 | 65.1 | | | | | 1985 | 30 | 1.4 |
| Japan | 38,074 | 41,511 | | 50,441 | 342 | 110.8 | 1983 | 220,548 | 494 | 594.5 | 1983 | 768 | 2.1 |
| Korea, Republic of | | | 15,746 | | 679 | 160.7 | 1981 | 7,030 | 274 | 71.7 | | | |
| *Europe* | | | | | | | | | | | | | |
| Austria | 1,407 | 1,560 | | 4,783 | 216 | 19.4 | 1990 | 31,801 | 197 | 60.8 | 1990 | 616 | 1.2 |
| Belgium | 2,900 | 3,082 | | 3,410 | | 205.2 | 1988 | 27,000 | 196 | 242.4 | 1980 | 915 | 27.7 |
| Bulgaria | | | 6,773 | | 757 | 0.6 | | | | | | | |
| Czechoslovakia | | | | 2,600 | | | 1987 | 39,604 | | 647.3 | 1987 | 8,317 | |

| Country | | | | | | | | | | |
|---|---|---|---|---|---|---|---|---|---|---|
| Denmark | 2,046 | 2,430 | 399 | 48.7 | 1985 | 2,304 | 804 | 19.4 | 1990 | 106 | 2.1 |
| Finland | | 3,100 | 247 | 3.9 | 1990 | 10,160 | 137 | 45.9 | 1987 | 314 | 0.4 |
| France | 1,400 | 20,320 | 260 | 25.6 | 1990 | 50,000 | 172 | 59.0 | 1990 | 3,958 | 3.7 |
| Germany, Republic of | 20,423 21,417 27,544 | 21,172 | 447 | 112.9 | 1990 | 81,906 | | 215.0 | 1990 | 6,000 | 20.1 |
| Greece | 7,000 | 3,000 | 259 | 19.1 | 1990 | 4,304 | | | 1990 | 450 | |
| Hungary | | 4,900 | 658 | 76.1 | 1989 | 45,000 | 2,509 | 229.8 | 1989 | 4,000 | 77.0 |
| Iceland | 93 | 80 | 388 | 0.9 | 1990 | 135 | | 1.1 | 1989 | 5 | |
| Ireland | 1,270 | 1,100 | 359 | 15.9 | 1984 | 1,580 | 346 | 22.9 | 1990 | 3,246 | 0.3 |
| Italy | | 20,033 | 249 | 47.8 | 1991 | 34,710 | 207 | 119.0 | 1980 | 2,000 | 6.8 |
| Luxembourg | 190 | 170 | 514 | 76.0 | 1990 | 1,300 | | 38.0 | 1990 | 1,040 | 6.0 |
| Netherlands | 7,242 | 7,430 | 500 | 21.3 | 1990 | 7,665 | 97 | 121.7 | 1990 | 200 | 8.2 |
| Norway | 1,700 | 2,000 | 280 | 7.1 | 1990 | 2,000 | 93 | 7.1 | 1990 | 64 | 0.4 |
| Poland | 7,900 | 12,806 | 212 | 25.9 | 1990 | 58,732 | 1,110 | 901.3 | 1987 | 1,043 | 11.4 |
| Portugal | 2,246 | 2,538 | 233 | 24.4 | 1990 | 662 | | 121.7 | 1987 | 1,708 | |
| Spain | 10,600 | 12,546 | 275 | 21.2 | 1990 | 13,800 | 102 | 3.0 | 1985 | 500 | |
| Sweden | | 3,200 | 301 | 6.1 | 1990 | 3,200 | | 9.7 | 1990 | 520 | 1.3 |
| Switzerland | | 3,000 | 336 | 53.7 | 1990 | 1,000 | | | 1990 | 2,540 | 2.5 |
| United Kingdom | | 20,000 | 291 | 67.8 | 1990 | 56,000 | 327 | 206.6 | 1989 | | 6.2 |
| USSR | | | | | | | | 13.8 | | | |
| *Oceania* | | | | | | | | | | | |
| Australia | 1,160 | | 681 | 1.3 | 1980 | | | 2.6 | 1980 | | |
| New Zealand | | | 653 | 4.3 | 1990 | | 38 | 1.1 | 1990 | 110 | 0.2 |

*Source:* OECD (1993)

approach have been discussed extensively in a World Health Organization report (WHO 1982). Furthermore, international organizations such as OECD and CEC are attempting to develop a cross-reference list of hazardous wastes as a first step toward harmonization of waste definitions.[1]

According to the present interpretation, hazardous industrial wastes can be categorized according to the nature and degrees of risk, such as toxicity, flammability, explosivity, infectivity and corrosivity. An illustrative example of the classification of hazardous wastes by the nature of risks is given in Table 3.11. National data on hazardous wastes are scarce and incomplete. Even if available, they are not comparable because of variations in the definitions and classification schemes of hazardous wastes adopted by different countries. Table 3.12 provides incomplete information on hazardous and special wastes (excluding nuclear waste) along with chemical and non-chemical wastes in OECD countries in the mid-1980s. Bearing in mind the severe limitations of making international comparisons, it is estimated that OECD countries generate about 300 million tons of hazardous wastes, including 265 million tons reported by the United States, around 1 million tons from Pacific OECD countries, and 20–24 million tons from European OECD countries. About 88 percent of these hazardous wastes are generated in the United States. France, the former Federal Republic of Germany, Italy and the United Kingdom are the main generating countries in Europe. Data from non-OECD countries, especially developing countries, are not available. Some sources of those wastes are given in Table 3.13. In Hungary, 3.5 million tons of hazardous wastes are generated annually (Kosponti 1986). Serious hazardous waste problems are likely to exist in some developing countries such as Brazil, China, India, and the Republic of Korea, given the industrial structure of those countries.

By far the largest portion of the total hazardous wastes generated tends to be produced by industrial production, with some minor exceptions. For instance, in the United States over 85 percent of hazardous waste is accounted for by the manufacturing sector (Piaseck and Gravander 1985, p. 43). On the

*Table 3.11     Category and source of hazardous wastes*

| Category | Source |
| --- | --- |
| Toxic chemicals | Chemical industry, heavy industries, coal-based thermal power plants, pharmaceuticals, pesticides, plastic and polymers |
| Flammable | Oil sludges, solvents, plasticizers, light metal discards |
| Explosives | Ordnance factories, oil tankers, safety matches, pyrotechnics |
| Corrosives | Acid slurries |
| Infective, biologicals | Hospital wastes, wastes from vaccine and serum institutes, fermentation industries, biotechnology |

*Source:*   OECD (1989)

*Table 3.12*   *Industrial waste and hazardous and special wastes in selected countries, 1980–87 ('000 tons)*

| Country | Year | Chemical waste | Non-chemical waste | Total | Hazardous and special wastes[a] |
|---|---|---|---|---|---|
| Austria | 1983 | 525 | 12,733[b] | 13,258 | 200 |
| Australia | 1980 | — | — | 20,000[c] | 300 |
| Belgium | 1980 | — | — | 8,000 | 915 |
| Canada | 1980 | — | — | 61,000 | 3,290[d] |
| Denmark | 1985 | 78[e] | — | 1,317 | 125 |
| Finland | 1985 | — | — | 15,000 | 124 |
| France | 1985 | — | — | 50,000 | 2,000[f] |
| Germany, Fed. Rep. of | 1984 | 10,419 | 45,513 | 55,932 | 5,000[g] |
| Greece | 1985 | — | — | 3,904 | — |
| Ireland | 1984 | — | — | 1,580 | 20 |
| Italy | 1985 | — | — | 35,000[c] | 1,000–3,000 |
| Japan | 1985 | — | — | 312,000 | 666[h] |
| Luxembourg | 1985 | — | — | 135 | 4 |
| Netherlands[i] | 1986 | — | 3,942 | — | 1,500[i] |
| New Zealand | 1982 | — | 300 | — | 30–60 |
| Norway | 1980 | 2,186 | — | — | 120 |
| Portugal | 1980 | — | — | 11,200 | 1,049[h] |
| Sweden | 1980 | 500 | 3,500 | 4,000 | 500 |
| Switzerland | 1987 | — | — | — | 120[j] |
| Spain | 1986 | — | — | 5,108 | 1,708[k] |
| United Kingdom | 1984 | — | — | 50,000 | 3,900[h,l] |
| United States | 1985 | 93,000[e] | — | 628,000 | 265,000 |

*Notes*
a. Special wastes that are considered hazardous.
b. Organization for Economic Co-operation and Development Secretariat estimates based on national definitions.
c. Organization for Economic Co-operation and Development Secretariat estimate.
d. Wet weight.
e. Hazardous chemical wastes only.
f. Amount of toxic or hazardous waste. The total amount of special waste is 18 million tons.
g. 1985.
h. 1986.
i. Data refer to enterprises of more than 10 employees, office and canteen wastes included.
j. Excluding ship cleaning residuals.
k. 1987.
l. England and Wales only; year ending 31 March 1987; excluding mine and quarry waste.

*Source:* OECD (1989)

*Table 3.13    Selected hazardous wastes in developing countries*

| Waste | Source |
|-------|--------|
| Cyanide wastes | Electroplating, metal processing, chemicals |
| Metal-finishing wastes | Cutting oils, acid slurry |
| Solvents | Vegetable oil recovery, chemical industry |
| Mercury wastes | Chloralkali plants |
| Fluoride | Bauxite, fertilizers |
| Arsenic | Fertilizers, wood-processing |
| Pesticides | Manufacture and formulation, outdated disposal |
| Plastics, monomers | Plastics |
| Phenols | Iron and steel, petrochemicals |
| Asbestos | Asbestos cement, insulation industry, building industry |

*Source:*   OECD (1989)

other hand, in Hungary, the mineral industry is responsible for 66 percent of the hazardous waste, with the chemical industry accounting for only 17 percent (Kosponti 1986). Recent United States data show that among United States industries, chemical and allied products accounted for almost 50 percent of the total industry hazardous waste of 266 million tons generated in 1983 (Egger 1989, p.66). Trailing far behind the chemical industry are primary metals (18 percent), petroleum and coal products (11.8 percent), fabricated metal products (9.6 percent), and rubber and plastic products (5.5 percent).

At more disaggregated industrial classification levels, industrial organic chemicals tend to be the highest-volume generator of hazardous wastes in the United States, according to a survey (EPA 1989), as shown in Table 3.14. In fact, the top ten industries generating hazardous waste in the United States in 1987 are dominated by various chemicals.

Needless to say, the type and volume of hazardous waste generated depends on the composition and size of an industry. A case in point is the electronics industry in Malaysia, one of the most important industries with an MVA share of nearly 15 percent. According to a 1983–84 hazardous waste survey by the Department of Environment of Malaysia, 52 percent of toxic and hazardous waste generation is accounted for by the electronics industry, 14 percent by the metals and electroplating industries, and the rest by the chemical, rubber, plastic, printing, packaging, tannery and pharmaceutical industries (Uriarte 1989).

*Table 3.14*    *Top ten industries producing hazardous waste in the*
*United States, 1995*

| US SIC | SIC category | Total release of hazardous waste ('000 tons) |
|---|---|---|
| 28 | Chemicals and allied products | 356.90 |
| 33 | Primary metal industries | 150.20 |
| 26 | Paper and allied products | 105.70 |
| 30 | Rubber and miscellaneous plastic products | 50.80 |
| 37 | Transport equipment | 49.90 |
| 20 | Food products | 39.10 |
| 34 | Fabricated metal products | 37.20 |
| 28 | Petroleum and coal products | 26.80 |
| 25 | Furniture and fixture | 18.20 |
| 32 | Stone, clay and glass products | 16.40 |

*Source:*   EPA (1996)

## 3.6   TOXIC CHEMICALS

Chemicals have become such an indispensable part of modern life that almost all products contain them, or are processed with or packaged by means of them. More than seven million chemicals are now known and several thousand new ones have recently been added to this long list. At present, about 80,000 chemicals are known to be used in the manufacture of a wide range of products to satisfy the ever-expanding range of consumer products. Over $1,000 billion worth of chemical products are today produced and sold all over the world. The United States and Europe each produce over $200 billion worth of chemical products (UNIDO 1990, p.185). Each one of these chemicals used in manufacturing processes is potentially hazardous if wrongly applied or if released in large quantities by design or accident. They also tend to remain in some form as polluting agents long after their original job is done. Moreover, not only has the number of chemicals been expanding rapidly over the last 20 years, but also the volumes produced have seen phenomenal growth. Global production of organic chemicals, for example, made quantum jumps from about 1 million tons a year in the 1930s to 7 million in 1950, 63 million in 1970 and about 250 million in 1985 (UNEP 1989).

Because of the overwhelming importance of chemical pollutants in terms of the quantities generated and the potential health risks and threats to the environment, chemical industry pollution in general and toxic chemicals wastes in particular would seem to warrant separate treatment. As in the case of hazardous wastes in the foregoing analysis, it is difficult to estimate exactly how

*Figure 3.1    Total TRI releases and transfers in the United States, 1987*

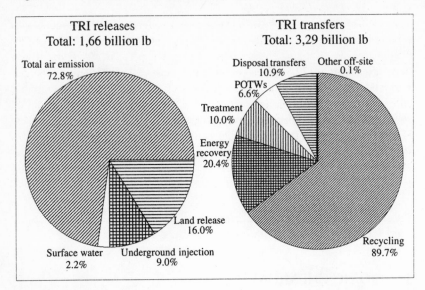

TRI releases
Total: 1,66 billion lb

Total air emission
72.8%

Land release
16.0%

Surface water
2.2%

Underground injection
9.0%

TRI transfers
Total: 3,29 billion lb

Disposal transfers
10.9%

Other off-site
0.1%

POTWs
6.6%

Treatment
10.0%

Energy
recovery
20.4%

Recycling
89.7%

*Source:*   EPA (1989)

much hazardous chemical waste is produced every year partly because of problems of defining the term 'hazardous,' as discussed earlier. Recent United States data will be largely relied on below to identify the types and industrial sources of major chemical pollutants and toxic chemicals and to quantify them, since United States data on chemical pollution appear to be by far more comprehensive and complete than any other country data available. Normally, toxic chemicals discharged from a manufacturing or processing operation consist primarily of two categories of toxic substances, namely heavy metals and organic compounds. The sources of these toxic chemicals are found in many varied manufacturing industries as well as in the chemical industry.

Now we present a more detailed review of sources and quantities of a wide range of important potentially toxic chemicals from various industries based on the 1987 United States survey data. In 1987, the United States Environmental Protection Agency (EPA) initiated the Toxics Release Inventory (TRI) program under which manufacturing establishments reported to the EPA information on more than 300 chemicals used or released to the environment. According to the first TRI survey, manufacturing establishments reported the release of 18.0 billion lb of 328 TRI chemicals into the air, water, land or underground wells, in addition to 4.6 billion lb of TRI chemicals transferred off-site to other facilities, such as public sewage systems or incinerators for treatment or disposal. The most important 328 TRI chemicals along with their industry emission sources and quantities are given in more detail in appendix Table A-11.

A total of 4.95 billion lb in releases and transfers of TRI chemicals was reported in 1995. Figure 3.1 shows that 2.2 percent of the total releases of TRI chemicals was discharged into surface water, 9.0 percent was injected into underground wells, 72.8 percent emitted into air, and 16.0 percent discharged into land. Now turning to industrial patterns of chemical releases, Figure 3.2 shows that the chemical industry tops the list by producing about 855.8 million lb, followed by primary metals (359.8 million lb) and paper products (153.4 million lb). The rest include petroleum and coal (65.1 million lb), textiles (19.3 million lb), transport equipment (33.1 million lb), rubber and plastics (121.9 million lb), electrical machinery (25.2 million lb) and food products (93.4 million lb) (see Figure 3.2).

*Figure 3.2   Amount of all categories of chemical releases and transfers by type of industry in the United States, 1987*

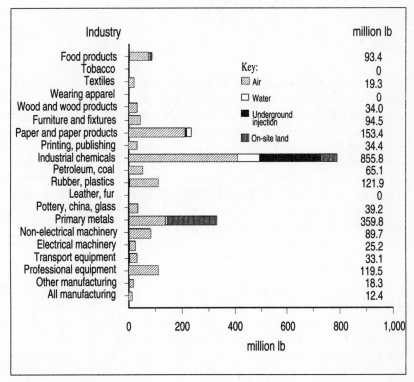

*Source:*   As for Figure 3.1

Table 3.15  Chemical pollution coefficient by industry in the United States, 1987–92

| ISIC code | US SIC | Industry | Year | Total release discharge ('000 lb) | $ million | | | Manufacturing value added coefficient (lb/$1000) | Manufacturing value added coefficient rank | Gross output coefficient (lb/$1000) | Gross output coefficient rank |
|---|---|---|---|---|---|---|---|---|---|---|---|
| | | | | | Manufacturing value added | Cost of materials | Gross output | | | | |
| 311/2/3 | 20 | Food products | 1987 | 287,012 | 121,608.7 | 208,754.4 | 329,725.4 | 2.35 | 13 | 0.87 | 14 |
| | | | 1992 | | 156,843.4 | 247,202.7 | 403,836.0 | | | | |
| 314 | 21 | Tobacco products | 1987 | 10,462 | 14,263.6 | 6,490.6 | 20,757.0 | 0.73 | 18 | 0.50 | 17 |
| | | | 1992 | | 27,167.1 | 7,993.8 | 35,136.7 | | | | |
| 321 | 22 | Textiles | 1987 | 349,911 | 25,660.0 | 37,565.3 | 62,786.5 | 13.45 | 5 | 5.47 | 6 |
| | | | 1992 | | 29,862.1 | 41,048.9 | 70,694.2 | | | | |
| 322 | 23 | Wearing apparel | 1987 | 4,770 | 9,879.2 | 32,515.5 | 32,005.4 | 0.14 | 20 | 0.07 | 20 |
| | | | 1992 | | 10,801.7 | 36,357.0 | 35,605.8 | | | | |
| 331 | 24 | Wood and wood products | 1987 | 35,961 | 28,664.4 | 41,259.1 | 69,746.5 | 1.26 | 15 | 0.52 | 16 |
| | | | 1992 | | 33,352.4 | 48,637.3 | 81,797.6 | | | | |
| 332 | 25 | Furniture and fixtures | 1987 | 59,715 | 20,310.3 | 17,324.0 | 37,461.9 | 2.95 | 11 | 1.60 | 11 |
| | | | 1992 | | 22,820.8 | 20,915.5 | 43,688.4 | | | | |
| 341 | 26 | Paper and paper products | 1987 | 2,807,409 | 50,488.8 | 58,753.1 | 108,989.0 | 56.46 | 2 | 25.87 | 2 |
| | | | 1992 | | 59,922.7 | 73,181.5 | 132,954.4 | | | | |
| 342 | 27 | Printing and publishing | 1987 | 62,936 | 90,162.3 | 46,372.1 | 136,195.6 | 0.71 | 19 | 0.47 | 18 |
| | | | 1992 | | 113,244.3 | 53,965.3 | 167,284.1 | | | | |
| 351 | 28 | Industrial chemical | 1987 | 12,088,830 | 120,777.5 | 109,230.9 | 229,546.0 | 99.71 | 1 | 52.42 | 1 |
| | | | 1992 | | 165,134.8 | 141,509.8 | 305,761.0 | | | | |

| | | | | | | | | | | | |
|---|---|---|---|---|---|---|---|---|---|---|---|
| 353/4 | 29 | Petroleum refining | 1987 | 762,361 | 18,518.4 | 112,776.7 | 130,414.0 | 41.43 | 4 | 5.79 | 5 |
| | | | 1992 | | 23,797.2 | 125,890.8 | 149,960.8 | | | | |
| 355/6 | 30 | Rubber and plastic products | 1987 | 277,097 | 44,418.0 | 42,504.5 | 86,603.2 | 6.26 | 7 | 3.20 | 7 |
| | | | 1992 | | 58,477.0 | 55,256.1 | 113,543.9 | | | | |
| 323 | 31 | Leather and fur products | 1987 | 52,087 | 4,377.9 | 4,754.9 | 9,082.4 | 12.18 | 6 | 5.82 | 4 |
| | | | 1992 | | 4,516.7 | 5,206.8 | 9,676.5 | | | | |
| 361/2 | 32 | Pottery, china and earthenware | 1987 | 116,987 | 33,375.1 | 28,147.6 | 61,479.6 | 3.54 | 9 | 1.92 | 9 |
| | | | 1992 | | 34,557.8 | 27,977.0 | 62,479.1 | | | | |
| 371/2 | 33 | Primary metals (iron and steel) | 1987 | 2,593,238 | 46,120.9 | 74,692.2 | 120,248.3 | 55.80 | 3 | 21.48 | 3 |
| | | | 1992 | | 51,816.4 | 85,903.8 | 138,333.2 | | | | |
| 381 | 34 | Fabricated metal products | 1987 | 306,289 | 74,957.9 | 72,668.6 | 147,366.1 | 4.06 | 8 | 2.06 | 8 |
| | | | 1992 | | 83,870.8 | 82,991.9 | 167,015.0 | | | | |
| 382 | 35 | Non-electrical machinery (industrial machinery) | 1987 | 99,091 | 118,187.7 | 99,569.5 | 217,669.5 | 0.83 | 11 | 0.45 | 19 |
| | | | 1992 | | 132,143.6 | 125,119.6 | 258,273.1 | | | | |
| 383 | 36 | Electrical machinery | 1987 | 297,117 | 95,815.3 | 76,194.7 | 171,286.2 | 3.10 | 10 | 1.72 | 10 |
| | | | 1992 | | 121,949.6 | 95,589.9 | 217,905.7 | | | | |
| 384 | 37 | Transport equipment | 1987 | 332,397 | 137,076.4 | 198,854.1 | 332,935.3 | 2.45 | 12 | 0.99 | 13 |
| | | | 1992 | | 161,058.4 | 234,776.7 | 401,213.9 | | | | |
| 385 | 38 | Professional and scientific equipment | 1987 | 81,141 | 70,974.5 | 37,211.5 | 107,324.9 | 1.14 | 16 | 0.75 | 15 |
| | | | 1992 | | 89,805.8 | 4,787.3 | 135,479.2 | | | | |
| 390 | 39 | Other manufacturing industries | 1987 | 36,324 | 17,409.3 | 14,621.3 | 31,925.9 | 2.08 | 14 | 1.13 | 12 |
| | | | 1992 | | 22,009.7 | 17,728.5 | 39,625.6 | | | | |
| | | Total | 1987 | 22,519,044 | 1,165,682.7 | 1,319,750.9 | 2,475,786.6 | 19.30 | | 9.05 | |
| | | | 1992 | | 1,428,707.4 | 1,571,289.2 | 3,006,275.2 | | | | |

*Source:* US Bureau of the Census (1994)

The environmental burden of the chemical industry in the United States is further underscored by the fact that the chemical industry accounted for 48 percent of total chemical discharges into surface water, 24 percent by underground injection and 41 percent to public sewage treatment plants. The chemical industry also heads the list for toxic chemical emissions, even when these are measured against the industry's output. Whether measured in terms of emissions per $1,000 of MVA or gross output, the chemical pollution coefficient for industrial chemicals is almost twice as large as the second-highest coefficient for paper products (see Table 3.15). Little change in ranking can be noted between the MVA coefficients and the gross output coefficients. It is also worth noting that there is a close rank correlation between total emissions and unit output coefficients in most industries producing basic industrial materials, but a weaker correlation in capital goods industries. For instance, industrial chemicals, paper products and primary metals ranked among the top, both in terms of total emissions and of unit output measurement. By contrast, transport equipment and electrical machinery ranked seventh and ninth, respectively, in total chemical emissions, but twelfth and tenth in terms of emissions per $1,000 of MVA.

Regarding specific chemicals, the TRI system requires the reporting of 308 individual chemicals and 20 chemical categories. The chemicals cover a gamut of toxicity, ranging from the acutely lethal to the mildly toxic, which may be subject to removal from the TRI list as part of the ongoing review process of the Environmental Protection Agency. It should be cautioned, therefore, that the large reported releases of chemicals of relatively low toxicity may be less environmentally damaging than the smaller quantity of highly toxic chemicals. TRI chemicals cover a wide range including well-known chemicals such as ammonia, benzene and copper, as well asobscure ones such as t-dimentylamino-axobenzene. TRI chemicals are produced not only as products, but are also used as raw materials for other products such as solvents, disinfectants, dyes and catalysts. Although more than 300 chemicals are included in the TRI list, the top 20 chemicals account for about 94 percent of total 1987 releases and transfers (see Figure 3.3). It was noted earlier that sodium sulphate alone represented 54 percent of all TRI releases and transfers in 1987. It is not surprising to find that, apart from emitting the greatest amount of total chemicals among industry groups, the industrial chemicals group generates also the greatest variety of chemicals. Other industry groups which discharge a relatively large number of different chemicals are iron and steel, non-ferrous metals, paper products, other chemical products, wood products, electrical machinery and transport equipment. By contrast, some light industry groups, namely food products, beverages, tobacco, leather products and footwear, seem to generate a far narrower range of chemicals than other industry groups. The table may serve as a rough checklist of the types of

*Figure 3.3    Top 20 chemicals with the largest releases and transfers in the United States, 1987*

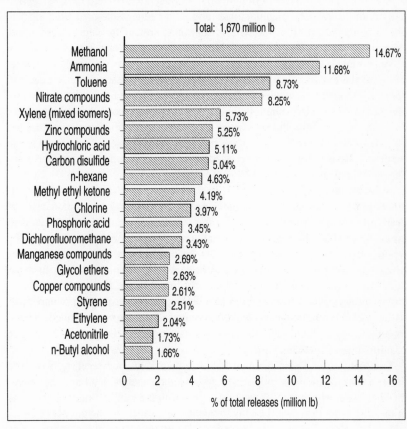

Total: 1,670 million lb

| Chemical | % of total releases |
|---|---|
| Methanol | 14.67% |
| Ammonia | 11.68% |
| Toluene | 8.73% |
| Nitrate compounds | 8.25% |
| Xylene (mixed isomers) | 5.73% |
| Zinc compounds | 5.25% |
| Hydrochloric acid | 5.11% |
| Carbon disulfide | 5.04% |
| n-hexane | 4.63% |
| Methyl ethyl ketone | 4.19% |
| Chlorine | 3.97% |
| Phosphoric acid | 3.45% |
| Dichlorofluoromethane | 3.43% |
| Manganese compounds | 2.69% |
| Glycol ethers | 2.63% |
| Copper compounds | 2.61% |
| Styrene | 2.51% |
| Ethylene | 2.04% |
| Acetonitrile | 1.73% |
| n-Butyl alcohol | 1.66% |

% of total releases (million lb)

*Source:    EPA* (1989)

chemicals and their quantitative significance associated with the development of a given manufacturing industry in developing countries.

## 3.7    THE EXAMPLE OF KATOWICE

Industrial pollution problems encountered in the Katowice province of Poland, situated 250 km south of Warsaw, adjacent to the Czech border, may typify the severity of environmental damage caused by industrial pollution in other highly industrialized regions of Eastern Europe. The largest number of the so-called 'dirty-process plants' in Poland are concentrated in the Katowice province. The bulk of these plants still use out-of-date technologies. This province accounts for nearly all the zinc and lead minerals mined and processed in Poland, 98 percent of hard coal produced, 52 percent of the steel and 31 percent of the coke manufactured, and 32 percent of the coal-fired electric power generated. All these activities occur in an area that covers 2.1 percent of Poland with a population share of 10 percent, or slightly over 3.5 million in 1980 (Wojewozki 1981).

Under the existing conditions, about 30 percent of gaseous substances and about 35 percent of total particulate matters of global emissions are discharged in to the atmosphere by about 3,500 large sources. As a result, more than 20 out of 54 pollutants listed by the Council of Ministers exceeded national standards in the Katowice province and, worse yet, many of these pollutants have annual average concentrations 5 to 20 times the national standards (Kapala and Herman 1987, pp. 99–107).

Water pollution is equally serious in this region. The Vistula river is so polluted that it is not suitable for industrial or agricultural use, much less for drinking. The major pollution source is salt contamination from a dozen coal mines located in the region that discharge 250 million liters of salt-laden waste water into the river each day. The high salinity of the river water contributes to the corrosion of pipes and boilers in those plants which have no other sources of water (*Business Week* 1990, pp. 20–24).

Air and water pollutants in the Katowice province contain a large variety of hazardous substances such as dust, sulphur dioxide, nitrogen oxides, carbon monoxides, soot, hydrocarbons including carcinogenic compounds, hydrogen cyanide, phenol and heavy metals.

The Institute of Environmental Protection in Katowice recently measured the exposure of the local population to two toxic metals, lead and cadmium, through the consumption of vegetables grown in the metal-contaminated soils in the Katowice Province. Lead is known to be harmful to the circulatory system and to cause neurological disorders. The main source of lead emission is non-ferrous metallurgical plants, mainly zinc and lead smelters in this region. Other sources such as iron and steel plants (mainly open-hearth furnaces) and automobiles are also important. Cadmium is also known to damage the lungs, blood, liver and kidneys. The main source of cadmium emission is the zinc smelting plants in this area, as cadmium is a trace element of zinc blend. Not surprisingly, the highest concentrations of cadmium are found around zinc processing plants in Katowice province.

In order to estimate the average weekly per capita intake of lead and cadmium through vegetable consumption by the population of the Katowice region, a study was conducted covering 431 vegetable plots on the basis of a random sample of the most commonly consumed vegetables from each plot; that is, carrots, parsley, celery, red beets and potatoes. From each selected plot,

30 to 50 sample vegetables were picked, washed as normally done in households, dried, ground and mineralized, and then the metal content for each vegetable was measured. The results for three districts in the Katowice province are summarized in Table 3.16 (Kucharski and Marchwinska 1990).

The sample results show that vegetable leaves are, not surprisingly, more readily exposed to metal contamination than roots. Thus, the highest concentration was found in celery leaves and parsley leaves, followed by celery roots, carrot roots, red-beet roots, parsley roots and potatoes. The study group also estimated the average weekly per capita consumption of selected vegetables from a sample survey of 205 households in the Katowice Province to arrive at the weekly intake of lead and cadmium through vegetable consumption. The estimates of weekly vegetable consumption and weekly metal intake are given in Table 3.16. Particularly notable is the very high per capita consumption of potatoes, around 2 kg per week.

According to the maximum concentration limits recommended by the Food and Agriculture Organization of the United Nations (FAO) and WHO, about 3 mg per week of lead and 0.4–0.5 mg of cadmium, the estimated lead intake of the local population exceeded the desired limits except in the Katowice district, and cadmium intake is almost twice the maximum limits for all districts. It should be noted that these estimates of metal intake are based on the measurement of metal concentrations in a small number of selected vegetables grown in the region; they exclude local consumption of many other vegetables grown there, and of many other vegetables and fruits that may be exposed to metal contamination, let alone intake from other sources such as inhalation of air-borne pollutants and consumption of contaminated livestock products. They are, therefore, likely to be considerably underestimated.

These results are much more shocking than comparable results obtained from Western European countries. Investigations carried out in Austria, Belgium, Denmark, France and the former Federal Republic of Germany in the period 1979–82 showed that the weekly per capita intake of cadmium through the consumption of vegetables, fruit and corn products was estimated to range between 0.11 and 0.34 mg, and between 0.5 and 1.5 mg of lead (*Business Week* 1990, p. 5). The intake of cadmium and lead in the Katowice province is several times higher than comparable figures in Western European countries.

It is worth noting that the thorough washing of vegetables in tap water reduced their lead content by over 20 percent but had little effect on their cadmium content. Peeling root vegetables can, however, be an effective way of removing some of the metal content; for instance, a 20 percent decrease in lead content and a 20–30 percent reduction of cadmium content in meals prepared from these vegetables. Moreover, over 90 percent of lead and cadmium was removed from potatoes and deposited in the waste when potatoes are subjected to alcoholic fermentation. These contaminated wastes

Table 3.16  *Metal concentrations in selected vegetables from allotments in Katowice, Chorzow and Zabkowice Bedzinskie*

| Place of sampling | Metal | Metal content in fresh vegetables (mg/kg) | | | | | | | Metal intake (mg/kg) |
|---|---|---|---|---|---|---|---|---|---|
| | | Parsley | | Carrot | Celery | | Red beet | Potatoes | |
| | | Leaves | Root | | Leaves | Root | | | |
| Katowice | Lead | 13.20 | 5.40 | 2.70 | 13.00 | 4.10 | 2.40 | 0.50 | 2.80 |
| | Cadmium | 0.44 | 0.40 | 0.48 | 2.66 | 2.07 | 0.67 | 0.20 | 0.71 |
| Chorzow | Lead | 8.50 | 3.50 | 4.00 | 9.80 | 6.00 | 2.00 | 0.80 | 3.30 |
| | Cadmium | 0.84 | 0.75 | 1.38 | 3.05 | 2.83 | 0.73 | 0.13 | 0.81 |
| Zabkowice | Lead | 12.20 | 6.60 | 4.70 | 5.10 | 1.10 | 2.10 | 0.80 | 3.50 |
| | Cadmium | 1.41 | 2.90 | 1.64 | 3.25 | 0.25 | 0.52 | 0.20 | 0.99 |
| Average weekly consumption per capita[a] | | 35.00 | 35.00 | 190.00 | 22.00 | 22.00 | 145.00 | 1,900.00 | — |

*Notes*
Maximum allowable concentration limits recommended by FAO and WHO are 3 mg of lead and 0.4–0.5 mg of cadmium per week.
a.  Based on the results of a 1989 survey of 205 households in Katowice district, conducted by the Institute of Environmental Protection at Katowice.

*Source:*  Kucharski and Marchwinska (1990)

are, however, often fed to livestock as fodder in the Katowice region (Kucharski and Marchwinska 1990, p. 6).

Given the relatively large quantities of potatoes consumed in Poland as a staple food—2–5 kg per capita per week (nearly twice the consumption in other countries)—scientists at the Institute of Environmental Protection at Katowice conducted an investigation of lead and cadmium concentration in raw potato samples from 13 regions in Poland (Kucharski and Marchwinska 1990, pp. 113–18). Four of these regions, including the Katowice province, are highly industrialized centers, while the remaining nine regions have less industrial intensity. As expected, all the districts within Katowice province as well as Katowice province as a whole, which are noted for their high concentration of heavy polluting industries, showed much higher concentrations of lead and cadmium than other regions. In fact, most of the districts in Katowice province greatly exceeded the maximum tolerance limits set by the government of Poland for lead and cadmium concentrations in potatoes, respectively 0.4 mg/kg and 0.06 mg/kg of potatoes. By contrast, lead and cadmium concentrations in raw potatoes in other regions of Poland appear to be less serious with few exceptions.

## 3.8 CONCLUSIONS

This case-study of lead and cadmium concentrations in potatoes in Poland illustrates forcefully one of the numerous links between industrial pollution and health hazards, and once again underscores the importance of environmentally sound industrial development. We attempt to recapitulate the salient points concerning industrial pollutants generated in the course of manufacturing activities below.

### Industrial Air Pollution

In general, manufacturing is not responsible for the emissions of most pollutants. Each major pollutant has its own major sources. Most importantly, electricity generation accounts for the bulk of anthropogenic emissions of sulphur dioxide, transport activities for nitrogen oxides and carbon monoxide, and motor vehicles for hydrocarbons and lead. Industry, however, is a major source of particulate emissions in different countries. Some estimates suggest that industrial sources contribute about 20 percent of total air pollution, but this may be an understatement. Many manufacturing industries consume a large quantity of electricity, and power generation is a major source of pollution, particularly of sulphur dioxide. The manufacturing sector should also be held responsible for some of the air pollution problems caused by electricity generation.

Data on air pollutants by disaggregated industry sources are not easy to come by. Not surprisingly, the fragmentary available data consistently show that the heavy polluters are those industries producing basic industrial materials; namely, chemicals, primary metals, paper, petroleum and coal products, fertilizers and building materials, whether measured in terms of the total quantity of emissions or the quantity of emissions per unit value of output.

**Industrial Water Pollution**

Industry is responsible for a fairly large share of waste-water discharge of a number of traditional water pollutants. In addition, contributions to water pollution are made by domestic sources, agricultural run-off and many diffuse sources such as the precipitation of air pollutants, soil pollution caused by applications of fertilizers and pesticides, intensive animal husbandry, landfill disposals and urban run-off. Moreover, in most countries industry is also discharging into municipal waste-water systems. These factors make it extremely difficult to estimate industry's share of total waste-water generated. Fragmentary data indicate a significant share of industry in total waste-water discharge, roughly around 20 percent.

While almost all industrial activities generate some pollution, a relatively small number of industrial processes are responsible for the bulk of the industrial water, air and solid waste loads generated in a given area. For instance, a small number of industries, including paper, chemicals, petroleum and coal and primary metals, together accounted for about 85 percent of the total volume of waste-waters generated in the United States' manufacturing sector in 1983. Moreover, according to the United States Environmental Protection Agency inventory of toxic chemical releases in 1987, five industries accounted for over 90 percent of total industry releases of toxic chemicals into surface water in 1987, estimated at 4,355 billion kg. These top five industries are chemicals, paper products, petroleum refining, textile mill products and primary metals.

**Industrial Solid Wastes**

A cross-country comparison of waste generation may be difficult owing to the different definitions used by different countries for each category of wastes. Available international data, nevertheless, make it possible to gauge the relative quantitative importance of industrial waste compared with that from other sources. For instance, the solid waste production in the United States in 1985 was almost 4 billion tons per year, and agriculture and mining accounted for the bulk of this total: about 38 percent and 35 percent respectively; the industry share of total waste production was less, at about 17 percent. Likewise, in France agricultural waste claimed the lion's share of about 70 percent of total waste generation amounting to 600 million tons in 1985, followed by 17 percent by the mining sector, compared with an industry share of about 9 percent. In contrast, agriculture and mining generated about 17 percent and 5 percent of slightly over half a billion tons of the total wastes generated in 1985 in Japan, while industrial wastes accounted for almost 60 percent. These results are not surprising because of the dominant position of industry over agriculture and mining in Japan, while agriculture and mining are more important in the United States and France.

Data on solid wastes generated by various industries are very scarce, and average data, even if available, tend to be less useful because of wide variations in process technologies, production efficiencies and waste recycling among different industries. However, the types of waste that are expected to be generated by various industries are known, and they have been identified in this chapter.

**Hazardous Industrial Wastes**

National data on hazardous wastes are scarce and incomplete. Even when available, they are not comparable because of wide variations in the definitions and classification schemes of hazardous wastes that are adopted by different countries. Bearing in mind these limitations, the fragmentary data show that by far the largest portion of the total hazardous wastes generated tends to be produced by industrial production, with some minor exceptions. For instance, in the United States over 85 percent of the hazardous waste is accounted for by the manufacturing sector. Recent data show that among United States industries, chemical and allied products were responsible for almost 50 percent of the total industrial hazardous waste of 266 million tons generated in 1983. Trailing far behind the chemical industry are primary metals (18 percent), petroleum and coal products (11.8 percent), fabricated metal products (9.6 percent), and rubber and plastic products (5.5 percent). At more disaggregated levels, industrial organic chemicals tend to be the highest-volume generator of hazardous wastes in the United States.

**Toxic Chemicals**

It is difficult to estimate the exact amount of toxic chemicals produced in different countries every year partly because the term 'toxic' is defined differently in different countries. Only recent United States data seem to be sufficient to permit the identification and quantification of the types and industry sources of toxic chemicals.

According to the first Toxic Release Inventory of the Environmental Protection Agency in 1987, manufacturing establishments reported the release of 8.2 billion kg of 328 TRI chemicals into the air, water, land or underground wells, in addition to 2.1 billion kg of TRI chemicals transferred off-site to other facilities such as public sewage systems or incinerators for treatment or disposal. Out of this total, the chemical industry topped the list, producing about 5.4 billion kg, or 54 percent of the total releases and transfers of TRI chemicals, followed by paper products and primary metals. The rest of the top-ten list includes petroleum refining, textiles, transport equipment, metal products, electrical machinery and food products.

The chemical industry accounted for 48 percent of total chemical discharges into surface water, 24 percent by underground injection and 41 percent to public sewage treatment plants. The chemical industry tops the list for toxic chemical emissions, even when these are measured against industry output. Whether measured in terms of emissions per $1,000 of MVA or gross output, the chemical pollution coefficient for industrial chemicals is almost twice as large as the second-highest coefficient, for paper products.

**Policy Prescriptions**

As pointed-out by Afsah *et al.* (1996), many obstacles exist in applying traditional environmental regulatory schemes to industries in developing countries. This is mainly because these schemes depend primarily on interactions between the state or government and the industry or plant. The main suggestion is that this interaction should be expanded to include two additional 'players': the community and the market. Afsah *et al.* believe that factories should deal directly with community leaders, social organizations and religious institutions in order to meet social environmental norms or else suffer a variety of sanctions. In the latter case, markets can reduce the volume of sales from the factories because of their 'bad' environmental reputation. A system of multiple agents and multiple incentives would thus serve to reduce active industrial pollution.

## CHAPTER NOTES

1. For a detailed discussion on establishing a practical classification scheme for hazardous wastes adapted to the needs of a country, see World Bank (1989).

# 4. Processes and Pollution in Selected Industries

## 4.1 THE PROBLEM

When considering industrial pollution at the plant and process levels, many different processes that generate many different types of pollutants and many possible methods for pollution control and waste management must be taken into account. The existence of numerous process technologies within an industry may preclude generalization of industrial pollution characteristics at the process levels. There are, however, cases where the processes are similar. This permits a discussion of a 'typical' pollution.

For illustrative purposes, we attempt to search out several such 'representative' processes from selected industries and to identify the major pollutants associated with each process. An example of these pollutants has been provided in Table 4.1. Among the industries included here are electronics, iron and steel, textiles, motor vehicles, petroleum refining, leather tanning, pulp and paper mills, and electric lamp manufacturing.

## 4.2 ELECTRONICS MANUFACTURING

High-technology industry is generally perceived as clean; for example, electronics manufacturing requires strict cleanliness at the workplace, because it is essential in the production of microelectronic devices, and at the same time it appears to generate little of the traditional pollutants such as sulphur dioxide and carbon monoxide. This is not the case: a large quantity of solvents and cleaners are released into the environment. Even more serious, the electronics industry is highly chemical-intensive, using a wide range of toxic chemicals in the various phases of the manufacturing processes such as cleaning, diffusion, chemical vapor deposition and etching, in the case of semiconductor manufacture.

The electronics manufacturing industries include a wide variety of processes and products. They include electron tubes, X-ray tubes, cathode ray tubes, semiconductors, integrated circuits (ICs), diodes, memory chips, transistors,

Table 4.1  Major process-related pollutants in selected industries

| Industry | Process | Major pollutants |
|---|---|---|
| Iron and steel | Sintering | Sulphur dioxide, oil, greases, hydrocarbons |
| | Cokemaking | Sulphur dioxide, hydrocarbons, hydrogen cyanide, ammonia, pheno, sulphide, BDO, oil, greases, acid, fluoride |
| | Open-hearth furnace | Oxide scale formation, dust |
| | Basic oxygen furnace | Heat, airborne fluxes, slag particles, carbon dioxide, oxides of submicron iron dust |
| | Electric-arc furnace | Various particulates |
| | Direct reduction | Various airborne solid and gaseous wastes, noise pollution |
| Motor vehicle | Stamping | Oils, metals, contaminated process and cooling water, contaminated power-house water |
| | Assembly | BOD, COD, hexavalent chromium, suspended solids, trivalent chromium, zinc |
| Petroleum refining | Drilling | Mud, salt water, free emulsified oil, tank-bottom sludge, natural-gas and oil spills |
| | Storage | Sodium chloride, sulphurous compounds, tetraethyl lead, sand particulates, hydrocarbons |
| | Crude separation | Carbon monoxide, ammonia, hydrogen sulphide, hyrdocarbon, sulphur dioxide, phenols, desalted water, spent amine solutions, contaminated condensates |
| | Light hydrocarbon processing | Phosporic acid, particulates, carbon monoxide |
| | Middle- and heavy-distillate processing | Spent caustics, phenols, acetaldehyde, ammonia, spent catalyst fines, acid sludges, waste caly, carbon monoxide |
| | Residual hydrocarbon processing | Malodorous vent gas from waste water and particulates |
| | Petroleum refining | Oil, sulphides, mercaptans, cyanides, ammonia, phenols, organic salts, phosphates, heavy metals |

| Leather tanning | Beamhouse process (washing, soaking, liming, unhairing, etc.) | BOD, suspended soils, dissolved salts, alkalinity, sulphides, sulphur dioxide, sulphuric acid, putrescible organic matter, hair lime-containing sludge |
| | Drying operation | Solvents, ammonia formaldehyde |
| | Tanning | BOD, COD, oils, ammonia nitrogen |
| Pulp and paper | Pulp mill | Sulphite liquor, fine pulp, bleaching chemicals, mercaptans, sodium sulphides, carbonates, hydroxides, sizing, casein, clay, ink dyes, waxes, grease, oils, fibers |
| | Wood preparation | Suspended and dissolved solids, bark refuse, wood particles, sand dust |
| | Chemical pulping | BOD, suspended solids, alkalines, acids |
| | Kraft pulping | Suspended particulates, malodorous gases, sulphur compounds |
| | Papermaking | Suspended solids, dissolved solids, BOD |
| Soda-lime glass (incandescent lamp envelopes) | Cullet quenching | Oils, suspended solids, COD |
| Textiles | Raw wool scouring | BOD, grease, suspended solids, pH |
| | Yarn and fabric manufacture | BOD, total solids, pH |
| | Wool finishing | BOD, COD, settled solids, chlorine, suplhate, phosphate, ammonia, pH, total solids |
| | Woven fabric finishing | BOD, suspended solids, total dissolved solids, suspended solids, pH, oil, grease, sodium hydroxide |
| | Knit fabric finishing | BOD, total dissolved solids, suspended solids, pH, oil, grease, acetate, dye carrier |
| | Carpet manufacture | Similar to those listed under woven fabric finishing and knit fabric finishing |

*Sources:* For iron and steel: OECD (1977); for motor vehicles: Nemerow (1987); for petroleum refining: WHO (1983)

85

capacitors, resistors, thermistors, varistors, printed-circuit boards (PCBs) and flexible circuits. Of particular importance here is the components sector, which includes semiconductors and printed-circuit boards manufacturing. An integrated circuit is a number of semiconductor devices interconnected on a single chip.

The assessment of toxic wastes from PCB and IC manufacture is complex because of certain unique features of the manufacturing process. First, sub-tractive processing, which involves coating a board or wafer with a layer of materials, then etching and removing or dissolving unwanted materials, gener-ates large quantities and varieties of toxic wastes. Second, numerous special-ized chemicals and chemical mixtures are being developed to meet the strict quality control requirements of the more sophisticated electronic components emerging in the market. Third, literally thousands of proprietary chemical for-mulae are now being used in the industry, and the composition of these chem-icals is often kept confidential (Reynolds 1986, p. 242). The waste streams associated with each process step of the manufacture of PCBs and ICs are depicted in Figure 4.1. Major waste streams of concern are of spent organic solvents or metals containing wastes. Major constituent chemicals in waste streams from PCBs are identified and their concentration ranges quantified in Tables 4.2 and 4.3. Organic solvents are used for wafer and board cleaning and for the developing and stripping of photoresist materials used in the image transfer and circuit fabrication processes. Major hazardous wastes generated in substantial quantities by semiconductor manufacture include chlorinated solvents, unchlorinated solvents, ferons, photoresist developers and strippers, and contaminated vacuum pump oils. Toxic wastes that may be generated by printed-circuit board manufacture include solvents, developers, strippers, cop-per etchant, electroless copper overflow, chromic and fluoroboric acids, solder strippers, fluxes, fusing fluids and wave oils.

The primary pollutants in the manufacture of printed-circuit boards and other electronic devices are copper and lead. To a lesser extent cyanide, silver, chromium nickel and some precious metals are also present. In addition, tin and fluorides also pose potential problems in direct discharge to waterways. Typically, rinses after plating or etching account for about a half of the pollut-ants generated. The rest come from dumping spent stripping solutions, etchants, cleaners, activators, and so on.

The high volume of wastes generated by electronics manufacturing processes is caused by the extreme purity required in process chemicals, which leads to a relatively high volume of waste generation per unit of output (compared with, for instance, the fabrication and zinc-electroplating of fasteners). But what is more important than the volume at plant level is the diversity of waste streams generated by these processes, as illustrated earlier (Foeke 1988, p. 285).

*Figure 4.1   Subtractive printed-circuit board production flowsheet and waste generation*

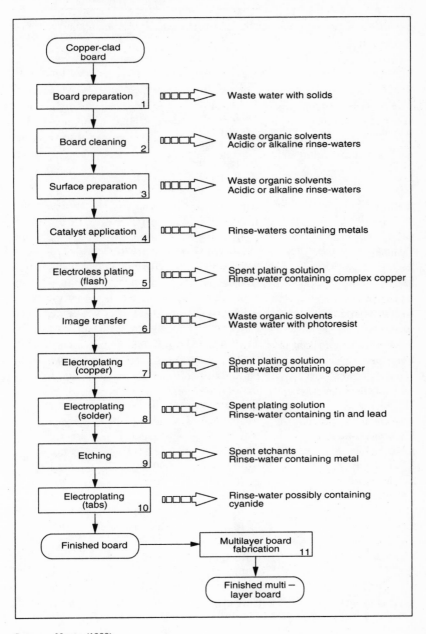

*Source:*   Nunno (1988)

*Table 4.2    Characteristics of raw waste streams from the manufacture of semiconductor devices*

| Parameter | Concentration range (mg/l) | Mean concentration (mg/l) | Industry-wide pollutant discharge (kg/day[a]) |
|---|---|---|---|
| Antimony | 0.001–0.187 | 0.021 | 13.2 |
| Arsenic | 0.003–0.067 | 0.018 | 13.2 |
| Beryllium | 0.001–0.015 | 0.002 | 1.9 |
| Cadmium | 0.001–0.008 | 0.003 | 1.9 |
| Chromium | 0.001–1.150 | 0.129 | 99.9 |
| Copper | 0.005–2.588 | 0.570 | 540.7 |
| Cyanide | 0.005–0.010 | 0.005 | 3.8 |
| Lead | 0.040–1.459 | 0.145 | 61.5 |
| Mercury | 0.001–0.051 | 0.004 | 5.7 |
| Nickel | 0.005–4.964 | 0.502 | 655.6 |
| Selenium | 0.002–0.045 | 0.021 | 6.9 |
| Silver | 0.001–0.013 | 0.005 | 3.8 |
| Thallium | 0.001–0.012 | 0.015 | 11.3 |
| Zinc | 0.001–0.289 | 0.093 | 46.5 |
| Phenols | 0.002–6.100 | 0.630 | 812.6 |
| Oil and grease | ND–20.8 | 5.058 | 2,778.3 |
| Total suspended solids | ND–203 | 31.610 | 30,470.6 |
| Total organic carbon | ND–80 | 55.676 | 17,094.2 |
| Biochemical oxygen demand | 9–202 | 52.768 | 38,848.1 |
| Fluoride | ND–330 | 62.000 | 35,909.0 |
| 1,2,4,-trichlorobenzene | 0.010–27.10 | 4.643 | 257.5 |
| 1,1,1-trichloroethane | 0.010–7.700 | 1.395 | 928.2 |
| Chloroform | 0.010–0.050 | 0.015 | 15.7 |
| 1,2-dichlorobenzene | 0.010–186.0 | 15.972 | 499.3 |
| 1,3-dichlorobenzene | 0.010–14.80 | 1.450 | 174.0 |
| 1,4-dichlorobenzene | 0.010–14.80 | 1.341 | 156.4 |
| 1,1-dichloroethylene | 0.010–0.071 | 0.029 | 9.4 |
| 2,4-dichlorophenol | 0.010–0.017 | 0.012 | 9.4 |
| Ethylbenzene | 0.010–0.107 | 0.021 | 6.3 |
| Methylene chloride | 0.010–2.400 | 0.244 | 276.1 |
| Naphthalene | 0.010–1.504 | 0.214 | 19.5 |
| 2-nitrophenol | 0.010–0.039 | 0.024 | 27.6 |
| 4-nitrophenol | 0.010–0.180 | 0.061 | 15.1 |
| Phenol | 0.014–3.500 | 0.519 | 203.5 |
| Di-n-octyl phthalate | 0.010–0.010 | 0.010 | 6.3 |
| Tetrachloroethylene | 0.010–0.800 | 0.122 | 363.0 |

*Table 4.2    Continued*

| Parameter | Concentration range (mg/l) | Mean concentration (mg/l) | Industry-wide pollutant discharge (kg/day[a]) |
|---|---|---|---|
| Toluene | 0.010–0.140 | 0.018 | 33.9 |
| Trichloroethylene | 0.007–3.500 | 0.322 | 177.1 |

*Notes*
ND = not detected.
a.   Flow rate weighted.

*Source:*   Nunno (1988)

*Table 4.3    Characteristics of raw waste streams from printed-circuit board manufacturing*

| Constituent | Range (mg/l) |
|---|---|
| Total suspended solids | 0.998–408.7 |
| Cyanide (total) | 0.002–5.333 |
| Cyanide (amenable to chlorination) | 0.005–4.645 |
| Copper | 1.582–535.7 |
| Nickel | 0.027–8.440 |
| Lead | 0.044–9.701 |
| Chromium (hexavalent) | 0.004–3.543 |
| Fluorides | 0.648–680.0 |
| Phosphorus | 0.075–33.80 |
| Silver | 0.036–0.202 |
| Palladium | 0.008–0.097 |
| Gold | 0.007–0.190 |
| Ethylene diamine tetra-acetic acid | 15.8–35.8 |
| Citrate | 0.9–1342 |
| Tartrate | 1.3–1108 |
| Nitrilotriacetonitrile | 47.6–810 |

*Source:*   As for Table 4.2

In sum, the high-technology industry is not pollution-free despite the image of its clean working environment. It is true that high-technology industry does not release highly visible traditional pollutants into the environment as do the smoke-stack industries, but it is beset by an ever-increasing discharge of a wide array of toxic wastes and of numerous proprietary chemical mixtures whose toxicity and dangers to human health and the environment are as yet unknown. On the other hand, the electronics industry is not only expected to play the central role in the progress and diffusion of information technology and in revolutionizing the telecommunications industry, but also such micro-electronics-based information technology is expected to be increasingly applied to better pollution control and protection of the environment. The practical applications of microelectronics technology are numerous, including environmental and monitoring systems for air, water and land pollutants, optimal waste management, low-waste and clean technologies, and environmental audit and impact assessment systems.

## 4.3   IRON AND STEEL

The iron and steel manufacturing process consumes large quantities of coke and iron ore, and is characterized by the multistage processes of coking, sintering, iron oxide reduction, steel manufacture, casting and steel product preparation. The nature of this process makes pollution control crucial. Since emissions and effluents from each separate process stage and the quantities of them depend on a multitude of factors such as raw materials, equipment and other inputs used as well as output produced, it is not possible to derive a representative figure of the raw residual pollutant loads from the various operations.

Pollutants generated from the sintering process include, among other airborne residuals, sulphur dioxide which varies between 15 kg and 25 kg per ton of sinter, oils and greases and hydrocarbons. Generally, no waterborne residuals are discharged from new sinter plants. Airborne pollutant control capital expenditures for a sinter plant of 700,000 tons per year have been estimated at $4.74–7.49 per ton of sinter (1972 dollars) (OECD 1977). The additional costs for the same plant was $1.13–2.03 per ton of sinter product.

Airborne residuals generated by coke-making include suplhur dioxide, hydrocarbons, hydrogen cyanide and waterborne pollutants, of which ammonia, phenol, sulphide, BOD, oil and grease and acids are components. Hydrogen sulphide, which tends to be the principal gaseous emission in coke-making, is efficiently treated by modules such as hoods and baghouses. A coking plant of 879,000 tonnes per year spends $2.59 per ton of coke product (1972 dollars) for the treatment of airborne pollutants. The large bulk of waterborne pollutants, such as ammonia, fluoride and phenols, are emitted from gas scrubbers. Solid residuals are also generated from molten slag during the expansion and contraction process.

There are three major processes for the manufacture of raw steel: (a) the open hearth furnace (OHF); (b) the basic oxygen furnace (BOF); and (c) the electric arc furnace. The OHF is known to cause some oxide scale formation on the cold scrap and dust from gas combustion. Leakages from gaseous combustion are extremely difficult to control. The BOF emits heat, airborne fluxes, slag particles, carbon monoxide, carbon dioxide and oxides of submicro-iron dusts. An electric arc furnace generates various types of particulates.

A wet Venturi scrubber for air cleaning is expected to entail capital expenditures of \$25.75–46.75 (1972 dollars) and an associated annual cost of \$3.60–14.20 per tonne of steel produced. The steel finishing process, entailing such operations as continuous casting, hot forming and cold finishing, generates some substantial airborne and waterborne residuals. Most of the waterborne residuals are caused by the pickling, electroplating, galvanizing and coating operations.

Direct reduction plants generate airborne pollutants in the form of both solid and gaseous wastes. Noise pollution, sometimes reaching over 100 decibels, is also associated with this technology. The cost of pollution control using the direct reduction process is expected to rise considerably as the best grade ores become depleted and poorer quality ores with greater impurities in concentration have to be mined. Also, the development of the direct reduction process will depend on the costs and the supply of various sources of energy. The direct reduction route has, however, several advantages over the classical method and the integrated steelworks; it is less labor-intensive, smaller in operational scale, and eliminates solid waste problems (but increases them in the mine). It is particularly suited to energy-rich developing countries because of its size.

## 4.4 TEXTILES

Textile production consists of several processes with interlinked unit operations by which a variety of initial material inputs are converted into a multitude of products. The unit operations may be carried out either batchwise or continuously. The OECD (1981) classifies textile manufacturing processes into the following eight sub-processes: (1) raw wool scouring; (2) yarn and fabric manufacture; (3) wool finishing; (4) woven fabric finishing; (5) knitted fabric finishing; (6) carpet manufacture; (7) stock and yard dyeing and finishing, and (8) commission finishing. Basically, each of these sub-processes together with their various unit operations pose immense waterborne pollution problems, partly because of the large quantities of chemicals and water used. Wet treatments of wool, flax and silk, for example, generate high levels of waterborne pollutant load, whereas the opening and carding of cotton causes airborne pollution that is equally damaging to human health.

Raw wool scouring (cleansing) entails extremely high waterborne residual loads such as BOD, grease, suspended solids and acidity. Suint, wax and detergent usage generate large quantities of BOD per tonne of wool processes. Base-level, intermediate and advanced-level abatement methods involving equipment and systems such as equalization basis, ultrafiltration, activated carbon treatment, clarifiers, rapid gravity filters, and so on, are used to deal with pollutants generated in all of the sub-processes mentioned. A capital expenditure option for a plant capacity of 21.7 tons of greasy wool per day in an advanced-level waterborne residual treatment (activated carbon) has been estimated at $185.7 per ton. The total annual operating cost estimate for the same treatment was $48.8 per ton (1977 dollars). Yarn and fabric manufacture essentially concerns dry-unit operations such as spinning, texturizing, weaving and knitting; it generates relatively small effluent load quantities. Manufacturers such as PVC (polyvinyl chloride) or rubber-coated fabrics, tyre cord materials and carpets are included in this sub-process.

A common distinguishing feature of sub-process (3)—wool finishing—is the number and variety of chemicals used and the consequent abnormal high waste loads. It consists of the following unit operations: (a) scouring; (b) carbonizing; (c) milling; (d) crabbing; (e) bleaching; (f) dyeing; (g) decasting, and (h) finishing. Scouring removes substances (carding and spinning oils, weaving sizes, and so on.) deliberately added to wool to assist processing, but it also generates high organic waste loads. In using dilute sulphuric acid as a medium for cleansing vegetable impurities in wool and for carbonizing operational solid wastes, sulphate, acidity and BOD are discharged. Milling is employed on its own or as a joint operation with scouring in order to stabilize wool, using acids or alkalines. It leads to the discharge of BOD, total solids and acidic waste water. Dyeing involves the use of acids. Wool fabric, for example, is dyed in jigs and winches (becks). Besides BOD, total solids and acidity, chromium and other non-biodegradable effluents result from wool and polyester dyeing. The use of relatively large quantities of toxic dye carriers, such as salicyclic acid, diphenyl, trichlorobenzene, butyl benzoate and methyl-naphthalene, poses apparent pollution dangers, especially to the aquatic environment. The toxic effluents of the dyeing operation listed above need to be absorbed in activated sludges (secondary treatment) and treated physico-chemically.

Woven fabric finishing is the fourth important sub-process; it involves desizing, scouring, mercerizing, bleaching, dyeing, printing and special finishing operations. Implicitly, desizing removes chemical glazes used on starch and synthetic materials such as polyvinyl acetate (PVA) and carboxymethyl cellulose (CMC). By using strong caustic soda solutions to improve the lustre and affinity of cotton for dyes in mercerizing, grease and wax impurities are discharged. The fifth, sixth, seventh and eighth sub-processes are similar in terms of their multiunit operations and effluents discharged.

In summary, it should be noted that the characteristics of the finishing operations are similar in all the selected sub-processes. They require the use of a large quantity of water and produce a large volume of aqueous effluent.

Although air pollution problems are secondary, some level of control is required (for example, cyclone collectors) since heating and mechanical dusting during carbonizing generate fine carbon particles, and smoke and fumes are released to the atmosphere. Odors of acetic acid, formaldehyde, acids and other organic discharges may be so strong as to make necessary the use of masks, wet scrubbing and absorption using activated carbon (Kucharski and Marchwinska 1990).

## 4.5   MOTOR VEHICLE MANUFACTURING

Motor vehicle production can be broken down into the following operations: (a) stamping; (b) body assembling; (c) painting; (d) trimming; and (e) final assembly operations (Nemerow 1987). Sheet steel or strip (initial material inputs) are cut to the required sizes, stamped by hydraulic presses and welded together ready for body assembling (Reynolds 1986). Relatively small amounts of waterborne residuals are released during the initial and crucial process operations because only small amounts of water are directly used. Some oils (lubricating and hydraulic), anywhere between 50 mg and several thousands mg per liter waste-water are, however, discharged. Solid wastes in the form of metals, contaminated process and cooling water, and contaminated power-house water (including boiler blowdown, softener regenerants, flyash) are significant stamping operation discharges.

The assembly operation usually entails several sequential processes. Stamped metal parts are initially constructed and painted. Interior and exterior trim (including fabric, plastic, glass, metal components, and so on.) produced in the parts plants are put together in the trim shop. The body-assembly plant fits ancillaries (such as wheels, engine, electrical components, and so on.) which have been manufactured elsewhere, and also fenders, hood and other front-end parts produced in the stamping operation. Finally, a painted and waxed finished motor vehicle emerges as a final output.

Effluents from motor vehicle plant operations are mainly organic waste-waters containing significant amount of BOD (biological oxygen demand), COD (carbon oxygen demand), and suspended solid loads. The latter, which is composed of zinc and chromium, originate from metal treating (borderizing) operations. Painting and paint-sanding also produce an appreciable amount of suspended solids and organic materials. These effluents seem to pose a major environmental pollution problem. With an innovative electrostatic painting process, reductions in pollution loads should be expected.

In conclusion, body assembly and final assembly are on average expected to generate for each batch of 100 motor vehicles produced the following major effluent loads: BOD (322–23 lb per 100 cars), COD (100.77 lb per 100 cars), hexavalent chromium (4.50 lb per 100 cars), suspended solids (360.30 lb per 100 cars), trivalent chromium (2.08 lb per 100 cars), and zinc (1.12 lb per 100 cars).

## 4.6   PETROLEUM REFINING

Although our analysis is confined to pollution problems associated with petroleum refining, it is worth noting that petroleum drilling (in-land and off-shore) itself creates significant environmental problems, generating waste loads such as drilling mud, salt water, free emulsified oil, tank-bottom sludge, natural-gas and oil spills (WHO 1983). In petroleum refining, crude oil is stored and distilled into hydrocarbon mixtures which are finally treated to give a variety of refined products. Petroleum refining can be divided into the following processing operations: (a) crude and refined product (storage); (b) crude separation; (c) light carbon processing; (d) middle and heavy distillate processing; and (e) residual hydrocarbon processing (Nelson 1985).

Petroleum refining, like iron and steel, rubber and glass manufacturing, uses very large quantities of water for processing and cooling, but since it is a closed-system operation, fugitive emissions from pump seals, valves, relief vents and leaks appear to be the major pollution sources. During the processing of crude oil and refined oil, product storage in cone-roofed or floating-roofed tanks may emit hydrocarbons. This emission is the apparent result of tank breathing due to temperature oscillations, and to evaporation and displacement during filling. Sodium chloride, sulphurous compounds, tetra-ethyl lead and sand particulates tend to be the important waterborne residuals from storage.

Various airborne pollutants such as carbon monoxide, ammonia, hydrogen sulphide, hydrocarbons, sulphur dioxide and phenols may be released during crude separation involving desalting, atmospheric distillation, hydrogen sulphite removal, sulphur recovery, gas processing, and so on. Desalted water, spent amine solutions and contaminated condensates may also be present.

Aqueous wastes from neutralization, washing contaminants containing phosphoric acid, airborne pollutants including particulates and carbon monoxide constitute the major pollutants in light hydrocarbon processing. Catalytic regeneration remains a typical pollution source in the mid and heavy distillate processing stage. Associated are spent caustics, acetaldehyde, phenols, ammonia, spent catalyst fines, acidic sludges and waste clay (all waterborne residuals), and carbon monoxide (the predominant airborne pollutant). Highly odoriferous vent gas from waste-water and particulates may be generated by the asphalt-blowing coking operation in residual hydrocarbon processing.

Waste-water discharge is generally the dominant pollutant problem in petroleum refineries. It contains a large number of pollutants at low concentrations, such as oil, sulfides, mercaptans, cyanides, ammonia, phenols, organic salts, phosphates, heavy metals, and so on. It is unclear which effluent contributes most to overall potential toxicity, but biological treatment and oxidation lagooning may reduce toxicity (OECD 1985).

## 4.7    LEATHER TANNING

The tanning process converts animal skins and hides into leather. It involves the suspension for long periods of hide and skins in vats containing the solution of tanning agents. Three processes of tanning may be identified: (a) the beam house; (b) the tanhouse; and (c) the finishing processes (Carmichael and Strezepek 1987). With multiple unit operations, pollutants generated by each process create serious environmental problems.

Washing and soaking, and liming and unhairing (all operations of the beam house process) produce substantial amounts of waste-water heavily contaminated with organic matter: BOD, suspended solids, dissolved salts, alkalinity and sulfides are well-known pollutants. Airborne pollutants such as sulphur dioxide and malodorous gas and sulphuric acid are released. Also generated are solid wastes including putrescible organic matter, hair and lime-containing sludge.

Tanhouse and finishing process operations produce airborne and water-borne pollutants and solid wastes. Drying operations release solvents, ammonia and formaldehyde into the atmosphere. Tanning generates a large amount of waste-water, of which BOD, COD, oils and ammonia nitrogen are significant components. Waste-water effluents constitute the major pollution factor in the tanning industry. They may be treated biologically and physico-chemically to reduce pollution loads (JEC 1978).

## 4.8    PULP AND PAPER MILLS

Pulp and paper manufacturing is a dual-phase operation, namely pulping and papermaking. The main aim of the pulping process is to disintegrate suitable prepared woods (soft or hard) to free the cellulose fibres from the lignin and carbohydrates that bind the fibres together. Other non-wood raw materials commonly used in developing countries for pulp are bagasses, straw, bamboo, reed, hemp, jute, flax, cotton and sometimes recycled paper.

There are two main pulping technologies, mechanical and chemical. The mechanical process breaks down the lignin bond in wood fibres. Mechanically prepared (groundwood) pulp made from wood that is grounded, screened and cooked, is mainly used for non-durable paper products, such as newspaper.

The chemical pulping technology breaks down the lignin and carbohydrate bonds, releasing the cellulose fibres. This is carried out in three main ways: (a) kraft pulping with a mixture of sodium hyrdoxide and sodium sulphite; (b) sulphite pulping with an acidic liquor containing a bisulphite; and (c) neutral sulphite semi-chemical pulping with a neutral mixture of sodium sulphite and sodium carbonate followed by mechanical disintegration.

A typical pulping process involves wood or non-wood resource preparation (including debarking), pulping, screening, washing, thickening, and bleaching with an oxidizing agent. For papermaking, the fiber slurry is finally dewatered to form wet sheet and then finally smoothed and dried.

Papermaking involves stock preparation, paper-machine operations, converting and finishing. During these operations, the pulp mixture is disintegrated, mixed with various fillers and dyes, washed and sometimes chemicals added, screened, and finally rolled to give different quality grades of paper.

Traditionally, the pulp and paper industry has been a heavy user of water. However, it has responded recently to environmental regulations by reducing usage to lower waste-water discharges. Most of the water is used in process water operations. Pulp mill wastes originate from wood preparation, pulping, digester cooking, washing, bleaching, thickening, drinking, and so on, and may contain sulphite liquor, fine pulp, bleaching chemicals, mercaptans, sodium sulphides, carbonates, hydroxides, sizing, casein, clay, ink, dyes, waxes, grease, oils and fibers. Wood preparation gives rise to waste-waters containing suspended and dissolved solids, to evaporation loss, and to solid wastes including bark refuse, wood particles and sand dust.

In contrast to mechanical pulping, all three chemical pulping processes produce relatively high contaminated waste-waters, the loads of which include BOD, suspended solids, alkalinity and acidity. Suspended particulate matter emissions, malodorous gases and materials originating from sulphur compounds may be produced in kraft pulping. Sulphur dioxide is the main gaseous pollutant related to both sulphide and neutral sulphite semi-chemical processes.

Effluents from papermaking processes generally contain suspended solids, dissolved solids, and BOD (mostly from bleaching). Although contaminated waterborne pollutants constitute the main pollution source, solid waste generation is common to almost all the pulp and paper-milling processes.

## 4.9   ELECTRIC LAMP MANUFACTURING

Commercial glass manufactures are of five basic types: (a) soda-lime; (b) lead; (c) fueled silica; (d) barosilicate; and (e) silica. The soda-lime type of glass is common. Incandescent glass, flat glass, auto glass, tumblers and tableware are typical examples. Incandescent lamp envelop glass, like other types of glass

manufacture, is characterized by mass production in large, direct-fired, continuous melting furnaces using silica sand, cullet (broken scrap glass), soda ash,
limestone, niter, salt cake, arsenic and decolorizer. The flow process begins
when raw materials are withdrawn from storage bins, batch weighed and
blended in a mixer. The mixed batches are continuously fed to the furnace, and
then passed through a forming machine (ribbon) which blows the molten glass
into clear incandescent lamp envelopes. Many of the clear envelopes are then
frosted or etched with hydrofluoric acid solution.

Water is used predominantly as process water for cullet quenching and for
rinsing frosted bulbs. Non-contact cooling water from batch feeders, melting
furnaces, ribbon machines and other auxiliary equipment is used as a source
of quench water. Cullet quenching alone contributes about 57 percent of the
total waste-water flow in a typical plant. It is contaminated with pollutants
such as oils, suspended solids and COD.

Frosting gives the inside surface of an etched lamp envelope certain light-
diffusing capabilities. Solutions containing hydrochloric acid, fluoride compounds and ammonia are often used in etching. But in so doing, waste-water
streams with high concentrations of fluoride and ammonia as pollutants are
generated. Ammonia is also added to plant waste-water as a result of frosting
solution carry-over and the discharge from fume scrubbing equipment. It is
worth noting that waste-water from frosting operations consist of relatively
higher concentrations of oil, suspended solids and COD pollutant loads compared to culleting operations. Furthermore, frosting produces high fluoride
and ammonia contaminants which may at certain concentration levels be
toxic. Fluoride in frosting waste-water may be reduced by using sand filtration
followed by activated alumina filtration. Such control technology may require
an investment of $624,000 and a total annual cost of $279,000 (1987 dollars).

In sum, incandescent lamp envelop manufacturers produce predominantly
waterborne pollutants; but airborne emissions such as dust and fumes, particulates and gaseous fluorides, and hydrocarbons emanating from raw material
mixing, melting, blowing and annealing process operations can also be found.


## 4.10  CONCLUSIONS

In this chapter we have provided rough indicators of the types of pollution
generated by manufacturing processes in a small sample of industries. What is
needed to more fully describe the pollution generated among a wide group of
industries in developing countries is a much larger database. Such a base could
then be used to model pollution outputs resulting from a full range of industrial
waste inputs. Most recently, Hettige *et al.* (1994) have suggested a framework
for such a modeling system. They begin by broadening the pollution emissions

database to include the United States EPA database, the human health and ecotoxicity database, and the longitudinal research database. The level of pollution emitted across industries is aggregated by constructing pollution intensity indices and then introducing risk weights to produce toxic pollution risk intensity indices. At this point, they have constructed indices which measure industrial pollution for some 74 four-digit ISIC codes. Even so, utilizing such indices in individual developing countries has certain limitations because of cross-country variations in regulatory, economic and technological conditions. Nonetheless, the ever-growing cost of waste disposal dictates that some measures of total industrial pollution activity be established. The limits of sustainable development can then be more accurately assessed.

# 5. Economic Implications of Industrial Pollution Abatement

## 5.1 THE PROBLEM

The economic costs of environmental protection are at least as important as its technological and engineering aspects. Environmental protection and particularly pollution control require substantial investment and other resource commitments. The impact of environmental expenditure on such economic factors as output, price levels, employment and trade has become an increasingly important issue for policy-makers as well as academic researchers, as environmental degradation becomes increasingly serious and menacing. Particularly controversial among environmental issues is how much should be spent on environmental protection and whether environmental expenditure is a major factor contributing to the recent decline in the productivity of developed countries. The question of whether economic growth and environmental protection are compatible has been studied extensively. The issue has important policy implications for developing countries, since the implementation of environmental regulations and safeguards would represent a new and competing demand for the limited productive resources available to those countries. At the same time, there is reason to believe that many of the new pollution-abating manufacturing technologies can overcome this dilemma by improving efficiency and reducing costs.

In this chapter, we briefly describe the economics of environmental protection, followed by an analysis of investment data on pollution abatement in selected countries. Empirical findings on the economic impacts of pollution abatement expenditure are then assessed at the following levels: aggregate macroeconomic impacts; industry impacts, and selected process-specific cost effects of pollution abatement. Finally, tentative conclusions are drawn and policy implications derived.

## 5.2   ENVIRONMENTAL ECONOMIC PRINCIPLES

In theory, the elementary economic principle of marginal cost pricing may apply equally to the question of how much should be spent on pollution abatement.[1] Namely, the optimal level of expenditure is found where an additional dollar cost (marginal cost) of pollution abatement is equal to the additional dollar benefit (marginal benefit) of pollutant removal. In practice, this marginal principle is sometimes difficult to apply, because of the nature of public goods and the attendant externalities inherent in environmental protection. For instance, what economic value should be placed on a damaged ozone layer or an extinct species? The principle of equating marginal cost to marginal benefit breaks down when both of the two variables cannot be easily quantified. Furthermore, the law of diminishing returns applies to the costs of pollution control, making the matter more complicated; that is to say, the costs of pollution abatement typically rise very slowly at low levels of removal until a critical point, say 70 percent removal, is reached. Then they rise sharply. By contrast, the benefits increase rapidly at first and then taper off. Therefore, each additional dollar spent brings a smaller benefit. To make a rational decision regarding optimal expenditure on pollution control, the incremental costs and benefits need to be compared rather than looking only at totals. Little is known about the shapes of those incremental costs and benefits in quantitative terms. This also explains why the reduction to zero of environmentally damaging emissions does not often make sense.

There are many different ways of financing pollution abatement, such as through subsidies, general taxes and the 'polluter-pays' mechanism, all of which directly affect the cost structure of a firm. If the firm makes the necessary capital investment to abate its pollution without an outside subsidy, the firm is said to 'internalize' its costs, or to bear its full costs. In the case of internalized costs, the effects of capital expenditure on output and prices will critically depend on the type of technology embodied in the capital investments, a distinction being made between plant and equipment designed to abate pollutants through add-on or end-of-line techniques and those through changes in production processes. If the end-of-line techniques are applied, costs will rise as industries internalize costs that they have not borne before. An increase in costs shifts the industry supply curve to the left, and output is reduced, as depicted in Figure 5.1. Some of the important reasons for raising the industry supply curve are that the pollution abatement equipment installed at the end of the existing production process represents not only additional capital costs, but also requires additional labor to operate and maintain it without raising output. As a result, productivity declines. In addition, those investments in pollution abatement may compete with other output-augmenting investments in plant and equipment, thus reducing the potential output of other productive investments.

*Figure 5.1 Industry equilibrium before and after pollution abatement*

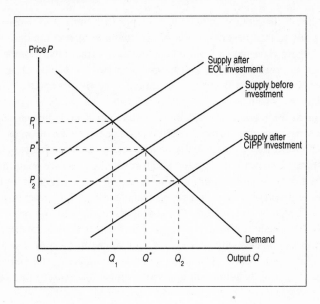

*Notes*
EOL = end of line.
CIPP = changes in production processes.

On the other hand, if the old process technology is replaced by the new clean or low-waste technology, in some cases the per unit production costs of the firm may go down and shift the industry supply curve in Figure 5.1 to the right, increasing industry output and lowering prices at the same time. The reasons are that low-waste process technologies may be typically designed to eliminate or reduce not only one but multiple sources of pollution simultaneously and, more importantly, to economize on energy, scarce raw materials and even labor inputs so that the initial increase in investment costs may be more than offset by those factor cost savings. Ultimately, the question of what impact environmental expenditures may have on output, productivity, employment, price levels and trade may have to be determined empirically, as explained below.

## 5.3 INVESTMENT IN POLLUTION ABATEMENT IN SELECTED COUNTRIES

The relative quantitative importance of environmental expenditure could have a significant bearing on its final impact on the economic activity of a given economy. Data on environmental expenditure for developing countries are rarely available, but there are some available in developed countries, which suggest that environmental expenditure is very small relative to other comparable expenditures on 'public goods' such as defense and public education. Expenditure on industrial pollution abatement has accounted for only a small percentage of total industry investment, as shown in Table 5.1. Except in Japan, the share of environmental expenditure in total industry investment was less than 7 percent.

Turning to the relative importance of individual manufacturing industries, the cumulative data for the former Federal Republic of Germany during the period 1971–77 clearly points to the preponderance of basic industrial materials producing industries in the relative share of total investment expenditure (see Figure 5.2). Among manufacturing industries, high spenders ranked in percentages are oil refining (19.9), chemicals (11.1), steelmaking (10.7), pulp and paper (9.6), non-metallic ores (9.2), steel and malleable iron smelting (8.5) and non-ferrous metals (8.4). As discussed earlier, the basic industrial materials producing industries are the heaviest polluters. In fact, as a whole they

*Table 5.1  Environmental expenditures as a percentage of total investment, 1975–90*

| Country | Year | Private environmental investment as % of total private investment | Industry environmental investment as % of total industrial investment |
|---|---|---|---|
| Austria | 1975 | — | 5.1 |
|  | 1985 | 2.7 | — |
|  | 1990 | — | 1.0 |
| Germany, Federal Republic of | 1975 | — | — |
|  | 1985 | 1.9 | 1.6 |
|  | 1990 | 2.1 | 1.4 |
| Japan | 1975 | 4.6 | 17.1 |
|  | 1985 | 2.9 | 0.5 |
|  | 1990 | 2.6 | 0.3 |
| France | 1975 | — | — |
|  | 1985 | 0.8 | 0.4 |
|  | 1990 | 0.7 | 0.4 |
| United States | 1975 | 3.4 | 5.8 |
|  | 1985 | 1.1 | 2.0 |
|  | 1990 | 1.4 | 2.0 |

*Source:*  OECD (1993)

*Figure 5.2　Industrial pollution control investment as a percentage of*
*total industrial investment expenditures in the*
*Federal Republic of Germany, 1971–77*

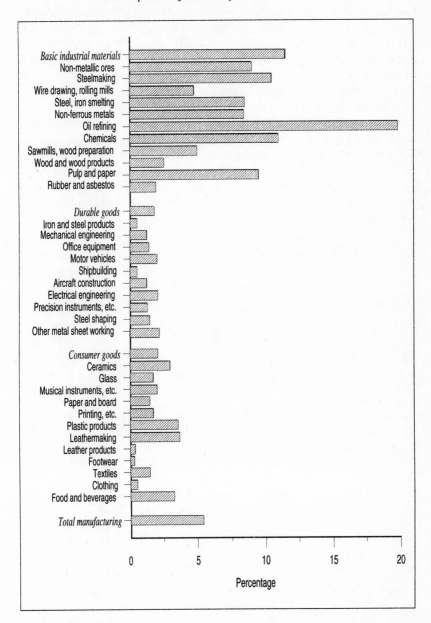

*Source:*　OECD (1982)

spend on pollution abatement almost six times more than durable goods or consumer goods industries as a percent of their total investment expenditures.

Japanese industry data also reveal pollution-control investment concentrated in basic materials industries (for example pulp and paper, chemicals, petrochemicals, oil, iron and steel) between 1973 and 1976, but their share of total investment sharply declined between 1977 and 1980 except for cement and thermal power plants (see Table 5.2). The possible reason for the high investment share of pollution control in 1972–76 is a short-term concentration of investment required to meet the sharply increased requirements of environmental legislation enacted in the early 1970s.

The most comprehensive and recent data available for environmental expenditure are survey results published by the United States government, as shown in Figure 5.3. The United States manufacturing sector as a whole spent $7,178 million for pollution abatement capital goods in 1985. Of this total, 57 percent was for air, 32 percent for water and 11 percent for solid wastes. Moreover, operating costs associated with pollution abatement activities (including

*Table 5.2*    *Pollution control investment in Japanese industry, 1973–80*[a]
          *(% of total investment)*

| Industry | 1973 | 1975 | 1976 | 1977 | 1978 | 1979 | 1980 |
|---|---|---|---|---|---|---|---|
| All industries | 10.6 | 17.7 | 13.5 | 7.2 | 5.4 | 4.9 | 5.3 |
| Iron and steel | 17.3 | 18.4 | 21.1 | 11.5 | 10.9 | 11.5 | 4.9 |
| Oil | 18.5 | 41.7 | 31.4 | 5.9 | 4.5 | 4.8 | 7.7 |
| Pulp and paper | 26.4 | 47.1 | 44.0 | 35.1 | 28.0 | 22.1 | 32.0 |
| Non-ferrous metals | 22.1 | 22.7 | 17.6 | 9.1 | 6.8 | 5.8 | 3.6 |
| Chemicals (except petrochemicals) | 17.1 | 32.8 | 17.6 | 8.7 | 5.0 | 3.7 | 3.5 |
| Engineering | 4.0 | 5.2 | 3.5 | 2.5 | 2.2 | 1.9 | 1.6 |
| Petrochemicals | 15.7 | 18.4 | 13.8 | 9.9 | 7.2 | 3.2 | 2.8 |
| Mining (except coal) | 24.4 | 37.9 | 37.6 | 26.2 | 14.5 | 15.7 | 3.0 |
| Textiles | 10.1 | 20.4 | 7.4 | 4.0 | 2.4 | 1.9 | 2.2 |
| Cement | 11.2 | 15.0 | 12.2 | 11.4 | 15.8 | 14.8 | 10.2 |
| Ceramics (except cement) | 9.9 | 10.2 | 8.2 | 5.8 | 10.3 | 3.7 | 11.4 |
| Gas | 2.3 | 2.1 | 1.5 | 1.1 | 1.2 | 2.1 | 2.4 |
| Coal | 4.0 | 8.2 | 2.7 | 2.1 | 0.9 | 1.6 | 1.2 |
| Other | 8.6 | 9.1 | 4.9 | 3.7 | 1.8 | 1.0 | 1.6 |
| Construction equipment | 5.9 | 7.2 | 4.4 | 6.1 | 4.6 | 2.6 | 1.9 |
| Electricity (except thermal power plants) | 1.1 | 1.1 | 0.9 | 0.8 | 0.8 | 0.7 | 0.9 |

*Note:*    a.    Estimates based on industrial engineering studies.

*Source:*    UNIDO (1990)

*Figure 5.3*   *Pollution-abatement capital expenditures and operating costs,*
               *by source of pollution, United States, 1985*

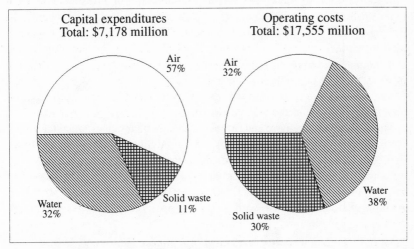

*Source:*   US Department of Commerce (1993)

payments to government units) amounted to $17,555 million, more than twice
the capital expenditure. Of this total 32 percent was for air, 38 percent for water
and 30 percent for solid wastes.

One crucial variable in assessing the economic impact of environmental
expenditure is the extent of the diffusion of clean technologies, a key factor
that affects the cost structure of a firm and has broader implications for the
nature of relationships between industrialization and the environment. Fortu-
nately, in the United States data a distinction is made between plant and equipment designed to abate pollutants through add-on or end-of-line techniques
and those that rely on changes-in-production processes (CIPP) (see Figure
5.4). It is evident that the diffusion of clean technologies is quite considerable
in a small number of industries, particularly petroleum and coal, and petroleum chemicals, although it is limited overall.

The industry average, however, conceals considerable variations among
individual industries (see Figure 5.5). Among industries spending heavily on
three types of pollution abatement in 1993 are again material processing
industries, namely, chemicals, petroleum, paper and pulp, primary metals.
Other non-material processing industries with heavy pollution abatement
expenditures are food products and transport equipment. The rest of industries
are relatively insignificant in terms of anti-pollution expenditure.

Unfortunately, comparable statistics for other countries are not available.
There is, however, some scattered anecdotal evidence. For instance, one

*Figure 5.4    Pollution-abatement capital expenditures on end-of-line and changes-in-production processes in the United States, 1993*

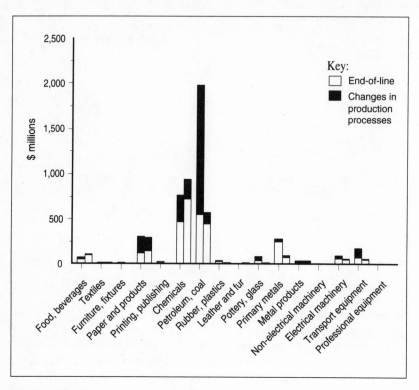

*Source:*    As for Figure 5.3

detailed study found no significant spread of clean technologies in the Federal Republic of Germany during the period 1975–84. The share of clean technologies in total environmental protection investments by industry increased from 19.6 percent in 1975 to 24 percent in 1980, only to drop to 16.3 percent in 1982, but rising again to 23 percent in 1983 (Leiper and Simonis 1988, p. 44). An OECD study (1985b, p. 83) also mentioned the limited diffusion of clean technologies in France; but in Denmark, about one-third of firms adopted new production processes for pollution abatement between 1975 and 1980. None of these studies provided detailed statistics on clean technologies by industry.

On the other hand, many process-specific technical and engineering case-studies are available on new technologies in different countries, some of which will be highlighted for illustrative purposes shortly. But these isolated pieces of information do not provide a clue to the extent of diffusion of new technologies which abate industrial pollution without reducing output and can

*Figure 5.5*     *Pollution-abatement capital expenditures and operating cost of abatement for major industries in the United States, 1993*

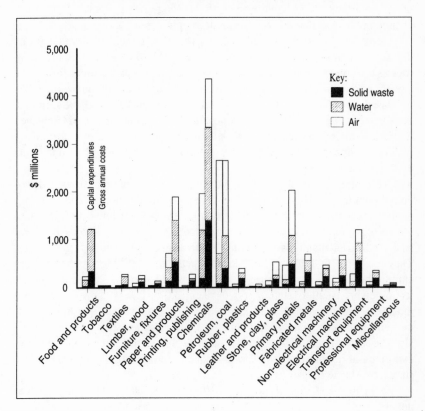

*Source:*     As for Figure 5.4

in some cases even lower production costs. More importantly, they underscore an urgent need for the diffusion of clean technologies. Finally, it must be noted that although the diffusion of clean technologies commands priority, add-on technologies could also be innovative and even necessary where alternative technologies cannot easily be developed.

## 5.4 ECONOMIC IMPACTS OF LONG-TERM STRUCTURAL CHANGES

The question whether or not conflict exists between output or productivity and environmental protection will probably have major implications for the future industrialization of developing countries. Some of the empirical evidence on this question will be examined shortly. We explore here possible environmental implications of the continuance of the long-term patterns of structural change in the manufacturing sector in developing countries.

Figure 5.6 shows the overall patterns of MVA growth in developed and developing countries over the period 1970–88. The MVA of developing countries as a whole grew at an average annual rate which was 2.5 times faster than developed countries, and the share of developing countries in world MVA increased from 6.88 percent to 11.56 percent between 1970 and 1988. In fact, the share of developing countries almost doubled during the period. However, the actual rate of progress in the developing countries' share of world manufacturing output falls far short of the rate required to achieve the Lima target of 25 percent by the year 2000.

At disaggregated industry levels, the ten fastest-growing industries in developing countries relative to their counterparts in developed countries are mainly concentrated in the following two groups: a labor-intensive light manufacturing group using renewable natural resources; and a capital-intensive basic industrial materials producing group using largely mineral resources. They are listed in Table 5.3. In addition, petroleum refining should be noted among the latter group because of its large world share (37 percent), despite its somewhat smaller relative growth-rates (3.07). It was shown earlier that most water-intensive industries as measured by requirements per unit of output tend to be concentrated in industries that process basic industrial materials. The manufacture of basic industrial materials is shown to be most energy- and material-intensive among various manufacturing activities. It was further shown that those industries are the heaviest polluters.

The 1990–91 Global Report published by UNIDO (1990) discussed in detail the global industrial growth process in the period 1975–85. One of the most significant findings from the standpoint of the environment was a clear reorientation of industrial structure between the South and the North in the traditional smokestack industries, which were drastically as a result of their massive restructuring efforts, while those regions have consolidated their dominance of the capital goods industry in both absolute and relative terms. The South as a whole has made significant headway in expanding its share of MVA in light industry and basic industry, but has made few gains in the capital goods industry.

If the trend towards the rapid expansion of smokestack industries in the South continues to accelerate, the environmental burdens of such an industrial transformation, in particular the problems posed by various traditional industrial pollutants associated with smokestack industries, may reach crisis proportions in the near future unless the diffusion of clean technologies occurs on a massive scale across industries. Severe industrial pollution problems

*Figure 5.6*   *Manufacturing value added (MVA) share and average annual*
                *growth rates of MVA, 1970–88*

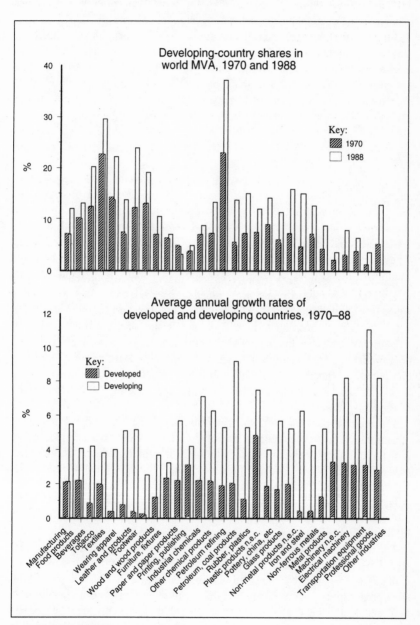

*Source:*   UNIDO (1990)

*Table 5.3    Top ten fastest-growing industries in developing countries*

| Type of manufacturing | Ratio of South–North annual growth rates 1970–88 | Share of South in world MVA, 1988 |
|---|---|---|
| Light manufacturing | | |
| Leather products | 15.91 | 24.71 |
| Footwear | 14.05 | 19.83 |
| Textiles | 7.96 | 21.26 |
| Wearing apparel | 6.13 | 14.07 |
| Beverages | 4.42 | 20.26 |
| Basic materials | | |
| Iron and steel | 13.96 | 15.46 |
| Non-ferrous metals | 5.79 | 12.66 |
| Plastic products | 4.13 | 15.92 |
| Petroleum and coal products | 3.85 | 14.99 |
| Metal products | 3.84 | 9.34 |

*Source:*   UNIDO (1990)

encountered now in many rapidly industrializing developing countries may foreshadow what is to come on a much greater scale in other developing countries. On the other hand, the severity of industrial pollution in the North may taper off or even steadily decline as a result of the rationalization of smokestack industries coupled with the enforcement of increasingly stringent environmental regulations. But as we saw earlier, high-technology industries create new industrial pollution problems, particularly toxic wastes, and industrial pollution problems are likely to continue in the North for the foreseeable future.

The regional incidence of industrial pollution in the South varies markedly, depending upon the regional patterns of industrialization. For example, industrial pollution may become a major problem in rapidly industrializing countries of East and South Asia, the Indian subcontinent and China, while tropical Africa, paralyzed by chronic stagnation, has yet to see any visible signs of industrial pollution problems. Another influencing factor is the ability of the ecosystem of different regions to process or to support different levels and different kinds of pollution.

The need for industrialization in developing countries is a foregone conclusion. The key issue is the sustainability of industrialization in terms of the constraints imposed by the natural resource base and the environmental absorptive capacity. Continued rapid industrial growth in developing countries may accelerate the depletion of natural resources accompanied by serious damage to the environment, and cause direct environmental degradation through unchecked industrial pollution to such an extent that the process of industrialization cannot be sustained. The environmental regulations of industrial activity may become increasingly important. But environmental protection requires heavy capital investments and additional resource commitments that developing countries cannot well afford. Environmental protection may thus put a brake on the process of industrialization, as described earlier. The question of the existence of potential conflict between environmental protection and industrial growth is of vital importance to those developing countries embarking on a course of industrialization. An examination of some of the empirical evidence on this issue is therefore in order.

## 5.5   ECONOMIC IMPACTS AT THE MACROECONOMIC LEVEL

In recent years, as environmental expenditures have begun to increase sharply in response to a rising interest in environmental problems in many countries, the economic impact of rises in environmental spending has also attracted the attention of many economists and policy-makers. In fact, the literature on the empirical investigation of the economic impact of environmental measures is already considerable.[2] But the empirical findings of the studies are not easily comparable due to marked differences in model structure, database and period, assumptions used in simulation exercises, statistical reliability and many other factors, so it is not possible to provide a comprehensive survey of existing empirical studies. We focus instead on the results of a recent OECD survey of comparative environmental impacts in selected countries.

The countries selected for the OECD study were Austria, Finland, France, the Netherlands, Norway and the United States, plus Italy and Japan (see Table 5.4). Although all the studies used macroeconomic models, there are considerable variations in the major characteristics of the models and their databases. Irrespective of the structural differences of country models, all studies compared the macroeconomic impacts of additional environmental expenditure to those without additional spending. Several significant observations are in order. First, the results suggest that although the short-term effects of increased environmental expenditure on GDP are all positive, albeit very small, the long-term effects are mixed: the estimates are all negative for some countries such as the Netherlands and the United States, negative and positive for others (Austria and Italy), and all positive for the remainders (Japan, Finland, France and Norway). The short-term impact is, however, likely to be more favorable than the long-term effects. In the short run, environmental investment may have positive effects on output and employment, but some of

*Table 5.4  Effects of additional environmental programs on selected economic variables*

| Country | GDP (%) | | Consumer prices (%) | | Unemployment ('000) | |
|---|---|---|---|---|---|---|
| | First year | Final year | First year | Final year | First year | Final year |
| Austria (1979–85) | — | −0.6/0.5 | — | 0.4/1.7[a] | — | — |
| Finland (1976–82) | 0.3 | 0.6 | 0.2 | 0.2 | −3.5 | −7.5 |
| France (1966–74) | — | 0.1/0.4 | — | 0.1 | −0.2/−1.1 | −13.2/−43.5 |
| The Netherlands (1979–85) | 0.1 | −0.3/−0.6 | 0.2/0.4 | 0.8/4.3 | −1.4/−2.3 | −3.8/6.9 |
| Norway (1974–83) | — | 1.5 | — | 0.1/0.9 | — | −25.0 |
| United States (1970–87) | 0.2 | −0.6/−1.1 | 0.2 | 5.0/6.7 | −80.0 | −150.0/−300.0[b] |
| Memorandum items[c] | | | | | | |
| Italy (1971–80) | — | −0.2/0.4 | — | 0.3/0.5 | — | — |
| Japan (1972–9) | 1.2/2.6 | 0.1/0.2[d] | — | 2.2/3.8 | (lower) | (lower) |

*Notes*
a.  GDP deflator.
b.  Partly estimated by Secretariat.
c.  Published OECD (1978).
d.  For period as a whole, suggesting negative results for final year.

*Source:*  OECD (1985c)

112

those short-term gains may be dissipated over the longer run because of rising prices or declining productivity.

Additional environmental expenditure seems to raise consumer prices. But the inflationary impact appears to be small in most cases, and less than 1 percent increase in the final year. The major exceptions are the United States and Japan, which show a 5–7 and 2–4 percent rise in consumer prices in the final years. On the other hand, environmental expenditure, although quantitatively small, reduces unemployment levels with few exceptions.

One important conclusion emerging from those results is that the macroeconomic impacts of environmental expenditure tend to be quantitatively insignificant, usually in the range of a few tenths of a percentage point per year, with the exception of some of the results for consumer prices. The results are not surprising, because environmental expenditure as a percentage of total investment and also relative to other public expenditure such as on education, health and welfare and defense are very small in these countries, as discussed earlier, and hence the overall effects of such expenditures on the economy are also likely to be small.

One significant corollary to the results is the adverse effect of environmental measures on labor productivity. This implication is drawn because environmental regulations tend either to lower or increase GDP at a rate slower than that at which they increase labor inputs. The nature of the relationship between productivity and environmental regulation is central to the question of complementarity (or conflict) between economic growth and the environment. This is because the decline in productivity caused by environmental regulation means that unit production costs will increase and prices may also rise, leading to a reduction of output. On the other hand, if environmental investments are of a change-in-process type, environmental expenditure may have a favorable impact on productivity, with consequent implications of compatibility between growth and the environment. Only microeconomic process-level empirical investigations provide more definitive clues as to the overall net effects of environmental expenditure on the economy. Aggregate empirical investigations may fail to capture cost-saving potential at the firm level. It must be noted also in this regard that macroeconomic empirical studies tend to show a conflict between growth and environmental control because the spread of clean or low-waste technologies economy-wide is still limited in most countries.

Environmental regulation may be one small factor responsible for the recent decline in productivity in the industrialized world. It could be said that environmental regulation may retard economic growth because it intervenes in market processes, adversely affecting rational decision-making at the firm level. But any government or environmental regulations are only a small part of the overall regulatory system. Moreover, there are many important causes of declining productivity growth other than environmental regulation. They include increases in energy prices, a slow-down in capital investment, the changing composition of the labor force (more young people and women workers), the changing composition of output (more services and less manufacturing), a decline in the work ethic, expanded social welfare programs, and regulatory activities including environmental regulation. An empirical study of the slow-down in manufacturing productivity growth in the United States shows that between 12 and 25 percent of the slow-down in productivity growth in the private sector between the early 1960s and the mid-1970s can be attributed to the widening scope of federal regulations, of which environmental regulations are only a small part (Christiansen and Haveman 1981).

Apart from data limitations and other conceptual and technical problems associated with econometric modeling, there are more fundamental limitations to a macroeconomic approach to the impact assessment of environmental expenditure. For instance, GDP is not an adequate measure of social welfare, and most of the benefits of environmental policies are not reflected in GDP or other national income accounts. The benefits of environmental protection are manifold and can be classified into the following three broad categories for analytical convenience: 'utility-increasing' benefits; 'cost-reducing' benefits; and 'output-increasing' benefits. Some examples of utility-increasing benefits are improvements in physical well-being derived from the availability of clean air, and reduced incidence of death or illness related to pollution. Cost-reducing benefits include reduced costs for municipal and industrial water treatment and less property and material damage to producers as a result of better air quality. Examples of output-increasing benefits are to be found in increased output, productivity and earnings attributable to the improved health conditions arising from a cleaner environment, the reduction in agricultural crop damage from air pollution, and the greater commercial fishery yields because of cleaner water (Freeman 1979).

All those benefits are quite substantial, but macroeconomic studies do not take into consideration such GNP-augmenting benefits of pollution abatement expenditure, mainly because of the enormous difficulties in estimating them. For instance, Freeman (1979) estimated that the realized benefits of air and water pollution control in 1978 were $2.8 billion and that the utility-increasing benefits were $24.8 billion. If these utility-increasing benefits were included in 1978 aggregate private output, the adjusted growth rate would be 4.11 percent instead of the actual growth rate of 3.92 percent. True productivity change could be roughly 0.19 percent or about one-fifth of a percentage point higher than that arrived at by the conventional measure.

In sum, while the macroeconomic effects of environmental expenditure have probably not been small, neither have the accompanying regulations been a major cause of the decline in productivity in the 1970s and 1980s, nor will they be a constraining factor on economic expansion in the future. Moreover, as a result of the failure to consider the beneficial effects of pollution control, the negative impact of environmental regulation has been somewhat overstated.

Many empirical studies on the industry impact of environmental programs have also appeared in recent years (Walter 1975; OECD 1982). Most studies used macroeconometric models linked to an input–output table to assess differential economic impacts of environmental expenditure on various industries. The empirical results of those studies are fairly similar to those obtained from the macroeconomic impact analysis. Environmental regulation tends to raise costs and prices and to reduce output in different industries, although the magnitude of change varies considerably from industry to industry. The employment effects are mixed, being positive for some industries and negative for others. Those results are subject to the same limitations associated with the macroeconomic analysis described earlier, and hence should be interpreted with great caution.

Consider the United States as an example. Results concerning the impacts of its 31 major industries were obtained using the Chase Econometric macroeconomic and input–output models to analyze differential industry effects. The effects of pollution-control expenditure on these industries are given in Table 5.5 which summarizes the percentage changes for prices, output and employment between the baseline forecast and the simulation with pollution-abatement expenditures. These differences are shown as at 1978 and 1983, cumulating from 1970.

Not surprisingly, those industries most directly subjected to environmental regulation showed the largest increases in prices. They include utilities, non-ferrous metals, paper, automobiles, iron and steel, stone, clay and glass, chemicals and petroleum. But it is worth noting that all industries showed price increases, including those not directly affected by pollution abatement expenditures, mainly through inter-industry linkages.

A decline in output was observed consistently in all industries except non-electrical machinery. The employment change is mixed for some industries, down for others, but the magnitude of the percentage change in employment seems to be generally smaller than that of output, thus implying declining productivity of labor across industries. Finally, it should be noted that the average annual percentage change of those figures should be much smaller, since they are cumulative from 1970.


## 5.6   ECONOMIC IMPACTS AT THE PROCESS LEVEL

Some of the weak economic impact results reported above are partly due to the failure of the underlying studies to capture the benefits of environmental activities (for example, improved health and productivity of workers) in the

*Table 5.5    Estimated impact of pollution-abatement expenditure on individual industries in the United States*

| Industry | By 1978 | | | By 1983 | | |
|---|---|---|---|---|---|---|
| | Prices | Output | Employ-ment | Prices | Output | Employ-ment |
| Agriculture | 0.3 | −0.8 | +0.6 | 0.6 | −1.3 | +1.3 |
| Mining | 0.4 | −1.2 | −0.1 | 0.7 | −2.5 | −0.4 |
| Construction | 0.1 | −2.1 | −0.4 | 0.2 | −3.5 | −0.2 |
| Food | 0.7 | −0.5 | +0.7 | 1.2 | −1.5 | +1.2 |
| Tobacco | 0.2 | −1.0 | +0.6 | 0.4 | −2.7 | +0.9 |
| Textiles | 0.5 | −1.4 | −0.1 | 0.9 | −2.5 | −0.2 |
| Apparel | 0.3 | −1.2 | −0.2 | 0.5 | −2.2 | −0.6 |
| Lumber | 0.6 | −4.4 | −1.3 | 1.5 | −4.4 | −0.6 |
| Furniture | 0.3 | −1.5 | −0.7 | 0.5 | −3.1 | −1.3 |
| Paper | 3.0 | −1.3 | −0.2 | 6.2 | −2.9 | −1.0 |
| Printing | 0.2 | −1.2 | −0.1 | 0.3 | −3.1 | −1.3 |
| Chemicals | 1.7 | −1.2 | −0.3 | 4.8 | 2.8 | −1.1 |
| Petroleum | 1.6 | −1.0 | +0.4 | 2.3 | −2.0 | +0.7 |
| Rubber | 0.6 | −1.6 | −0.5 | 1.0 | −4.2 | −1.4 |
| Leather | 0.4 | −0.8 | 0.0 | 0.9 | −1.4 | −0.3 |
| Stone, clay and glass | 2.0 | −2.0 | −0.7 | 3.2 | −3.4 | −1.0 |
| Iron and steel | 2.3 | −1.4 | −0.2 | 4.1 | −2.9 | −0.3 |
| Non-ferrous metals | 5.4 | −0.7 | +0.4 | 8.1 | −2.4 | +0.3 |
| Fabricated metals | 0.4 | −1.2 | 0.0 | 0.8 | −3.1 | −0.6 |
| Non-electrical machinery | 1.0 | +0.2 | +1.1 | 2.8 | −1.6 | +0.3 |
| Electrical machinery | 0.5 | −1.4 | −0.3 | 1.2 | −3.5 | −1.0 |
| Automobile | 2.5 | −2.1 | −0.5 | 5.5 | −5.6 | −2.4 |
| Other transport equipment | 0.3 | −1.0 | +0.2 | 0.6 | −0.9 | +0.8 |
| Professional instruments | 0.2 | −0.7 | +0.4 | 0.4 | −2.7 | −0.4 |
| Miscellaneous manufacturing | 0.2 | −0.9 | +0.3 | 0.4 | −1.7 | −0.7 |
| Transport services | 0.3 | −1.1 | +0.4 | 0.5 | −2.7 | +0.5 |
| Communications | 0.2 | −1.2 | −0.1 | 0.4 | −4.0 | −1.5 |
| Utilities | 15.2 | −0.7 | +0.5 | 27.8 | −1.8 | +0.6 |
| Trade | 0.3 | −1.0 | +0.2 | 0.6 | −2.7 | −0.8 |
| Finance, insurance and real estate | 0.2 | −0.8 | +0.1 | 0.8 | −2.4 | −0.1 |
| Other services | 0.4 | −1.1 | +0.8 | 0.7 | −2.6 | +1.6 |

*Source:*    OECD (1982)

cost-benefit calculations. More importantly, macroeconomic studies can be faulted for their inability to distinguish between end-of-line investment for pollution control and change-in-process investment for pollution prevention.

At the individual plant level, this distinction may be a critical determinant of the profitability of environmental expenditure. Most aggregate studies assume investment in end-of-line pollution-control equipment. In such a case, additional expenditure for the purchase, operation, and maintenance of new equipment with increased labor requirements will add to production costs and reduce pollutant emission, but will not increase measured output. As a result, labor productivity may decline under this assumption.

On the other hand, the introduction of low-waste or clean technologies through process modifications and material substitutions may not only achieve significant environmental improvements, but also lower production costs at the same time through substantial savings of energy and raw materials, and even of labor inputs. More specifically, the following potential benefits have been identified, one or more of which an enterprise adopting clean technologies may realize while reducing industrial pollution (Huisingh 1989, pp. 4–8):

1.  savings in raw materials and energy;
2.  decreased waste management costs;
3.  improved product quality;
4.  enhanced productivity;
5.  decreased down-time;
6.  reduced worker health risks and environmental hazards;
7.  decreased long-term liability for clean-up of waste materials that might otherwise have been buried;
8.  improved public image of the company.

The evidence that pollution-control measures can reduce rather than increase per unit production costs and hence improve productivity is still fragmentary and cannot be generalized across industries and countries, since it only applies to a relatively small fraction of total environmental investments, as shown by the United States data. Nevertheless, numerous case-studies at the plant level do suggest that pollution-prevention investment in clean technologies can lower production costs and at the same time reduce emissions.[3] We will highlight below several selected case-studies of such new production processes.

In the electroplating processes of zinc and cadmium with the basic material (mostly steel or iron), large quantities of waste-water, exhaust air and sludge are emitted; pollution occurs because of the presence of heavy metals and salts (UNEP and Federal Republic of Germany 1985). Conventional processing technologies are zinc electroplating and cadmium electroplating. New and clean technologies involved a low-waste zinc electroplating plant, which is now marketable, and a low-waste cadmium electroplating plant, which is in its pilot stage.

Comparative data from conventional and clean zinc and cadmium electro-plating processes on materials and energy requirements, and on the generation of air-borne, water-based and solid residuals are given in Table 5.6. It was

*Table 5.6    Schematic comparison of conventional and clean technologies for zinc and cadmium electroplating processes*

| Material/energy | Conventional technology | Clean technology | Difference clean–conventional |
|---|---|---|---|
| 1.   *Zinc electroplating per 10 kgs of zinc deposit* | | | |
| Fresh water, total | 13.4 m$^3$ | 1.2 m$^3$ | −12.2 m$^3$ |
| Required chemicals: | | | |
| Hot degreasing | — | — | — |
| Pickling degreasing | 8.8 kg | 3.4 kg | −5.4 kg |
| Electrolyte degreasing | 4.1 kg | 1.1 kg | −3.0 kg |
| Plating | 7.5 kg | 3.4 kg | −4.1 kg |
| Chromating | 0.9 kg | 0.3 kg | −0.6 kg |
| Waste water treatment | 42.8 kg | 5.6 kg | −37.2 kg |
| Thermal energy | 360.0 kcal | 396.0 kcal | +36.0 kcal |
| | (424.2 kWh) | (466.6 kWh) | (+42.4 kWh) |
| Electrical energy | 222.0 kWh | 288.0 kWh | +66.0 Kwh |
| 2.   *Cadmium electroplating per 10 kgs of cadmium deposit* | | | |
| Fresh water, total | 17.0 m$^3$ | 1.6 m$^3$ | −15.4 m$^3$ |
| Required chemicals: | | | |
| Hot degreasing | 2.0 kg | 0.7 kg | −1.3 kg |
| Pickling degreasing | 9.0 kg | 3.6 kg | −5.4 kg |
| Electrolyte degreasing | 4.4 kg | 1.1 kg | −3.3 kg |
| Plating | 9.0 kg | 4.3 kg | −4.7 kg |
| Chromating | 3.0 kg | 0.9 kg | −2.1 kg |
| Waste water treatment | 140.0 kg | 19.8 kg | −120.2 kg |
| Thermal energy | 400.0 kcal | 438.0 kcal | +38.0 kcal |
| | (−471.3 kWh) | (−516.1 kWh) | (−44.8 kWh) |
| Electrical energy | 238.5 kWh | 277.5 kWh | +39.0 kWh |
| *Residuals (airborne, waterborne and solid)* | | | |
| 1.   *Zinc electroplating per 10 kg of zinc deposit* | | | |
| Waste water | 13.0 m$^3$ | 0.4 m$^3$ | −12.6 m$^3$ |
| Zinc sludge | 35.0 kg | 1.8 kg | −33.2 kg |
| 2.   *Cadmium electroplating per 10 kgs of cadmium deposit* | | | |
| Waste water | 16.0 m$^3$ | 0.6 m$^3$ | −15.4 m$^3$ |
| Cadmium sludge | 80.0 kg | 2.3 kg | −77.7 kg |

*Source:*   UNEP and Federal Republic of Germany (1985)

reported that the construction of a low-waste electroplating plant would increase investment costs by approximately 20–30 percent compared with a conventional plant. But these increased costs are offset by cost savings of about 70 percent for chemicals and around 90–95 percent of emission fees.

**Waste-paper Production.**

Conventional technologies for waste-paper processing involve a process with an open water circuit or a process with a reduced water circuit. A new process technology is the closed water cycle system developed by Gissler and Pass in Germany.[4] Comparative data on materials and energy requirements and residuals in open, reduced and closed process water systems are given in Table 5.7. It should be noted that the comparison of energy consumption of the open and the closed system given in Table 5.6 is misleading. This is because installation of an open water system would today require final waste-water treatment, which would consume additional energy. The study did not provide comparative investment costs of new and conventional technologies.

*Table 5.7*   *Schematic comparison between conventional (open or reduced water system without water treatment) and clean (waste-water-free closed system) technologies in paper products from waste paper in the paper industry*

| Parameter | Unit | Conventional technology[a] | | Clean technology[b] | Difference |
|---|---|---|---|---|---|
| | | Open | Reduced | | |
| Water | m$^3$/t | 30 | 9.1 | 1 | −29 |
| Energy | kWh | 15 | | 38 | 23 |
| Amount of waste-water | m$^3$/t | 27 | 7.5 | 0 | −27 |
| Annual quantity of waste-water | m$^3$ | 594,000 | 172,500 | 0 | −594,000 |
| BOD | mg/l | 1,500 | 2,500 | 2,000 | |
| BOD-freight | t/a | 891 | 431 | 0 | −891 |
| COD | mg/l | 2,000 | 3,000 | 2,600 | |
| COD-freight | t/a | 1,188 | 518 | 0 | −1,188 |
| Sedimentary substances | | —[c] | —[c] | —[c] | |

*Notes*
BOD = biological oxygen demand.
COD = chemical oxygen demand.
a.   Open or reduced waste-water system without water treatmen.
b.   Waste-water-free closed systemt.
c.   With optimal operating sedimentation cone.

*Source:*   UNEP and Federal Republic of Germany (1985)

**Printed-circuit Board (PCB) Manufacturing.**

The Hewlett-Packard Company has replaced the conventional silk screen process by a dry-film photopolymer image transfer system, developed by Dupont, to obtain better printed circuit boards.[5] The original manufacturing processes were extremely chemical-intensive, resulting in the emission of pollutants and increased chemical disposal costs and liabilities, while the new processes use either fewer toxic chemicals or chemicals that produce fewer by-products for disposal. However, the cost savings in terms of chemicals and their disposal have not been sufficient to offset the increased costs of other inputs for the new processes. These results are summarized in Table 5.8. This example goes to show that not all clean technologies are necessarily economic or cost effective.

On the other hand, recent plant-level case-studies on waste minimization in the PCB industry in the United States by the Alliance Technologies Corporation (Bedford, Mass.) present both technically and economically favorable alternatives to existing technologies in waste minimization related to PCB manufacturing (Nunno 1988). One of the plant case studies is concerned with the economic viability of a new toxic solvent waste recovery system (Recyclene RX-35) compared with that of conventional off-site reclamation technologies. The results are summarized in Table 5.9. The operation of the two-stage solvent recovery system resulted in a 97.5 percent reduction in waste volume and a 99.8 percent recovery of solvent in the overhead. Moreover, the recycling of about 10,625 gallons (48,301 liters) of solvent at this particular plant in the first year of operation meant a disposal saving of

*Table 5.8    Cost comparison between the conventional (silkscreen process) and low-waste (dry-film image transfer process) technologies in printed-circuit board manufacturing in the electrical machinery industry ($)*

| Method | Conventional technology (silkscreen) | Low-waste technology (dry-film) | Difference |
|---|---|---|---|
| Treatment | 1,083 | 27,860 | 26,777 |
| Disposal | 40,101 | — | −40,101 |
| Water | 261 | 977 | 716 |
| Sewer | 20 | 75 | 55 |
| Energy | 4,631 | 53,306 | 48,675 |
| Chemicals | 88,860 | 31,898 | −56,962 |
| Dry-film | — | 157,762 | 157,762 |
| Total | 134,956 | 271,878 | 136,922 |

*Source:*   Johnnie (1987)

Table 5.9    Annual cost savings and payback for Recyclene RX-35 waste
recovery system installation alternative to offset reclamation in
the printed-circuit board manufacturing industry

| Cost item | No. of units per year | Cost per unit ($) | Cost prior installation ($) | Cost after installation ($) |
|---|---|---|---|---|
| Contaminated solvent | 10,625 gallons | 0.35 | 3,719 | — |
| Recyclene bottoms | 3.2 tons | 200 | — | 640 |
| Differential solvent purchase | 10,602 gallons | 4.50 | 47,709 | — |
| Differential energy consumption | 20,092 kW | 0.60 | — | 1,205 |
| Replacement liners | | | | |
| Teflon | 52 bags | 45.15 | — | 2,348 |
| Nylon | 155 bags | 6.50 | — | 1,010 |
| Additional labor | 208 hours | 15.00 | — | 3,120 |
| Total cost | | | 51,428 | 8,323 |
| Annual cost savings (first year) | | | | 43,105 |
| Recyclene RX-35 purchase and installation cost | | | | 26,150 |
| Payback period | | | | 7.3 months |

*Source:*    Nunno (1988, p. 17)

$0.35 per gallon (4,546 liters) of solvent, or $3,720 per year. In addition, a saving of $47,709 per year resulted from not buying virgin solvents. The total savings of these two items amounted to $51,428, which represents a net first-year saving of $16,955 including total capital costs and an estimated investment payback period of 7.3 months (see Table 5.9).

**Corrosion Protection of Components**

The conventional process technologies for corrosion protection of small components such as screws, nuts and springs as connecting elements are cadmium electroplating processes. It is well known that such processes produce toxic wastes, in particular cadmium. A new process technology designed to avoid the toxic waste problem associated with the conventional technology is the Rotalyt-Alutop process (ECE 1985). The new process is not only capable of reducing toxic wastes, but may also prove to be an economic means of ensuring the corrosion protection of bulk components of iron and steel. A cost comparison of the conventional and the new process technologies is provided in Table 5.10. It is worth noting that the new process uses far less energy and raw materials, and the overall unit production cost of goods treated by the new process is 30 percent lower than those treated by the conventional process.

*Table 5.10    Schematic comparison between the conventional (cadmium plating) and the low and non-waste technologies (Rotalyt-Alutop process) in the non-electrical machinery, electrical machinery and transport equipment industries*

|  | Conventional (cadmium electroplating) | Low-waste (Rotalyt-Alutop) |
|---|---|---|
| Materials and energy requirements |  |  |
| Electrical energy | 920 kWh/t[a] | 140 kWh/t |
| Organic brightener | 10 1/t | — |
| Metal | 15 kg/t (cadmium) | 14 kg/t (A1) |
| Rinse water | 1,000 1/t | 200 1/t |
| Promotor (catalyst) | 0 | 5 kt/t |
| Pre- and post-treatment | 120 kg/t | 20 kg/t |
| Investment requirements and unit production costs:[b] |  |  |
| Cadmium plating plant | approx. DM 600,000 |  |
| Rotalyt-Alutop plant | approx. DM 500,000 |  |
| Process costs comparison per ton of treated goods (DM, provisional values): |  |  |
| Labor costs | 116 | 116 |
| Energy costs | 96 | 12 |
| Metal and chemical costs | 56 | 78 |
| Maintenance costs | 12 | 12 |
| Effluent costs | 42 | 21 |
| Amortization and interest (10 yrs, 10 %) | 66 | 55 |
| Total | 388 | 294 |

*Notes*
a.   Tons of plated parts
b.   Investment costs for a 100 tons per month plant.

*Source:*   UNESCO (1985, pp. 4–5)

## Textile Printing

In textile printing, a clean technology called 'transfer text-printing technology' was invented in the early 1960s by the French engineer Noel de Plase, and has been adopted world-wide. This new process is not only environmentally clean, but also offers considerable savings in terms of cost and time compared with the conventional method (UNEP and Federal Republic of Germany 1985). Some comparative data on materials and energy requirements in the use of conventional and clean technologies for textile printing are given in Table 5.11. Energy and cost savings with clean technology are substantial.

*Table 5.11    Comparative data for conventional and clean technologies for textile printing*

| Material/energy | Conventional technology | Clean technology | Difference clean– conventional technology |
|---|---|---|---|
| Water per kg (liters) | 50–150 | 0 | –(50–150) |
| Solid residuals per kg (g) | 100–400 | | |
| Printpaste/dyestuff per $m^2$ (g) | 130–135 | 73–81 | –(123–124) |
| Printing machines | | | |
|    Energy per $m^2$ (kWh) | 100–350 | | |
|    Energy per kg (kWh) | 300 | | |
| Drying steam per $m^2$ (kWh) | 50–60 | | |
| Oil conversion (g/$m^2$) | 40–60 | | |

*Source:* UNEP and Federal Republic of Germany (1985, p. R13)

More importantly, transfer printing with an organic solvent system does not generate any airborne or water-borne residuals, because used solvent is recovered and reused in a closed system. Only some solid residuals are collected for burning. Comparable investment requirements for the conventional and new processes are not available.

**Potato-starch Manufacturing**

The former USSR developed a low-waste technology for extracting potato starch in 1982. The process separates the potatoes into solid and liquid elements, which are then processed independently. As a result, potato powder is produced without washing potatoes (the dry method), with natural potato cell fluid with water as a by-product. In the conventional process technology, the diluted potato cell fluid containing proteins, sugars, and so on is discharged with the wastes (ECE 1990a). Cost data for energy and raw materials and investment requirements for the conventional and low-waste technologies are summarized in Table 5.12. It is worth noting that the new technology eliminates waste-water and results in considerable material and energy savings. Above all, the investment requirement for the new process is reduced, and the operational costs per ton of output are almost 30 percent lower.

**Preparation of Molding Sands in the Foundry Industry**

The cost-effectiveness of the traditional and low-waste process technologies for preparing sand molds for metal casting was studied by the government of Poland in 1981 and the results are summarized in Table 5.13.

*Table 5.12   Comparison of standard potato-starch process with low-pollution potato-powder process in the food industry*

| Item | Standard technique | Low-pollution technique | Differences |
|------|--------------------|-------------------------|-------------|
| Materials and energy requirements | 5 tons of potatoes per ton of starch; 0.3 GJ of electrical energy and 0.17 GJ in the form of steam per ton of end-product | 5 tons of potatoes per ton of potato powder: 0.2 GJ of electrical energy and 0.1 GJ in the form of steam per ton of end-product | Energy saving |
| Residuals generation | Diluted internal vegetation water | No waste | Elimination of wastes |
| Pollution control measures | Necessity for purification plants | Co-products: natural potato cell fluid and dry fodder | No pollution |
| Waste discharge | Wastes in the form of diluted internal vegetation water cause pollution | Non-polluting | No waste disposal |
| Investment requirements and unit production costs | 0.6 million roubles for purification plants | 0.2 million roubles for organization of potato powder production | |
| Miscellaneous | Operating costs: 530 roubles per ton of starch | Operating costs: 380 roubles per ton of potato powder | Reduction of unit production costs by 150 roubles per ton of end-product |

*Note:*   GJ = gigajoule.

*Source:*   ECE (1990a, p. 6)

Compared with the conventional technology, the low-waste technology yields substantial savings in energy and raw materials, while reducing the emission of pollutants. More importantly, the unit cost of molding sands per ton of castings was more than halved for different weight factors as a result of adopting the low-waste technology (ECE 1990b).

## Production of Semi-synthetic Antibiotics from Penicillin

In some cases, the end-of-line or add-on process technology for pollution abatement could also be profitable, largely through the recovery and recycling of useful by-products. The recovery of pyridine from the production of semi-synthetic antibiotics from penicillin, using a clean technology developed by Gist Brocades in the Netherlands, is a case in point (ECE 1990c). Semi-synthetic antibiotics are produced from penicillin by chemical process. In various processing stages several chemicals and solvents are used and effluents containing several inorganic and organic substances are produced. These are normally discharged into sewage systems. The new clean technology is an add-on technology for the recovery of pyridine from water and its reuse in production processes. Pyridine recovery facilities have been in operation since mid-1983. None of the wastes generated by this clean technology are directly discharged into the environment. More importantly, the economic value of the recovered pyridine more than compensates for the operational and capital costs of the new add-on technology, as shown in Table 5.14 which also gives a comparison of the conventional and the clean technologies.

## Summary of other Case-studies

Examples abound of profitable recovery and reuse of industrial wastes as secondary raw materials. This is reflected in the list given in Table 5.15 of selected non-waste technologies applied in France. In all cases, the market value of recovered waste products exceeds the operating costs of new process technologies, and the gross operating profits may provide a sufficient margin to cover annual capital costs. On the basis of a survey in the United States of more than 500 companies that adopted clean technologies, it was found that each company reduced industrial wastes by between 85 percent and 100 percent, and, even more importantly, the investment pay-back periods were short, about three years. These benefits accrued to old industries as well as to high-technology industries. The technological changes included: (a) the incorporation of advanced technologies, such as ion exchange and ultrafiltration; (b) process modifications involving the replacement of an old substance by a new, less-polluting material; and (c) the adoption of less chemical-intensive and more mechanical processes. The most dramatic case was an improved photo-

*Table 5.13   Comparison between conventional technology and low-waste technology with respect to sand use and reutilization in foundry molding technology*

| Item compared | Production parameters | | Conventional technology | Low-waste technology | Difference |
|---|---|---|---|---|---|
| New sand consumption per liter of castings | A. | Bentonite sands | | | |
| | | $m = 5$ $\quad u_{sp} = 50$ | 2.5 tons | 0.75 tons | 1.75 tons |
| | | $m = 5$ $\quad u_{sp} = 90$ | 0.5 tons | 0.15 tons | 0.35 tons |
| | | $m = 20$ $\quad u_{sp} = 50$ | 10.0 tons | 3.00 tons | 7.00 tons |
| | | $m = 20$ $\quad u_{sp} = 90$ | 2.0 tons | 0.60 tons | 1.40 tons |
| | B. | Self-hardening sands | 5.0 tons | 1.50 tons | 3.50 tons |
| Energy consumption per liter of castings | A. | Bentonite sands | | | |
| | | $m = 5$ $\quad u_{sp} = 50$ | 1,500 MJ | 450 MJ | 1,050 MJ |
| | | $m = 5$ $\quad u_{sp} = 90$ | 300 MJ | 90 MJ | 210 MJ |
| | | $m = 20$ $\quad u_{sp} = 50$ | 6,000 MJ | 1,000 MJ | 4,200 MJ |
| | | $m = 20$ $\quad u_{sp} = 90$ | 1,200 MJ | 360 MJ | 940 MJ |
| | B. | Self-hardening sands | 3,000 MJ | 900 MJ | 2,100 MJ |
| Emission of waste per liter of casting | A. | Bentonite sands | | | |
| | | $m = 5$ $\quad u_{sp} = 50$ | 2.5 tons | 0.75 tons | 1.75 tons |
| | | $m = 5$ $\quad u_{sp} = 90$ | 0.5 tons | 0.15 tons | 0.35 tons |

| | | | | |
|---|---|---|---|---|
| | $m = 20$ $u_{sp} = 50$ | 10.0 tons | 3.00 tons | 7.00 tons |
| | $m = 20$ $u_{sp} = 90$ | 2.0 tons | 0.60 tons | 1.40 tons |
| | B. Self-hardening sands | 5.0 tons | 1.50 tons | 3.50 tons |
| Type of omitted waste | Bentonite and self-hardening sands | Knocked-out sand | Knocked-out sand and rejects from reclamation plant | Not significant |
| Investment outlays for installation | Capacity $Q = 4$ tons/hour | | 8 million zl | 8 million zl |
| | $Q = 10$ tons/hour | | 20 million zl | 20 million zl |
| Unit cost of some molding sand components in relation to liters of casting | A. Bentonite sands $m = 20$ $u_{sp} = 50$ | 221 zl | 102.45 zl | 110.55 zl |
| | $m = 20$ $u_{sp} = 90$ | 882 zl | 400.90 zl | 472.20 zl |
| | B. Self-hardening sands | 1865 zl | 916.50 zl | 948.50 zl |

*Notes*

Factor $m = \dfrac{\text{molding sand weight}}{\text{casting weight}}$

$u_{sp}$ = sand recovery rate in used sand processing (%)
The monetary unit in Poland is the zloty (zl)
MJ = megajoule

*Source:* ECE (1990b, p. 11)

127

*Table 5.14   Comparison between conventional and low-waste add-on technologies for the production of semi-synthetic antibiotics from penicillin*

| Item | Conventional technology (1) | Low-waste technology (2) | Difference (2) – (1) |
|---|---|---|---|
| Materials and energy requirements (add-on technology): | | | |
| Sodium hydroxide 25% (effluent pH adjustment) | | 350 tons | 350 tons |
| Steam (distillation) | | 2,000 tons | 2,000 tons |
| Electricity (pumps etc.) | | 70,000 kWh | 70,000 kWh |
| Generation of waterborne residuals | 800 cubic meters per year of waste water containing 100 tons of pyridine 20 tons of a mixture of various organic compounds | Pyridine recovery, hence no pyridine in waste water | |
| Discharge of airborne, water-borne and solid wastes | | | |
| Effluent (population equivalents) | 3,000 | — | –3,000 |
| Benefits related to implementation of low-and non-waste technology | | | |
| Total investments (in Fl) | | 2,500,000 | 2,500,000 |
| Total elimination costs (in Fl) | 135,000 | –238,000 | –373,000 |
| Unit elimination costs (Fl per population equivalent) | 45 | –79 | –124 |
| Gross savings | | | 373,000 Fl per year (3,000 per population equivalent × Fl 124 per population equivalent)[a] |

*Note:*   a.   Fl = florin, Dutch currency.

*Source:*   ECE (1990, p. 4)

graphic process developed by PCA International, Inc. in North Carolina. The initial cost of $120,000 for the process modification was paid back in a few months by annual savings in the cost of several solutions: the developing solution ($360,000), the fixer solution ($25,000), the bleach solution ($780,000) and the silver recovery ($1,410,000). This amounts to total annual savings of $2,575,000 (Huisingh and Bailey 1986).

## 5.7 CONCLUSIONS

This evaluation of selected process-level case-studies suggests that industrialization and environmental protection need not be a zero-sum game in which one gain at the expense of the other when clean or low-waste technologies are adopted. More specifically, integrated approaches to process modification designed for pollution and waste reduction at source and economizing on factor inputs could result in both increased productivity, or lower production costs, and an improved environment. Such cost-cutting and pollutant-reducing technologies seem to be available in the market or are in the process of being developed in a sufficient quantity across industries. However, a key question remains: Why are most of the manufacturing industries still scarcely penetrated by such potentially profit-making clean technologies, and instead dominated by the end-of-pipe approaches to pollution controls, as empirically confirmed earlier?

There are numerous and diverse obstacles to the diffusion of new process technologies among individual firms. Any firm which explores the possibilities of adopting new environmental technologies usually faces a wide array of constraints of a technical, economic, financial and political nature. Consideration will now be given to selected technical, structural and regulatory aspects which may have an important bearing on explaining the slowness of industrial adoption of clean technologies. It must be cautioned at the outset that barriers to the diffusion of technical change are discussed largely in the context of developed economies, and that the magnitude of the problem may appear even greater when assessed against the social and economic conditions in developing countries.

The lack of technical information about clean technologies is often cited as an important obstacle to technical change. While knowledge about new technologies is essential, it is not, however, the most significant factor affecting manufacturing decisions today in developed countries. In fact, one United States study evaluated the various obstacles confronted and found that about 90 percent of them are political and financial (insufficient cash flows and financial capital regulatory problems, risk and uncertainty, competitive pressures, reluctance to change, an so on) and only 10 percent of a technical nature (lack of centralized and reliable information, low level of awareness

*Figure 5.15  Costs and benefits of selected non-waste technologies used in France*

| Process | Company | Cost of operating conventional pollution-control process (French francs) | | Profit from alternative recovery process (French francs) | |
|---|---|---|---|---|---|
| Recovery of hydrocarbon in an oil refinery | Raffinerie ELF Feyzin (Thone) | Investment<br>Operating costs | 2,438,000<br>— | Investment<br>Operating costs<br>Sales of recovered product | 11,000,000<br>2,644,000<br>5,356,000 |
| Recovery of methionine mother liquor by evaporation | Société alimentaire equilibrée de Commentry (Allier) | Investment<br>Operating costs | 9,600,000<br>960,000 | Investment<br>Operating costs<br>Sales of recovered product | 7,000,000<br>10,500,000<br>13,000,000 |
| Recovery of protein and potassium from a yeast factory | Société industrielle de la levure Fala (SILF), Usine de Strasbourg (Bas-Rhin) | Investment<br>Operating costs | 10,800,000<br>1,080,000 | Investment<br>Operating costs<br>Sales of recovered product<br>Gross operating profit | 5,200,000<br>860,000<br>1,015,500<br>155,500 |
| Recovery of lead and tin from furnace fumes | Société des allaiges d'etain et derives, montreuil (Seine-Saint Denis) | Investment<br>Operating costs<br>Sale of recovered product<br>Profit | —<br>—<br>4,400<br>4,400 | Investment<br>Operating costs<br>Sales of recovered product<br>Gross operating profit | 300,000<br>200<br>8,390<br>8,730 |
| Conversion of phosphoric acid waste into plasterboard | Rhône progil, Les roches de Condreu (Isère), Rouen (Seine-Maritime) | Investment<br>Operating costs | 9,000,000<br>5,000,000 | Investment<br>Operating costs<br>Sales of recovered product | 35,000,000<br>73,000,000<br>73,500,000 |

| | | | |
|---|---|---|---|
| Water recycling in fiberboard plant | Isorel, Castel jaloux (Tarn-et-Garonne) | Investment 5,000,000<br>Operating costs 500,000 | Investment 2,500,000<br>Operating costs 100,000<br>Sales of recovered product 350,000<br>Gross operating profit 250,000 |
| Recycling of effluents in glue and gelatine manufacture | Société des établissements George Alquier Bout-du-Pont- de-l'Ain, Mazamet (Tarn) | Investment 534,000<br>Operating costs 53,000 | Investment 248,000<br>Operating costs —<br>Reduced consumption of recovered product 18,000<br>Gross operating profit 18,000 |
| Recovery of iron dust in steelworks | Sacilor, Gandrange (Moselle) | Investment 3,700,000<br>Operating costs 1,850,000 | Investment 9,800,000<br>Operating costs 3,250,000 |
| Recovery of plum juice | Établissements Laparre Castelnaud de Gratecombe (Lot-et-Garonne) | Investment 768,000<br>Operating costs 77,000 | Investment 235,000<br>Operating costs 140,000<br>Sales of recovered profit 247,500<br>Gross operating profit 107,500 |
| Recovery of glycerine in a soap factory | Savonnerie de Lutterbach (Haut-Rhin) | Investment 600,000<br>Operating costs 60,000 | Investment 400,000<br>Operating costs 101,700<br>Sales of recovered product 280,000<br>Gross operating profit 178,300 |
| Recovery of quarry washings | Société d'exploitation de l'entreprise Mirsaint-Lary (Hautes-Pyrénées) | | Investment 188,000<br>Operating costs 3,200<br>Sales of recovered product 11,000<br>Gross operating profit 7,800 |

*Source:* UNEP (1982, pp. 425–6)

and availability of technology and alternatives, and so on) (OECD 1985b). The technological information gap, however, could be the single important initial obstacle to the diffusion of clean technologies in developing countries. Easy access to technical information is particularly important for small and medium-sized firms if they are to innovate.

One of the difficulties most often cited in the literature is related to the characteristics of firms and the structure of industry. In particular, the absorptive capacity of a firm for technical change is seen to be related to the size and maturity of a firm and industry. A firm in the early stages of its growth cycle tends to be flexible in choosing factor proportions in production methods, and hence can be receptive to new processes. In contrast, as the firm becomes mature it becomes molded to certain established manufacturing practices. As a result, production systems become more inflexible and technical changes tend to be marginal. For instance, sugar refining in the United Kingdom, leather tanning in the Netherlands, and paper and pulp manufacture in France are all seen to be mature industries; all have shown some resistance to new process technologies, and instead have preferred 'end-of-pipe' approaches to pollution abatement. However, resistance to technical change caused by the ossification of industry structure is less relevant in a large number of developing countries, where most of the manufacturing industries are at an embryonic stage of development or are yet to be developed.

One intervening influence is the size of firms, which may affect significantly their capacity to absorb new technologies regardless of the stage of development. The small size of some firms may prevent them adopting clean technologies, even if they are aware of such opportunities, since they cannot afford the capital outlay, the modernization required, or the attendant risks of using new technologies. They are not capable of undertaking any large-scale research and development, and hence become technically dependent on outside sources. These limitations of small and medium-sized firms are likely to be even more serious in developing countries.

Environmental regulation constitutes another frequently cited obstacle to technological change. In particular, the relationship between environmental regulation and technical change is a contentious issue. The scope, content and methods of enforcement of environmental regulation may directly affect the attitude and response of a firm to clean technologies. In all cases, it is imperative that the formulation and implementation of environmental regulation be adjusted to the individual characteristics of the firms and industries concerned.

In general, the stringency of environmental regulation can raise production costs, because of diminishing returns in improving environmental quality. It must be noted, however, that strict regulation can also provide a stimulus for research into efficient technological solutions leading to savings in energy, raw materials and labor inputs. One of the major lessons learned from a variety of industrial case-studies is, however, that the stringency of regulation is not a decisive factor. What is more important is the flexibility of regulation enforcement. It was shown earlier that the economic impact of environmental regulation varies considerably among industries, usually being more pronounced in certain heavy-polluting industries such as paper and pulp, chemicals, iron and steel and non-ferrous metals than in others. It is essential, therefore, that the degree of stringency and the form of regulation should allow sufficient response time to enable basic process changes to be made instead of a rush to hasty solutions such as an end-of-pipe adjustment. However, too much time allowed for the enforcement of environmental regulation may result in a certain laxity and diminished motivation for technical change on the part of firms.

There are many other regulatory aspects, such as uncertainty related to the implementation schedule, their content, their continuity and consistency over time, as well as financial factors. All these aspects could influence firms' technological choices. For instance, high pollution charges may act as a strong financial incentive for industry to find efficient technological solutions in some cases.

In essence, any program designed to promote the diffusion of clean technologies must focus on an array of issues much broader than just the technical aspects. In this regard, developing countries could benefit considerably from the rapidly accumulating experiences of developed countries when they attempt to formulate and implement their own environmental policy to promote the diffusion of clean technologies.

## CHAPTER NOTES

1. Readers interested in the theory and methods of environmental economics should consult Tietenberg (1992).
2. For simulation studies of environmental impacts using a macroeconometric model, see, for instance, Data Resources Inc. (1979); OECD (1982, 1985a); JEC (1978); Walter (1976). For an impact analysis based on the input–output table for Federal Republic of Germany, see Schaefer and Stahmer (1989).
3. For instance, see Bringer and Zoss (1984); Campbell and Glenn (1982); Chazelon (1982); ECE (1982); Gardner and Huisingh (1987); Royston (1979).
4. For full technical details, see UNEP and Federal Republic of Germany (1985).
5. For technical details, see Johnnie (1987).

# 6. Conclusions

Industrialization exerts inevitable stresses upon the environment. This study has sought to determine the stresses which arise at different stages of industrialization. In other words, it has attempted to delineate the environmental pressures emanating from the growth and expansion of different manufacturing industries. Environmental deterioration associated with industrial development occurs at both the input and the output sides of production activities. Industrial production requires the input of a wide variety of natural resources such as water, energy, minerals, forest products, and other raw materials whose rapid depletion may cause environmental damage and ecological disruption. On the output side, the manufacturing process generates myriad forms of waste that may create serious environmental hazards involving air, surface, and groundwater pollution, hazardous wastes and toxic chemical releases, soil contamination, thermal heat, carbon dioxide releases and noise. Also, the use of many manufactured end-products, such as pesticides, detergents, paints, plastics and combustion engines further contributes to these hazards.

There is an extensive literature on industrial pollution, as well as on its wider environmental effects. Most of it deals with certain specific aspects of industry and environment, such as industrial water pollution, air pollution from the iron and steel industry, toxic waste dumps at ground sites, acid rain and industrial hazardous wastes. Few studies have attempted to assemble a comprehensive picture covering all forms of environmental impact and industrial development, in particular the impact on air, land and water. Such a collective or overall assessment of the environmental stress arising from process transformation at different stages of industrialization is urgently needed, not only to place the industry–environment relationship in a proper perspective, but also, more importantly, to enable policy-makers and development planners in developing countries to derive a correct and comprehensive assessment of the environmental implications of pursuing alternative strategies of industrial development. For instance, with such a complete picture of the industry–environment link, it becomes possible to assess the particular environmental threats and the major pollution problems for land, air and water, both actual and potential, that may arise from alternative industrial development strategies. It also makes it easier to identify the key pollutants and the major sources of environmental damage. The present study has attempted to meet this need by providing a more integrated perspective on the environmental impact of industrial development.

Economic development through industrialization has been a historically well-trodden path to the achievement of higher standards of living and expanded economic development. Industrialization and economic development is today perceived as a major cause of environmental degradation in developed countries. This perception is not, however, shared by developing countries, which today cannot escape environmental problems. Without development, poverty-induced environmental degradation such as deforestation, desertification and environmental contamination caused by sub-standard living conditions will continue to plague developing countries. However, environmental problems will also arise out of the actual attempts to eradicate poverty through industrialization and development. From the perspective of developing countries, the primacy of industrialization is beyond dispute, despite its potential environmental costs. More importantly, industrialization could become a cure for their environmental problems, if an environmentally sound industrial development strategy is pursued.

In this regard, the importance of low-waste or clean technologies cannot be over emphasized in forging ahead with the industrialization process. A number of case-studies have been reviewed which substantiate the potential of new clean technologies not only to reduce industrial pollution drastically, but also to remain economically profitable in their own right. The substantial savings achieved in materials and labor costs are often more than sufficient to offset initial higher investment costs. Low-waste or clean technologies also point to a way out of a potential conflict between industrial growth and environmental protection. Growth and environmental protection can go hand in hand with clean technologies.

One important conclusion of the present study is that if the current patterns of structural change in world industry continue unchecked, environmental problems in developing countries will probably reach crisis proportions in the near future. More specifically, it has been shown that the world-wide stagnation during 1980–82 and the subsequent recession forced many developed countries extensively to restructure and trim down their traditional smokestack industries and caused them to shift to the development and expansion of high-technology industries. As a result, a considerable part of the traditional manufacturing activities in developed countries have been redeployed to developing countries. For instance, the fastest-growing industries in developing countries compared with their counterparts in developed countries during the period 1970–88 are mainly concentrated in two groups: the labor-intensive light manufacturing group (leather, footwear, textiles, wearing apparel and beverages), and the capital-intensive basic materials producing group (iron and steel, non-ferrous metals, plastics, petroleum and coal products, metal products, industrial chemicals and paper).

This study has shown that growth industries in developing countries are highly resource-intensive, they use large quantities of water, energy and raw materials, and at the same time are highly pollution-intensive, generating a large variety of pollutants and industrial wastes including toxic substances. It seems evident that the rapid expansion of smokestack industries in the South may become unsustainable sooner than expected, unless the diffusion of clean technologies occurs on a massive scale across industries and countries. Industrial pollution and the depletion of natural resources in developing countries may soon reach a critical level that will subsequently give rise to severe environmental disruption. It is true that industrial pollution represents more of a potential than an actual threat in many regions of the South, particularly in Africa; but severe industrial pollution problems encountered now in many rapidly industrializing developing countries may foreshadow what is to come on a far broader scale in other developing countries.

To recapitulate, the crux of the problem is the extent to which the drive to sustain industrialization in developing countries will be constrained by their natural resource base and their environmental absorptive capacity. To promote continued rapid industrial growth without also imposing environmental controls in developing countries may accelerate the depletion of natural resources, with serious ecological and environmental consequences, and cause direct environmental degradation through unchecked industrial pollution, to such an extent that the process of industrialization will no longer be sustainable.

This study has thus shown that the key to sustainable industrial development is clean technology. There are certain apparent advantages of adopting clean technologies in developing countries. While still at relatively early stages of industrialization, many developing countries have the option of selecting production techniques which are less disruptive to their environment than the existing technologies used in developed countries. Moreover, when a new plant is being built, the adoption of a clean process technology or the incorporation of pollution-abatement equipment is significantly cheaper than the installation and 'adding-on' of such equipment to an existing plant.

From the perspective of individual developing countries where industrial pollution is still far less serious than in developed countries, the principal approach is to adopt less costly and less effective industrial pollution-control methods, and to assume that technical progress will reduce pollution-abatement costs. Further economic growth may then make the costs of more effective methods much easier to bear in the future. The 'fallacy-of-composition' argument, however, may make this approach untenable. While the industrial pollution problem may be manageable by individual developing countries in isolation, the environmental pressure imposed by the simultaneous industrialization process of developing countries collectively may become unsustainable, not only for individual countries, but also for the global environment because of the transboundary migration of pollutants and their overall cumulative effects. These manifest themselves in broader ecosystem damage such as the 'greenhouse effect,' the depletion of the ozone layer, acid rain and other global threats.

The mutuality of interest between developed and developing regions in environmental protection seems to provide a compelling case for North–South co-operation to promote and sustain environmentally sound industrial development in developing countries, mainly through the diffusion of such technologies. There are, however, some major obstacles to the diffusion of clean technologies in developing countries. First of all, the bulk of clean technologies engineered in developed countries may not be appropriate for the ecological conditions of developing countries. Even if appropriate technologies are found, the urgent need still exists for technical co-operation, knowledge transfer, and the development of expertise in waste management and environmental regulations and policies. More importantly, environmental protection requires heavy capital investments and additional resource commitments that developing countries often cannot afford. The question of who pays for the higher costs arising out of an environmentally sound approach to industrialization in developing countries and how this burden is to be allocated between developed and developing countries is crucial. Given the present debt problems and resource constraints confronting most developing countries, the burden of additional resource mobilization may rest on the developed countries. The appropriate *modus operandi* for channeling such additional resources, whether through existing bilateral or multilateral machineries or through an entirely new avenue such as a special fund for environmental protection in developing countries, is an issue which warrants separate consideration. Otherwise, we will all pay dearly if we fail to act in this vital area of international co-operation.

Closely related to industrial pollution problems in developing countries is the fact that increased pollution-control costs in certain industrial processes in developed countries could give rise to a substantial differential in international manufacturing cost-competitiveness. This price and cost differential may in turn create pressures for increased generalized protectionism or the erection of non-tariff barriers against specific products manufactured in countries unencumbered by stringent environmental regulation. Such a shift in competitiveness may also accelerate the migration of polluting industries or processes to countries facing a less urgent pollution problem, mainly developing countries. This possibility of the export of pollution to developing countries appears to be particularly acute with hazardous products: faced with strict environmental regulation at home, many manufacturers in developed countries find it economically attractive to move hazardous manufacturing plants to less restrictive places. Empirical evidence of the international migration of highly polluting industries from developed to developing countries abound, particularly in the production of hazardous substances. The list of hazardous products and industries exported to developing countries includes asbestos, textiles and friction products, arsenic and refined copper from primary smelters, mercury mining, lead mining and smelters, primary refined zinc, pesticides, benzidine dyes, vinyl chloride and iron and steel.[1]

Given the accelerating trend toward the international redeployment of polluting industries to developing countries, the latter may face a difficult decision regarding whether to create a favorable climate for foreign investment at the cost of the environment, or to protect the environment at the cost of slowing down foreign capital inflows. So far, international co-operation on the promotion of clean industrial pollution has not yet reached a critical level. As a result, developing countries have failed to benefit from the experience of developed countries in avoiding the worst forms of environmental damage by not adopting preventive strategies for pollution control rather than reactive strategies involving clean-up after pollution. Such preventive strategies call for the integration of environmental policies into industrial development plans at the initial stages of formulation. Above all, it calls for massive financial support to promote clean technologies in developing countries. Ultimately, North–South co-operation will make it possible not only to create a cleaner global environment, but also to obviate the need for the North–South migration of polluting industries. In this regard, it is important that the increasing preoccupation with the environment in developed countries should not be allowed to detract from their support for the continued industrialization of developing countries, either by reducing resource transfers or by distorting aid priorities. Such support was recently witnessed in the 1997 Kyoto Agreement which granted developing countries exemptions in carbon-dioxide emissions. There is some hope that further co-operation will continue in the future.

## CHAPTER NOTES

1. For extensive documentation on the United States export of plants producing various hazardous products to developing countries, see OECD (1985d); for general surveys of the question of hazardous exports, see Castleman (1974); Gladwin and Walter (1980); OECD (1980); Street and Zorn (1983).

# Appendix: Statistical Tables

*Table A-1*  *International comparison of water requirements per unit of selected manufactured products*

| Industry, product and country | Unit of product (tons, except as specified) | Water required per unit (liters) |
|---|---|---|
| *Food products* | | |
| Bread, United States | | 2,100–4,200 |
| Bread, Cyprus | | 600 |
| Bread or pastry, Belgium | | 1,100 |
| Canned food | | |
| Fruit, Belgium | | 15,000 |
| Vegetables, Belgium | | 8,000–30,000 |
| Fruit and vegetables, Canada | | 10,000–50,000 |
| Vegetables, Israel | | 10,000–15,000 |
| Fruit, vegetables and juices (1965), United States | | 24,000 |
| Meat | | |
| Meat freezing, Cyprus | Ton of carcass | 500 |
| Meat freezing, New Zealand | | 3,000–8,600 |
| Meat packing, United States | Ton of prepared meat | 23,000 |
| Meat packing, Canada | Ton of carcass | 8,800–34,000 |
| Milk and milk products | | |
| Cheese | | |
| Cyprus | | 10,000 |
| New Zealand | | 2,000 |
| United States | | 27,500 |
| Milk | | |
| Belgium | 1,000 liters | 7,000 |
| Finland | | 2,000–5,000 |
| Israel | | 2,700 |
| Sweden | | 2,000–4,000 |
| United States | | 3,000 |

*Table A-1    Continued*

| Industry, product and country | Unit of product (tons, except as specified) | Water required per unit (liters) |
|---|---|---|
| Sugar | | |
| Denmark | Ton of sugar-beets | 4,800–15,800 |
| Finland | Ton of sugar-beets | 10,000–20,000 |
| Italy | Ton of sugar-beets | 10,500–12,500 |
| United States | Ton of sugar-beets | 3,200–8,300 (range) 6,000 (average) |
| France | Ton of sugar-beets | 10,900 |
| Germany, Federal Republic of | Ton of sugar-beets | 10,400–14,000 |
| Israel | Ton of sugar-beets | 1,800 |
| United Kingdom | Ton of sugar-beets | 3,200–8,300 |
| Beverages | | |
| Beer | | |
| Belgium | Kiloliter | 7,000–20,000 |
| Canada | Kiloliter | 10,000–20,000 |
| France | Kiloliter | 14,500 |
| United States | Kiloliter | 15,200 |
| Finland | Kiloliter | 10,000–20,000 |
| Israel | Kiloliter | 13,500 |
| United Kingdom | Kiloliter | 6,000–10,000 |
| *Pulp and paper* | | |
| Groundwood pulp, Finland | Ton of wood pulp | 30,000–40,000 |
| Sulphate pulp | | |
| Finland | Ton of pulp | 250,000–350,000 |
| Sweden | Ton of unbleached pulp | 75,000–300,000 |
| Sweden | Ton of bleached pulp | 170,000–500,000 |
| Sulphite pulp | | |
| Finland | Ton of bleached pulp | 450,000–500,000 |
| Finland | Ton of unbleached pulp | 250,000–300,000 |
| Sweden | Ton of bleached pulp | 300,000–700,000 |
| Sweden | Ton of unbleached pulp | 140,000–500,000 |
| Wood pulp | | |
| Industry average, United States | Ton of pulp and paper | 236,000 |
| Industry average, United Kingdom | Ton of paper and board | 90,000 |
| Industry average, France | Ton of pulp and paper | 150,000 |
| *Chemicals* | | |
| Ammonia, naphtha, reforming, Japan | | 255,000 |
| Ammonium nitrate, Belgium | | 52,000 |
| Ammonium sulphate, United States | | 835,000 |

*Table A-1   Continued*

| Industry, product and country | Unit of product (tons, except as specified) | Water required per unit (liters) |
|---|---|---|
| Caustic soda and chlorine, Canada | | 125,000 |
| Caustic soda, Solvay process, United States | | 60,500 |
| Caustic soda, dual process, Germany, Federal Republic of | | 160,000 |
| Soap, Belgium | | 37,000 |
| Soap, Cyprus | | 4,500 |
| Soap, laundry, United States | | 960–2,100 |
| *Textiles* | | |
| Dyeing and finishing | | |
| Cotton yarn, Israel | | 60,000–180,000 |
| Synthetic yarn, Israel | | 90,000–180,000 |
| Wool yarn, Israel | | 70,000–140,000 |
| Fabrics, Israel | | 60,000–100,000 |
| Mills | | |
| Cotton | | |
| Finland | | 50,000–150,000 |
| Sweden | | 10,000–250,000 |
| Wool | | |
| Finland | Ton of cloth or yarn | 150,000–350,000 |
| Sweden | Ton of wool | 400,000 |
| *Iron and steel products* | | |
| Belgium | | |
| Blast furnace, no recycling | | 58,000–73,000 |
| Blast furnace, with recycling | | 50,000 |
| Finished and semi-finished steel, no recycling | | 61,000 |
| Finished and semi-finished steel, with recycling | | 27,000 |
| Canada | | |
| Pig iron | | 130,000 |
| Open hearth steel | | 22,000 |
| France | | |
| Smelting | | 46,000 |
| Martin process (open hearth) | | 15,000 |
| Thomas process (Bessemer converter) | | 10,000 |
| Electric furnace steel | | 40,000 |
| Rolling mills | | 30,000 |

*Table A-1    Continued*

| Industry, product and country | Unit of product (tons, except as specified) | Water required per unit (liters) |
|---|---|---|
| United States | | |
| Fully integrated mills | | 86,000 (average) |
| Rolling and drawing mills | | 14,700 (average) |
| Blast furnace smelting | | 103,000 (average) |
| Electrometallurgical ferro-alloys industry, consumption use | | 72,000 (average) |
| *Miscellaneous products* | | |
| Automobiles, United States | Vehicle | 38,000 |
| Fertilizer plant, Finland | Ton of saltpetre (25% nitrogen) | 270,000 |
| Glass, Belgium | | 68,000 |
| Leather, South Africa | | 50,100 |
| Leather, Finland | Ton of hides | 50,000–125,000 |
| Leather tanning, United States | Square meter of hide | 20–2,550 |
| Leather tanning, Cyprus | Square meter of small animal skins | 110 |

*Note:*    Table based on data from the following countries: Belgium, Canada, Cyprus, Denmark, Finland, France, Federal Republic of Germany, Israel, Italy, Japan, Netherlands, New Zealand, South Africa, Sweden, United Kingdom, United States. Most of the data were provided by the respective governments in response to requests from the Secretary-General of the United Nations for such information in 1957 and 1968. The wide range of variations in specific water amounts reflects differences in technologies.

*Source:*    ECE (1975)

Table A-2  Selected environmental effects of the energy sector[a]

| Energy sources | Air | Waters (surface, underground/inland and marine) | Land and soils | Wild life | Other effects (solid waste, risks to human health, noise, visual impact, etc.) |
|---|---|---|---|---|---|
| Coal[b] | $SO_x$, $NO_x$, particulates | Acid mine drainage Mine liquid waste disposal Water availability Wash water treatment Water pollution from storage heaps | Land subsidence Land use for mines and heaps Land reclamation of open cast mines | Natural habitat disturbed Exploitation of wilderness or natural areas for surface mining | Noise of rail transport of coal Dust emission Visual impact of coal heaps Occupational risks |
| Petroleum products[b] | $H_2S$ production $SO_x$, $NO_x$, CO, $CO_2$, HC, ammonia, particulates, trace elements | Oil spills Water availability | Land use for facilities and pipes | Natural habitat disturbed Pipeline impact on wild life Wild life polluted through leaks or spills | Blow-outs Explosions and fires Pipeline leaks Spills (accidental and operational) Visual impact of pipelines |
| Gas[b] | HC emission (mainly methane) Trace metal emission $H_2S$ and combustion emissions | Liquid residual disposal | Land use for facilities and pipes | Natural habitat disturbed Impact of pipelines on wild life | Blow-outs High leak potential General safety Spills and explosions Visual impact of pipelines |
| Electricity generation from fossil fuels (excluding nuclear energy) | $SO_x$, $NO_x$, CO, $CO_2$, HC, trace elements, particulates, radionuclides Long-range transport and deposition of pollutants Climatic impact of cooling towers | Water availability Thermal releases | Land requirement | Secondary effects on water, air and land Solid wastes Ash disposal Noise | Visual impact of cooling towers and power lines |

*Table A-2 Continued*

| Energy sources | Air | Waters (surface, underground/inland and marine) | Land and soils | Wild life | Other effects (solid waste, risks to human health, noise, visual impact, etc.) |
|---|---|---|---|---|---|
| Uranium fuel cycle and electricity from nuclear power plants | Radioactive dust Gaseous effluent (radionuclides, F, No$_x$) Noble gas, H-3, I-131, C-14 Local climatic impact of cooling towers Decontamination and decommissioning of nuclear power plants | Mine drainage Underground water contamination Water availability Thermal releases Liquid radionuclide emission (H-3, CO-60, Sr-90, I-131, Ru-106, Cs-136 and 137) | Land subsidence (mine) Land reclamation of open cast mines Land use for mines | Secondary effects of impact on water, land and air (toxic metal liquid and solid chemical wastes, radiological wastes) Recycled fission products High-level radioactive wastes Visual impact of cooling towers and power lines Noise Occupational risks | Radioactive products Mine water Mill tailing water |
| Hydropower[c] | | Effect on hydrological cycles Water quality and resources | Land irreversibly flooded Landslide risks affected | Wild life habitat of rivers Change in ecosystems Fish migration | Visual impacts Risk of dam rupture |
| Others[c] Biomass, geothermal, wind and solar energies | Biomass combustion: air pollution, particulates Geothermal: air pollution | Biomass conversion: pollution water availability Geothermal: water pollution | Land use for energy plantations Land requirement of solar energy | Biomass: ecosystem disruption by energy plantations wind generators Biomass risk to workers Photovoltaic toxic pollution when decommissioning | Noise of wind generators Visual impact |

*Notes*

a. Excluding energy use in transport, agriculture and other activities (heating, etc.).

b. Fossil fuels, extraction, treatment, transport and waste disposal.

c. Renewable energy.

*Source:* OECD (1985b)

*Table A-3    Industrial use of raw materials*

| ISIC code | Industry | Raw materials |
|---|---|---|
| 311/2 | Food products | Livestock, fruits, vegetables, salt, glucose, water |
| 313 | Beverages | Fruits, malt, hops, glucose, water |
| 314 | Tobacco | Raw tobacco, paper wrappers and package, menthol |
| 321 | Textiles | Raw cotton, wool and silk, ethylene oxide and terephthalic acid (for polyester), water |
| 322 | Wearing apparel | Textile products |
| 323 | Leather and fur products | Animal hides and skin, chromium, sodium chloride |
| 324 | Footwear | Leather, plastic, wood |
| 331 | Wood products | Wood fibres |
| 332 | Furniture, fixtures | Wood products, plastic, metals |
| 341 | Paper and paper products | Pulp, aluminum sulphates |
| 342 | Printing, publishing | Paper, ink |
| 351 | Industrial chemicals | Inorganic and organic chemicals, limestone |
| 352 | Other chemical products | Inorganic and organic chemicals |
| 353 | Petroleum refineries | Crude oil |
| 354 | Miscellaneous petroleum products | Coal |
| 355 | Rubber products | Latex, polymers, chemicals |
| 356 | Plastic products n.e.c. | Polyvinyl chloride (PVC), polyethylene terephthalate (PET), recycled plastics |
| 361 | Pottery, china etc. | China clay, fireclay, ball clay, dolomite |
| 362 | Glass and products | Silica sand, limestone, soda ash, recycled glass |
| 369 | Non-metallic products, n.e.c. | Limestone, chalk, gypsum/anhydrite |
| 371 | Iron and steel | Iron ore, limestone, recycled scrap |
| 372 | Non-ferrous metals | Bauxite, copper, lead, zinc, cadmium |
| 381 | Metal products | Recycled scrap, metal sheet |
| 382 | Non-electrical machinery n.e.c. | Steel, recycled scrap |
| 383 | Electrical machinery | Tungsten, glass-ceramics, silicon, copper |
| 384 | Transport equipment | Glass steel fibre, reinforced plastic, aluminum, chrome |
| 385 | Professional and scientific goods | Silicon, steel, diamond, platinum |
| 390 | Other industries | Steel, other intermediate raw materials. |

*Sources:*    Highley (1984, p. 9); Sell (1981)

*Table A-4     Known significant water pollutants, selected industries*

| Categories of sources | Known significant pollutants |
|---|---|
| 1. Pulp and paper mills | BOD, COD, SS, bac, WSL, $NH_3$, DS biocides |
| 2. Paperbased, builder's paper and board mills | BOD, COD, SS |
| 3. Meat product and rendering process | BOD, DS, SS, N, $NO_3$, $NH_3$, O&G, P, bac |
| 4. Dairy product processing | pH, BOD, COD, DS, SS, set.s |
| 5. Grain mills | BOD, SS, pH, DS, N, P, heat |
| 6. Canned and preserved fruits and vegetables processing | BOD, SS, pH |
| 7. Canned and preserved seafood processing | BOD, COD, SS, DS, O, fecal coliform, Cl |
| 8. Sugar processing | BOD, COD, SS, DS, coli, $NH_3$, pH, heat |
| 9. Textile mills | BOD, COD, DS, color, SS, O&G, heavy metals (Cu, Cr, Zn) |
| 10. Cement manufacturing | DS, SS, pH, heat |
| 11. Feedlots | BOD, DS, SS, $NO_3$, P, coli |
| 12. Electroplating | Heavy metals (Cr, Zn, Ni, Cd, others), CN, acidity, pH, DS, SS |
| 13. Organic chemicals manufacturing | O, unreacted raw materials, BOD, COD, SS, acidity or alkalinity, heavy metals and heat |
| 14. Inorganic chemicals manufacturing | Divided into 22 discrete subcategories,[a] BOD, DS, COD, pH, heat |
| 15. Plastic and synthetic materials | BOD, COD, SS, heavy metals, pH (subcategories vary extensively) |
| 16. Soap and detergent manufacturing | BOD, COD, SS, O&G, surf, pH |
| 17. Fertilizer manufacturing | |
|    Subpart A - phosphate type | pH, P, F, Cd, As, V, U |
|    Subpart B - ammonia | pH, N, O |
|    Subpart C - urea | pH, N |
|    Subpart D - ammonium nitrate | ph, N, $NO_3$ |
|    Subpart D - nitric acid | ph, N, $NO_3$ |
| 18. Petroleum refining | O, S, Phen, $NH_3$, BOD, COD, heavy metals, alkalinity |
| 19. Iron and steel manufacturing | Phen, CN, $NH_3$, O, SS, heavy metals, (Cr, Ni, Zn, Sn), DS, acidity, heat |
| 20. Non-ferrous metals manufacturing | BOD, SS, DS, COD, CN, pH, color, turb, heavy metals, P, N, O&G, heat |
| 21. Phosphate manufacturing | F, As, P, $H_3PO_4$, $H_2SO_3$, $H_2SO_4$, HCl, SS, Cr, DS, $NH_3$ |
| 22. Steam electric power plants | BOD, SS, DS, COD, CN, pH, surf, color, O&G, phen, turb, heavy metals, VS, P, N, heat |
| 23. Ferroalloy manufacturing | |
|    Subpart A – open electric furnaces with wet air pollution control | SS, Cr, $Cr^{6+}$, CN, Mn, O, phen, $PO_4$ |

*Table A-4 Continued*

| Categories of sources | Known significant pollutants |
|---|---|
| Subpart B – covered electric furnaces with wet air pollution control | SS, Cr, $Cr^{6+}$, Mn, O, phen, $PO_4$ |
| Subpart C – slag processing | SS, Cr, Mn, O |
| Subpart D – non-contact cooling | Heat, SS, Cr, $Cr^{6+}$, O, $PO_4$ |
| 24. Leather tanning and finishing | BOD, COD, DS, alkalinity, hard, color, NaCl, $SO_3$, S, amines, Cr, $Na_2CO_3$, O&G |
| 25. Glass and asbestos manufacturing | |
| Glass | $NH_3$, pH, color, turb, heat, phen, BOD, COD, DS, SS, O&G |
| Asbestos | SS, BOD, pH, |
| 26. Rubber processing | BOD, COD, N, surf, color, Cl, S, O&G, phen, Cr |
| 27. Timber products | BOD, COD, SS, DS, color, TOC |

*Notes*
Definition of parameters:

| | | | | | | |
|---|---|---|---|---|---|---|
| 1. | alk | alkalinity | | 20. | hard | hardness |
| 2. | As | arsenic | | 21. | HCl | hydrochloric acid |
| 3. | bac | bacteria | | 22. | heat | thermal |
| 4. | BOD | biological oxygen demand | | 23. | Mn | manganese |
| 5. | Cd | cadmium | | 24. | N | nitrogen (organic or kjelhahl) |
| 6. | COD | chemical oxygen demand | | 25. | NaCl | sodium chloride |
| 7. | Cl | chlorine | | 26. | $Na_2Co_3$ | sodium carbonate |
| 8. | coli | total coliform | | 27. | $NH_3$ | ammonia |
| 9. | color | color (APHA) and/or dyes | | 28. | Ni | nickel |
| 10. | CN | cyanide | | 29. | $NO_3$ | nitrate |
| 11. | Cr | chromium (total) | | 30. | O | oil |
| 12. | $Cr^{6+}$ | chromium hexavalent | | 31. | P | phosphate |
| 13. | Cu | copper | | 32. | phen | phenols |
| 14. | DS | dissolved solids | | 33. | pH | acidity |
| 15. | F | fluoride | | 34. | S | sulphide |
| 16. | G | grease | | 36. | set.s | settleable solids |
| 17. | $H_2SO_3$ | sulphorous acid | | 36. | SS | suspended solids |
| 18. | $H_2SO_4$ | sulphuric acid | | 37. | surf | surfactants |
| 19. | $H_3SO_4$ | phosphoric acid | | 38. | turb | turbidity |

a. Inorganic chemicals manufacturing subcategories:

| | | | |
|---|---|---|---|
| 1. | aluminum chloride | 6. | chlorine, sodium, hydroxide, potassium, hydroxide |
| 2. | aluminum sulphate | 7. | hydrochloric acid |
| 3. | calcium carbide | 8. | hydrofluoric acid |
| 4. | calcium chloride | 9. | hydrogen peroxide |
| 5. | calcium oxide | 10. | nitric acid |

*Source:* Azad (1976, pp. 1–12)

*Table A-5    Industries by stressor type*[a]

---

*High stressor (pollutants to air and water)*

| | |
|---|---|
| Metal mines | Iron and steel mills |
| Coal mines | Smelting and refining |
| Crude petroleum and natural gas | Petroleum refining |
| Non-metal mines | Manufacturers of industrial chemicals |
| Pulp and paper mills | Electric power (thermal and nuclear) |

*Medium stressor (pollutants to air)*

| | |
|---|---|
| Quarries and sand pits | Concrete products manufacturers |
| Bakery products | Glass and glass products manufactures |
| Sawmills, planing and shingle mills | Abrasives manufacturers |
| Veneer and plywood mills | Lime manufacturers |
| Iron foundries | Miscellaneous non-metallic mineral products |
| Manufacturers of miscellaneous electrical products | Miscellaneous petroleum and coal products |
| Clay products manufacturers | Manufacturers of mixed fertilizers |
| Cement manufacturers | Manufacturers of plastics and synthetic resins |

*Medium stressor (pollutants to water)*

| | |
|---|---|
| Logging | Copper and copper alloy rolling, casting and extruding |
| Quarries and sand pits | Metal rolling, casting and extruding, n.e.s. |
| Meat and poultry products | Metal frabricating |
| Fruit and vegetable processing | Clay products manufacturers |
| Dairy | Cement manufacturers |
| Flour and breakfast cereal products | Ready-mix concrete manufacturers |
| Feed industry | Lime manufacturers |
| Beverage industry | Manufacturers of lubricating oils and greases |
| Tyre and tube manufacturers | Miscellaneous petroleum and coal products |
| Leather tanneries | Manufacture of mixed fertilizers |
| Textile industries | Manufacturers of synthetic plastics and resins |
| Asphalt roofing manufacturers | Manufacturers of pharmaceuticals and medicines |
| Steel pipe and tube mills | Paint and varnish |
| Iron foundries | Soap and cleaning compounds |
| Aluminum rolling, casting and extruding | Miscellaneous chemicals |

*Low stressor (pollutants to air)*

| | |
|---|---|
| Logging | Aluminum rolling, casting and extruding |
| Food and beverage industries | Copper and copper alloy rolling, casting and extruding |

## Table A-5 Continued

*Low stressor (pollutants to air) (Continued)*

| | |
|---|---|
| Tobacco products | Metal fabricating |
| Rubber and plastics products | Machinery |
| Leather industries | Transportation equipment |
| Textile industries | Electrical products |
| Knitting mills | Ready-mix concrete manufacturers |
| Clothing industries | Manufacturers of lubricating oils and greases |
| Wood industries | Manufacturers of pharmaceuticals and medicines |
| Furniture and fixtures | Paint and varnish |
| Asphalt roofing manufacturers | Soap and cleaning compounds |
| Paper box and bag manufacturers | Manufacturers of toilet preparations |
| Miscellaneous paper converters | Miscellaneous chemicals |
| Printing, publishing and allied products | Miscellaneous manufacturing |
| Steel pipe and tube mills | |

*Low stressor (pollutants to water)*

| | |
|---|---|
| Bakery products | Paper box and bag manufacturers |
| Miscellaneous food industries | Miscellaneous paper converters |
| Tobacco products | Printing, publishing and allied products |
| Rubber footwear | Machinery |
| Miscellaneous rubber products | Transport equipment |
| Plastic fabricating, n.e.s. | Electrical products |
| Shoe factories | Stone products |
| Leather glove factories | Concrete products |
| Luggage, handbag and small leather goods | Glass and glass products |
| Knitting mills | Abrasive manufacturers |
| Clothing industries | Miscellaneous non-metallic mineral products |
| Wood industries | Manufacturers of toilet preparations |
| Furniture and fixtures | Miscellaneous manufacturing |

*Note:* a. Including primary industries (excluding agriculture), manufacturing industries and the electric power generation industry.

*Source: Human Activity and the Environment* (1986)

*Table A-6*  *Major air pollutants*[a]

| Pollutant | Characteristics | Principal sources | Principal effects | Controls | National ambient standards (micrograms per m³)[b,c] |
|---|---|---|---|---|---|
| Carbon monoxide (CO) | A colorless, odorless gas with a strong chemical affinity for haemoglobin in blood | Incomplete combustion of fuels and other carbon-containing substances, such as in motor vehicle exhausts; natural events such as forest fires or decomposition of organic matter | *Health:* Reduced tolerance for exercise, impairment of fetal development, aggravation of cardiovascular diseases<br>*Other:* Unknown | Automobile engine modifications (proper tuning, exhaust gas recirculation, redesign of combustion chamber); control of automobile exhaust gases (catalytic or thermal devices); improved design, operation and maintenance of stationary furnaces (use of finely dispersed fuels, proper mixing with air, high combustion temperature) | Primary:<br>8-hour = 10,000<br>1-hour = 40,000<br>Alert:<br>8-hour = 17,000 |
| Hydro-carbons (HC) | Organic compounds in gaseous or particulate form; for example, methane, ethylene, and acetylene | Incomplete combustion of fuels and other carbon-containing substances, such as in motor vehicle exhausts: processing, distribution and use of petroleum compounds such as gasoline and organic solvents; natural events such as forest fires and plant metabolism; atmospheric reactions | *Health:* Suspected contribution to cancer<br>*Other:* Major precursors in photochemical oxidants through atmospheric reactions | Automobile engine modifications (proper tuning, crankcase ventilation, exhaust gas recirculation, redesign of combustion chamber); control of automobile exhaust gases (catalytic or thermal devices); improved design, operation and maintenance of stationary furnaces (use of finely dispersed fuels, proper mixing with air, high combustion temperature); improved control procedures in processing and handling petroleum compounds) | |

| Pollutant | Description | Sources | Effects | Control | Standards ($\mu g/m^3$) |
|---|---|---|---|---|---|
| Nitrogen dioxide ($NO_2$) | A brownish-red gas with a pungent odor, often formed from oxidation of nitric oxide (NO) | Motor vehicle exhausts, high-temperature stationary combustion, atmospheric reactions | *Health:* Aggravation of respiratory and cardiovascular illnesses and chronic nephritis. *Other:* Fading paints and dyes; impairment of visibility; reduced growth and premature leaf drop | Catalytic control of automobile exhaust gases, modification of automobile engines to reduce combustion temperature, scrubbing flue gases with caustic substance or urea | Primary: Annual =100 Alert: 24 hour = 282 11 hour = 1,130 |
| Photo-chemical oxidants ($O_x$) | Colorless, gaseous compounds which can comprise photochemical smog: for example, ozone ($O_3$), peroxyacetyl nitrate (PAN), aldehydes, and other compounds | Atmospheric reactions of chemical precursors under the influence of sunlight | *Health:* Aggravation of respiratory and cardiovascular illnesses, irritation of eyes and respiratory tract, impairment of cardiopulmonary function. *Other:* Deterioration of rubber, textiles and paints; impairment of visibility; leaf injury, reduced growth, and premature fruit and leaf drop in plants | Reduced emissions of nitrogen oxides, hyrdocarbons, possibly sulphur oxides | Primary: 1 hour = 160 Alert: 1 hour = 200 |
| Sulphur dioxide ($SO_2$) | A colorless gas with a pungent odor; $SO_2$ can oxidize to form sulphur trioxide ($SO_3$) which forms sulphuric acid with water | Combustion of sulphur-containing fossil fuels, smelting of sulphur-bearing metal ores, industrial processes, natural events such as volcanic eruptions | *Health:* Aggravation of respiratory diseases, including asthma, chronic bronchitis, and emphysema; reduced lung function; irritation of eyes and respiratory tract; increased mortality *Other:* Corrosion of metals; deterioration of electrical contacts, paper, textiles, leather, finishes and coatings, and building stone; formation of acid rain; leaf injury and reduced growth in plants | Use of low-sulphur fuels; removal of sulphur from fuels before use; scrubbing of flue gases with lime or catalytic conversion | Primary: Annual = 80 24 hour = 365 Alert: 24 hour = 800 |

*Table A-6 Continued*

| Pollutant | Characteristics | Principal sources | Principal effects | Controls | National ambient standards (micrograms per m$^3$)[b,c] |
|---|---|---|---|---|---|
| Total suspended particulates (TSP) | Any solid or liquid particles dispersed in the atmosphere, such as dust, pollen, ash, soot, metals, and various chemicals; the particles are often classified according to size as settleable particles: larger than 50 microns; aerosols: smaller than 50 microns; and fine particulates: smaller than 3 microns | Natural events such as forest fires, wind erosion, volcanic eruptions; stationary combustion, especially of solid fuels; construction activities; industrial processes; atmospheric chemical reactions | *Health:* Directly toxic effects or aggravation of the effects of gaseous pollutants; aggravation of asthma or other respiratory or cardiorespiratory symptoms; increased cough and chest discomfort; increased mortality<br>*Other:* Soiling and deterioration of building materials and other surfaces, impairment of visibility, cloud formation, interference with plant photosynthesis | Cleaning of the flue gases with inertial separators, fabric filters, scrubbers, or other electrostatic precipitators; alternative means for solid waste reduction; improved control procedures for construction and industrial processes | Primary:<br>Annual = 70<br>24 hour = 260<br>Secondary:<br>Annual = 60<br>25 hour = 150<br>Alert:<br>24 hour = 375 |

*Notes*

a.  Pollutants for which national ambient air quality standards have been established.

b.  Primary standards are intended to protect against adverse effects on human health. Secondary standards are intended to protect against adverse effects on materials, vegetation and other environmental values.

c.  The federal episode criteria specify that meteorological conditions are such that pollutant concentrations may be expected to remain at these levels for 12 or more hours to increase; in the case of oxidants, the situation is likely to recur within the next 24 hours unless control actions are taken.

*Source:* Council on Environmental Quality (1975, pp. 301–3).

*Table A-7   Nation-wide air pollution emissions by pollutant and source in the United States, 1970–86 (million tons, except lead in thousand tons)*

| Year and pollutant | Total | Controllable emissions | | | | | | Miscellaneous uncontrollable | Percent of total | | |
|---|---|---|---|---|---|---|---|---|---|---|---|
| | | Transport | | Fuel combustion[a] | | | Solid waste | | Transport | Fuel combustion[a] | Industrial |
| | | Total | Road vehicles | Total | Electric utilities | Industrial process | | | | | |
| **1970** | | | | | | | | | | | |
| Carbon monoxide | 98.7 | 71.8 | 62.7 | 4.4 | 0.2 | 9.0 | 6.4 | 7.2 | 72.7 | 4.5 | 9.1 |
| Sulphur oxides | 28.4 | 0.6 | 0.3 | 21.3 | 15.8 | 6.4 | — | 0.1 | 2.1 | 75.0 | 22.5 |
| Volatile organic compounds | 27.5 | 12.4 | 11.1 | 1.1 | — | 8.9 | 1.8 | 3.3 | 45.1 | 4.0 | 32.4 |
| Particulates | 18.5 | 1.2 | 0.9 | 4.6 | 2.3 | 10.5 | 1.1 | 1.1 | 6.5 | 24.9 | 56.8 |
| Nitrogen oxides | 18.1 | 7.6 | 6.0 | 9.1 | 4.4 | 0.7 | 0.4 | 0.3 | 42.0 | 50.3 | 3.9 |
| Lead | 203.8 | 163.6 | 156.0 | 9.6 | 0.3 | 23.9 | 6.7 | — | 80.3 | 4.7 | 11.7 |
| **1980** | | | | | | | | | | | |
| Carbon monoxide | 76.1 | 52.6 | 45.3 | 7.3 | 0.3 | 6.3 | 2.2 | 7.6 | 69.1 | 9.6 | 8.3 |
| Sulphur oxides | 23.9 | 0.9 | 0.4 | 19.3 | 16.1 | 3.8 | — | — | 3.8 | 80.8 | 15.9 |
| Volatile organic compounds | 23.0 | 8.2 | 6.9 | 2.2 | — | 9.2 | 0.6 | 2.9 | 35.7 | 9.6 | 0.4 |
| Particulates | 8.5 | 1.3 | 1.1 | 2.4 | 0.8 | 3.3 | 0.4 | 1.1 | 15.3 | 28.2 | 38.8 |
| Nitrogen oxides | 20.3 | 9.2 | 7.2 | 10.1 | 6.4 | 0.7 | 0.1 | 0.2 | 45.3 | 49.8 | 3.4 |
| Lead | 70.6 | 59.4 | 56.4 | 3.9 | 0.1 | 3.6 | 3.7 | — | 84.1 | 5.5 | 5.1 |
| **1986** | | | | | | | | | | | |
| Carbon monoxide | 60.9 | 42.6 | 35.4 | 7.5 | 0.3 | 4.5 | 1.7 | 5.0 | 70.0 | 11.8 | 7.4 |
| Sulphur oxides | 21.2 | 0.9 | 0.5 | 17.2 | 14.3 | 3.1 | — | — | 4.2 | 81.1 | 14.6 |
| Volatile organic compounds | 19.5 | 6.5 | 5.3 | 2.3 | — | 7.9 | 0.6 | 2.2 | 33.3 | 11.8 | 40.5 |
| Particulates | 6.8 | 1.4 | 1.1 | 1.8 | 0.4 | 2.5 | 0.3 | 0.8 | 20.6 | 26.5 | 36.8 |
| Nitrogen oxides | 19.3 | 8.5 | 6.6 | 10.0 | 6.6 | 0.6 | 0.1 | 0.1 | 44.0 | 51.8 | 3.1 |
| Lead | 8.6 | 3.5 | 3.3 | 5.0 | 0.1 | 1.9 | 2.7 | — | 40.7 | 5.8 | 22.1 |

*Note:*   a.   Stationary

*Source:*   US Bureau of the Census (1989, p. 200)

*Table A-8    Weighted direct emission coefficients of air pollution,
The Netherlands, 1973 (units of air pollution)*

| Rank | Industry | Process | Combustion | Transport | Total |
|---|---|---|---|---|---|
| 1. | Fertilizers | 2,646 | 179 | 34 | 2,859 |
| 2. | Other chemical basic products | 577 | 194 | 6 | 777 |
| 3. | Building materials | 435 | 76 | 67 | 578 |
| 4. | Other transport equipment | 530 | 10 | 6 | 546 |
| 5. | Other services | 477 | 7 | 10 | 494 |
| 6. | Primary metals | 186 | 151 | 4 | 342 |
| 7. | Fabricated metal products | 320 | 8 | 7 | 336 |
| 8. | Other agriculture | 0 | 247 | 16 | 262 |
| 9. | Machinery | 173 | 6 | 8 | 187 |
| 10. | Rubber and synthetic chemical products | 131 | 35 | 9 | 175 |
| 11. | Maintenance and repair | 155 | 17 | 2 | 174 |
| 12. | Automobile manufacture | 155 | 6 | 2 | 163 |
| 13. | Paper | 100 | 56 | 5 | 161 |
| 14. | Sea and air transport | 137 | 1 | 12 | 150 |
| 15. | Coal mining | 72 | 65 | 0 | 137 |
| 16. | Construction | 90 | 4 | 32 | 126 |
| 17. | Floor coverings and other textiles | 79 | 20 | 9 | 107 |
| 18. | Retail trade | 46 | 13 | 35 | 94 |
| 19. | Weaving | 62 | 26 | 5 | 92 |
| 20. | Printing and publishing | 64 | 12 | 14 | 90 |
| 21. | Other mining | 0 | 77 | 12 | 89 |
| 22. | Chemical final products | 64 | 12 | 8 | 85 |
| 23. | Sugar | 0 | 55 | 27 | 82 |
| 24. | Lumber and wood products | 26 | 17 | 23 | 66 |
| 25. | Wholesale trade | 43 | 3 | 18 | 64 |
| 26. | Other manufacturing | 0 | 50 | 4 | 54 |
| 27. | Grain mill products | 10 | 16 | 19 | 46 |
| 28. | Dairy products | 0 | 20 | 21 | 41 |
| 29. | Canning, preserving | 0 | 11 | 29 | 40 |
| 30. | Electric utilities[a] | 6 | 31 | 4 | 40 |
| 31. | Margarine, oil, other foods | 2 | 17 | 4 | 40 |
| 32. | Hotels, restaurants and bars | 0 | 23 | 13 | 36 |
| 33. | Confectionery products | 0 | 24 | 10 | 34 |
| 34. | Livestock (intensive) | 0 | 8 | 25 | 33 |
| 35. | Social services | 0 | 13 | 20 | 33 |
| 36. | Leather, shoes | 0 | 12 | 18 | 29 |
| 37. | Electrical products | 11 | 8 | 9 | 28 |

*Table A-8  Continued*

| Rank | Industry | Process | Combustion | Transport | Total |
|------|----------|---------|------------|-----------|-------|
| 38. | Knitting | 0 | 14 | 11 | 26 |
| 39. | Spinning | 0 | 13 | 12 | 26 |
| 40. | Banking, insurance | 0 | 11 | 15 | 26 |
| 41. | Beverages | 0 | 14 | 11 | 25 |
| 42. | Medical services | 0 | 12 | 11 | 23 |
| 43. | Bakery products | 6 | 10 | 7 | 23 |
| 44. | Paper products | 0 | 10 | 10 | 20 |
| 45. | Culture, recreation | 0 | 15 | 6 | 21 |
| 46. | Clothing | 0 | 9 | 10 | 19 |
| 47. | Water | 0 | 19 | 0 | 19 |
| 48. | Livestock (extensive) | 0 | 3 | 14 | 17 |
| 49. | Business services | 0 | 7 | 10 | 17 |
| 50. | Meat products | 0 | 5 | 8 | 13 |
| 51. | Petroleum and natural gas | 5 | 7 | 1 | 13 |
| 52. | Other transport | 2 | 8 | 5 | 15 |
| 53. | Communications | 0 | 8 | 3 | 11 |
| 54. | Tobacco | 0 | 4 | 6 | 10 |
| 55. | Petroleum and coal products[a] | 0 | 5 | 1 | 6 |
| 56. | Gas | 0 | 0 | 1 | 1 |
| 57. | Real estate | 0 | 0 | 0 | 0 |
| 58. | Fishing | 0 | 0 | 0 | 0 |
| 59. | Other | 0 | 0 | 0 | 0 |

*Note:*  a.  Pollution due to combustion in this sector has been imputed directly to users of products of this sector in order to arrive at calculated results consistent with the underlying physical flows

*Source:* James, Jansen and Opschoor (1978, pp. 140–41)

*Table A-9  Waste generation by types of industrial waste in selected countries, 1980–87 (tons)*

| Country | Year | Waste oil | Waste solvent | Paint | Concentrated acids | Metal finishing waste | Waste containing | | PCBs | Biocides | Plastics, rubber | Phenolic wastes |
|---|---|---|---|---|---|---|---|---|---|---|---|---|
| | | | | | | | Silver or zinc | Mercury | | | | |
| Austria | 1983 | 650,000[a] | 7,000 | 5,800 | 1,266,000 | 1,394,000 | 270 | 163 | 1,900 | 39 | 102,000 | 131,000 |
| Australia[b] | 1983 | 30,700 | 2,000 | 4,350 | 49,000 | 12,300[c] | 750[d] | — | 50[e] | 3,500 | 110[f] | 42,000[g] |
| Canada | 1985 | 367,000 | 262,000 | 72,700 | — | 186,200 | — | 200,000[h,i] | 8,000[j] | 4,500 | 74,000[h] | 19,100[h] |
| Finland | 1982 | 80,000[k] | 11,000 | 15,200 | 270,000[l] | 6,000 | 500 | — | 89 | 1,600 | 25,000[h] | 120 |
| France | 1982 | 250,000 | 250,000 | 90,000 | — | — | — | 450[h,m] | 2,000[h] | — | — | 23,000[n] |
| Germany, Federal Republic of | 1984 | 719,611 | 305,215 | 268,065 | 1,493,296 | 222,206 | 65,988 | — | 5,481 | — | 734,369 | — |
| Ireland | 1980 | 25,000 | 13,500 | — | — | 33,000 | 1,600 | — | — | 5 | 45,000 | — |
| Japan | 1985 | 2,800,000[o] | — | — | 4,237,000[p] | — | — | — | — | — | 2,042,000 | — |
| Luxembourg[q] | 1985 | 460 | 126 | 303 | 64 | 1,300 | — | 1,100 | 121 | — | — | — |
| New Zealand | 1983 | 900 | 50 | 10 | 1,000 | 900 | — | — | 800[r] | 30 | — | — |
| Norway | 1987 | 55,000 | 14,000 | 6,000 | 4,000 | 17,000 | — | 3,000 | 150[s] | 300 | 100,000[k] | 10[t] |
| Sweden | 1980 | 180,000 | 33,000 | 20,000 | 72,880 | 112,000 | 3,600 | 450 | 30 | 600 | 161,000[w] | — |
| United States | 1985 | 4,900,000[u] | 3,000,000[v] | 630,000[w] | 2,737,740 | 1,800,000[w,x] | — | 712,837[y] | 21,000[z] | 12,000 | | 366,000[y] |

*Notes*

a. Including refinery wastes containing mineral oils.
b. 1983, state of Queensland only, data given in kiloliters.
c. Metal finishing wastes plus neutral salts.
d. Oil-based inks.
e. 250 kiloliters being phased out.
f. Bituminous emulsions.
g. Organic chemicals.
h. 1980.
i. Mainly from pulp mills.
j. Including 6,500 tons of high level PCBs currently in storage in Canada and awaiting disposal.
k. 1985.
l. 1983.
m. Containing more than 1 percent of mercury.
n. 1978 estimate.
o. Includes solvent waste.
p. Includes dilute acids.
q. Amounts treated.
r. Estimated total of PCB-contaminated waste to be disposed in the next 10–15 years.
s. Organization for Economic Co-operation and Development Secretariat estimates.
t. 1984.
u. 1982.
v. 1981.
w. Hazardous wastes only.
x. Wastes originating from metal plating only.
y. 1977.
z. PCB-contaminated electric fluids (PCB = polychlorinated biphenyl).

*Source:* OECD (1989)

157

*Table A-10   Sources and types of industrial wastes*

| Industry groups | Waste-generating processes | Expected specific wastes |
| --- | --- | --- |
| Plumbing, heating, air conditioning, special trade contractors | Manufacturing and installation in homes, buildings, and factories | Scrap metal from piping and duct work; rubber, paper and insulating materials, miscellaneous construction and demolition debris |
| Ordnance and accessories | Manufacturing and assembling | Metals, plastic, rubber, paper, wood, cloth, and chemical residues |
| Food and kindred products | Processing, packaging and shipping | Meats, fats, oils, bones, offal vegetables, nuts and shells, and cereals |
| Textile mill products | Weaving, processing, dyeing and shipping | Cloth and fiber residues |
| Apparel and other finished products | Cutting, sewing, sizing and pressing | Cloth and fibers, metals, plastics and rubber |
| Lumber and wood products | Sawmills, mill work plants, wooden containers, miscellaneous wood products, manufacturing | Scrap wood, shavings, sawdust; in some instances metals, plastics, fibers, glues, sealers, paints and solvents |
| Furniture, wood | Manufacture of household and office furniture, partitions, office and store fixtures | Those listed under lumber and wood products, and in addition cloth and padding residues |
| Furniture, metal | Manufacture of household and office furniture, lockers, bedsprings and frames | Metals, plastics, resins, glass, wood, rubber, adhesives, cloth and paper |
| Paper and allied products | Paper manufacture, conversion of paper and paperboard, manufacture of paper-board boxes and containers | Paper and fiber residues, chemicals, paper coatings and fillers, inks, glues and fasteners |
| Printing and publishing | Newspaper publishing, printing, lithography, engraving and bookbinding | Paper, newsprint, cardboard, metals, chemicals, cloth, inks and glues |
| Chemicals and related products | Manufacture and preparation of organic chemicals (ranges from drugs and soups to paints and varnishes, and explosives) | Organic and inorganic chemicals, metals, plastics, rubber, glass, oils, paints, solvents and pigments |
| Petroleum refining and related industries | Manufacture of paving and roofing materials | Asphalt and tars, felts, asbestos, paper, cloth and fiber |

158

| | | |
|---|---|---|
| Rubber and miscellaneous plastic products | Manufacture of fabricated rubber and plastic products | Scrap rubber and plastics, lampblack, curing compounds and dyes |
| Leather and leather products | Leather tanning and finishing; manufacture of leather belting and packing | Scrap leather, thread, dyes, oils, processing and curing compounds |
| Electrical | Manufacture of electric equipment, appliances, and communication apparatus, machining, drawing, forming, welding, stamping, winding, painting, plating, baking and firing operations | Metal scrap, carbon, glass, exotic metals, rubber, plastic, resins, fibers, cloth residues |
| Transport equipment | Manufacture of motor vehicles, truck and bus bodies, motor vehicle, aircraft, ship and boat building parts, etc. | Metal scrap, glass, fibers, wood, rubber, plastics, cloth, paints, solvents, petroleum products |
| Professional and scientific controlling instruments | Manufacture of engineering, laboratory, and research instruments and associated equipment | Metals, plastics, resins, glass, wood, rubber, fibers and abrasives |
| Miscellaneous manufacturing | Manufacture of jewelry, silverware, plated ware, toys, amusements, sporting and athletic goods, costume novelties, buttons, brooms, brushes, signs, and advertising displays | Metals, glass, plastics, resins, leather, rubber, composition, bone, cloth, straw, adhesives, paints and solvents |
| Stone, clay and glass products | Manufacture of flat glass, fabrication or forming of concrete, gypsum and plaster products; forming and processing of stone and stone products, abrasives, asbestos, and miscellaneous non-mineral products | Glass, cement, clay, ceramics, gypsum, asbestos, stone, paper and abrasives |
| Primary metal industries | Melting, casting, forging, drawing, rolling, forming, and extruding operations | Ferrous and non-ferrous metal scrap, slag, sand, cores, patterns, bonding agents |
| Fabricated metal products | Manufacture of metal cans, hand tools, general hardware, non-electric heating apparatus, plumbing fixtures, fabricated structural products, wire, farm machinery and equipment, coating and engraving of metal | Metals, ceramics, sand, slag, scale, coatings, solvents, lubricants, pickling liquors |
| Machinery (except electrical) | Manufacture of equipment for construction, mining, elevators, moving stairways, conveyors, industrial trucks, trailers, stackers, machine tools, etc. | Clay, sand, cores, metal scrap, wood, plastics, resins, rubber, cloth, paint, solvents, petroleum products |

*Source:* Lederman (1976, Table 5)

159

*Table A-11  Toxic release chemicals by industry and by weight, United States, 1987 ('000 lb)*

| Chemical | 311/2 Food products | 313 Beverages | 314 Tobacco | 321 Textiles | 322 Wearing apparel | 323 Leather and leather products | 324 Footwear | 331 Wood products | 332 Furniture and fixtures |
|---|---|---|---|---|---|---|---|---|---|
| Acetone | | | | 2.6 (16) | | | | 49.2 (37) | 270.0(102) |
| Acrylamide | | | | | | | | | |
| Acrylonitrile | | | | | | | | | |
| Aluminum (fume or dust) | | | | | | | | | |
| Aluminum oxide | | | | | | | | | |
| Ammonia | 225.4(452) | 29.2 (76) | | 49.0 (48) | | 2,581.1  (9) | | 10.7 (19) | |
| Ammonium nitrate (soln) | | | | | | | | | |
| Ammonium sulphate (soln) | | 51.5  (2) | | 60.0 (50) | | 4,800.8 (20) | | | |
| Aniline | | | | | | | | | |
| Antimony | | | | | | | | | |
| Arsenic | | | | | | | | | |
| Asbestos (friable) | | | | | | | | 3.1 (47) | |
| Barium | | | | | | | | | |
| Benzene | | | | 34.0 (32) | | | | | |
| Biphenyl | | | | | | | | | |
| Bromomethane (methyl bromide) | 11.7  (5) | | | | | | | | |
| 1,3-Butadiene | | | | | | | | | |
| Butyl acrylate | | | | | | | | | |
| n-Butyl alcohol | | | | | | | | 9.0 (28) | 49.0 (85) |
| 1,2 Butylene oxide | | | | | | | | | |
| Cadmium | | | | | | | | | |
| Carbon tetrachloride | | | | | | | | | |
| Chlorine | 34.8(230) | | | | | | | | |
| Chlorine dioxide | | | | | | | | | |

| Chemical | | | |
|---|---|---|---|
| Chlorobenzene | | | |
| Chloroethane (ethyl chloride) | | | |
| Chloroform | | | |
| Chloromethane (methyl chloride) | | | |
| Chlorothalnii(1,3-benzedecarbo-nitrile, 2,4,5,6-tetrachloro-) | | | |
| Chromium | | | 0.2 (63) |
| Cobalt | | | 1.3 (40) |
| Copper | | 1,054.6 (20) | |
| Cumene | | | |
| Cumene hydroperoxide | | | |
| Cyclohexane | | | |
| 2, 4-D (acetic acid, 2, 4-dichlorophenoxy-) | | | |
| Decarbromodiphenyl oxide | | | |
| Di-(2-ethylhexyl) phthalate (DEHP) | | | 10.7 (4)   26.7 (25) |
| Dibtyl phthalate | | | |
| Dichlorobenzene (mixed isomers) | | | |
| 1,2-Dichloroethane (ethylene dichloride) | | | |
| Dichloromethane (methylene chloride) | 14.8 (10) | | |
| Diethanolamine | | | |
| Diethyl phthalate | | | |
| Dimethyl sulphate | | | |
| n-Dioctyl phthalate | | | |
| Ethyl acrylate | | | 406.4 (59) |
| Ethylbenzene | | | 156.8 (6) |
| Ethylene | | | |
| Ethylene glycol | | | 80.7 (6) |

## Table A-11  Continued

| Chemical | 311/2 Food products | 313 Beverages | 314 Tobacco | 321 Textiles | 322 Wearing apparel | 323 Leather and leather products | 324 Footwear | 331 Wood products | 332 Furniture and fixtures |
|---|---|---|---|---|---|---|---|---|---|
| Ethylene oxide | | | | | | | | | |
| Formaldehyde | | | | | | | | 4,300.6 (96) | |
| Freon 113 | | | | | | | | | |
| Hydrochloric acid | | | | | | | | | 144.6 (15) |
| Hydrogen cyanide | | | | | | | | | |
| Hydrogen fluoride | | | | | | | | | |
| Isopropyl alcohol | | | | | | | | 22.7 (18) | 198.3 (65) |
| Lead | | | | | | | | | |
| Manganese | | | | | | | | | |
| Mercury | | | | | | | | | |
| Methanol | | | 62.3 (3) | | | | | | |
| Methyl acrylate | | | | | | | | 22.2 (41) | 403.1(147) |
| Methyl ethyl ketone | | | | 96.0 (35) | | 12.9 (13) | | 45.1 (55) | 121.1(194) |
| Methyl isobutyl ketone | | | | | | 12.9 (8) | | 12.0 (25) | 138.6 (59) |
| Methyl methacrylate | | | | | | | | | |
| Methylenebis (phyeylisocyante) (MBI) | | | | | | | 4.8 (1) | | |
| Methylene bromide | | | | | | | | | |
| Molybdenum trioxide | | | | | | | | | |
| 2-Methoxyethanol | | | | | | | | | |
| Naphthalene | | | | | | | | | |
| Nickel | 27.0 (16) | | | | | | | 93.7 (89) | |
| Nitric acid | 126.5 (98) | | | | | | | | 12.3 (3) |

162

| Chemical | | | | | | |
|---|---|---|---|---|---|---|
| 2-Nitropropane | | | | | | |
| Phenol | | | | | | |
| P-Phenylenediamine | | | | | | |
| Phosphoric acid | 63.1(345) | | | | | |
| Phosphorus (yellow or white) | | | | | 10.7 (12) | |
| Phthalic anhydride | | | | | | |
| Polychlorinated biphenyls (BCPs) | | | | | | |
| Propylene (propane) | | | | | | |
| Propylene oxide | | | | | | |
| Sodium hydroxide (soln) | 1,306.9(789) | 68.6(204) | | 552.2(229) | 4,500 (16) | 4.6(121) |
| Sodium sulphate (soln) | | 503 (11) | | 1,421.2(153) | | |
| Styrene | | | | | 5.8 (10) | |
| Sulphuric acid | 37.6(239) | 55.4 (65) | | 102.9 (88) | 3,700 (30) | |
| Tetrachloroethylene (perchloroethylene) | 17.0 (2) | | | 46.8 (25) | | |
| Trade secret | | | | | 78.0 (9) | |
| 1,1,1-Trichloroethane (methyl chloroform) | | | 47.4 (58) | | 47.4 (58) | 138.2 (21) |
| 1,1,2-Trichloroethane | | | | | | |
| 1,2,4-Trichlorobenzene | | | 140.0 (2) | | | |
| Trichloroethylene | | | | | | |
| 1,2,4-Trimethylbenzene | | | | | | |
| Toluene | | | 83.3 (34) | | 83.3 (16) 122.0(100) | 698.7(239) |
| Toluene-2, 4-diisocyanate | | | | | 3.6 (3) | |
| o-Toluidine | | | | | | |
| Vinyl acetate | | | | | | |
| m-Xylene | | | 99.7 (4) | | | |
| Xylene (mixed isomers) | | | | | 101.7 (74) | 815.1(201) |
| Zinc (fume or dust) | | | | | | |

*Table A-11 Continued*

| Chemical | 341 Paper and paper products | 342 Printing, publishing | 351 Industrial chemicals | 352 Other chemical products | 353 Petroleum refining | 355 Rubber products | 356 Plastic products n.e.c. | 361 Pottery china, etc. | 362 Glass products |
|---|---|---|---|---|---|---|---|---|---|
| Acetone | 363.9(129) | | 65.0(281) | 1,765.6(312) | | | 1,131.0(203) | 24.3  (5) | |
| Acrylamide | | | 151.0 (30) | | | | | | |
| Acrylonitrile | | | 35.7 (80) | | | | | | |
| Aluminum (fume or dust) | | | | 322.7  (3) | | | | | |
| Aluminum oxide | | | 71.2(170) | | 3,118.5(116) | | 660.0 (25) | 9.0 (26) | |
| Ammonia | 10.7 (19) | | 1,726.4(606) | 10.5(123) | 11.7(102) | | | | |
| Ammonium nitrate (soln) | | | | 644.3 (31) | | | | | |
| Ammonium sulphate (soln) | | | | | | | | | |
| Aniline | | | 736.6 (54) | | | | | | |
| Antimony | | | 1.0 (16) | | | | | | |
| Arsenic | | | 1.3 (12) | | 7.6  (8) | | | | |
| Asbestos (friable) | 89.6  (6) | | | | | | | | |
| Barium | | | | | | | | | |
| Benzene | | | 90.2(128) | | 18.3(172) | | | 2.0  (3) | |
| Biphenyl | | | | | | | | | |
| Bromomethane (methyl bromide) | | | | | | | | | |
| 1,3-Butadiene | 23.6  (1) | | 93.9 (84) | | | | | | |
| Butyl acrylate | 3.0 (11) | 14 (11) | 1.0 (83) | 0.7 (48) | | | | | |
| n-Butyl alcohol | | | 26.2(134) | 228.7(161) | | | 1.7 (16) | | |
| 1,2 Butylene oxide | | | 98.9  (6) | | | | | | |
| Cadmium | | | 1.0  (1) | | | | | | |
| Carbon tetrachloride | | | | | | | | | |
| Chlorine | 30.0(220) | | 80.0 (56) | | | | | | |
| Chlorine dioxide | | | 59.6(449) | | | | | | |

| | 1 | 2 | 3 | 4 | 5 | 6 | 7 |
|---|---|---|---|---|---|---|---|
| Chlorobenzene | | 2,115.0 (45) | | | | | |
| Chloroethane (ethyl chloride) | | 153.0 (37) | | | | | |
| Chloroform | 290.0 (90) | 1,421.0 (55) | | | | | |
| Chloromethane (methyl chloride) | | 0.2 (5) | | | | | |
| Chlorothalnil(1,3-benzedecarbo-nitrile, 2,4,5,6-tetrachloro-) | | | | | | | |
| Chromium | | 1.0 (43) | | | | | |
| Cobalt | | | | | | | |
| Copper | | 37.6 (28) | | | | | |
| Cumene | | 0.3 (15) | | | | | |
| Cumene hydroperoxide | | | | | | | |
| Cyclohexane | | 28.2 (21) | 10.3 (17) | | | | |
| 2, 4-D (acetic acid, 2, 4-dichlorophenoxy-) | | | | | | | |
| Decarbromodiphenyl oxide | 6.0 (2) | | | | 4.0 (4) | | |
| Di-(2-ethylhexyl) phthalate (DEHP) | | 19.7 (44) | 6.0 (24) | | | | |
| Dibtyl phthalate | | | 3.6 (25) | | | | |
| Dichlorobenzene (mixed iso-mers) | | | 65.6 (5) | | | | |
| 1,2-Dichloroethane (ethylene dichloride) | | 16.7 (49) | | | | | |
| Dichloromethane (methylene chloride) | | 11,653.1(170) | 1,146.6 (279) | 640.0 (66) | 25.8 (34) | 238.8(121) | 1.0 (2) |
| Diethanolamine | | 1.8 (66) | | | | | |
| Diethyl phthalate | | 1.6 (10) | | | | | |
| Dimethyl sulphate | | 7.6 (16) | | | | | |
| n-Dioctyl phthalate | | | 24.5 (15) | | | | |
| Ethyl acrylate | | 440.4 (59) | | | | | |
| Ethylbenzene | | 54.3(111) | | | | | |
| Ethylene | | 264.6(122) | | | | | |
| Ethylene glycol | | 16.1(287) | 506.2(259) | | | | |

*Table A-11 Continued*

| Chemical | 341 Paper and paper products | 342 Printing, publishing | 351 Industrial chemicals | 352 Other chemical products | 353 Petroleum refining | 355 Rubber products | 356 Plastic products n.e.c. | 361 Pottery china, etc. | 362 Glass products |
|---|---|---|---|---|---|---|---|---|---|
| Ethylene oxide | | | 77.2 (72) | | | | | | |
| Formaldehyde | | | 119.7 (243) | 2.2(107) | | | | | |
| Freon 113 | | | 1,056.5 (39) | | | 11.8 (3) | | | |
| Hydrochloric acid | 2.0(145) | | 45,003.4 (550) | | | | | | |
| Hydrogen cyanide | | | 134.0 (28) | 40.8(254) | | | 169.0 (26) | | |
| Hydrogen fluoride | | | | | | | | | |
| Isopropyl alcohol | | 225.0 (60) | | | | | | | |
| Lead | | | | 94.3(109) | | | 30.0 (16) | | |
| Manganese | | | | | | | | | |
| Mercury | | 0.2 (21) | 10.8 (20) | | | | | | |
| Methanol | 606.6(159) | | 99.9 (499) | 176.6(371) | | | 100.0 (34) | | |
| Methyl acrylate | | | | | | | | | |
| Methyl ethyl ketone | 161.0 (84) | 102.2 (37) | 294.5 (136) | 974.2(335) | | | 532.3(120) | | |
| Methyl isobutyl ketone | 854.1 (19) | | | 186.3(164) | | | 4.0 (21) | | |
| Methyl methacrylate | | | 250.5 (88) | | | | 736.2 (18) | | |
| Methylenebis (phyeylisocyante) (MBI) | | | 2.0 (40) | | | | | | |
| Methylene bromide | | | 18.3 (3) | | | | | | |
| Molybdenum trioxide | | | | | 130.0 (21) | | | | |
| 2-Methoxyethanol | | | | | | | | | |
| Naphthalene | | | 7.0 (71) | | | | | | |
| Nickel | | | 3.0 (42) | | | 254.0 (1) | | | |
| Nitric acid | | | | | | | | | |

| | | | | | | | | |
|---|---|---|---|---|---|---|---|---|
| 2-Nitropropane | 12.9 (1) | | | | | | | |
| Phenol | 6.6 (21) | | 0.4 (168) | | | | | |
| P-Phenylenediamine | | | 0.1 (6) | | | | | |
| Phosphoric acid | | | | 1.6(190) | 470 (53) | | | |
| Phosphorus (yellow or white) | | | 35.0 (34) | | | | | |
| Phthalic anhydride | | | 1,750.0 (105) | | | | | |
| Polychlorinated biphenyls (BCPs) | 53.5 (14) | | 18.0 (18) | | | | | |
| Propylene (propane) | | | 6,400.0 (103) | | | | | |
| Propylene oxide | | | 64.0 (63) | | | | | |
| Sodium hydroxide (soln) | 71.8(377) | | 268.0(1,054) | 67.9(563) | | | 123.4 (38) | |
| Sodium sulphate (soln) | 97.2(149) | | 4,462.1 (404) | | | | | |
| Styrene | | | 364.2 (255) | 1.3(309) | | | 939.0(170) | |
| Sulphuric acid | 920.8 (23) | | 4,639.4 (931) | 82.0 (55) | | | | |
| Tetrachloroethylene (perchloroethylene) | | 38.3 (39) | 39.2 (62) | | | 1.5 (20) | | |
| Trade secret | 470.0 (4) | | | 1.2 (5) | | | | |
| 1,1,1-Trichloroethane (methyl chloroform) | 13.3 (51) | | 1,158.8 (135) | 50.4(247) | | 107.7(100) | 66.9(103) | |
| 1,1,2-Trichloroethane | | | 870.6 (16) | | | | | |
| 1,2,4-Trichlorobenzene | | | 1,058.8 (48) | 4.7 (8) | | | | |
| Trichloroethylene | | | 21.0 (22) | | | | | |
| 1,2,4-Trimethylbenzene | | | | | | | | |
| Toluene | 89.7(117) | 191.5(100) | 316.9 (360) | 1,312.3(574) | 56.1(163) | 192.0 (92) | 121.1 (91) | |
| Toluene-2, 4-diisocyanate | | | | 0.7 (27) | | | | 8.2 (2) |
| o-Toluidine | | | 16.4 (12) | | | | | |
| Vinyl acetate | | | 218.0 (88) | | | | | |
| m-Xylene | 42.0 (41) | | | | | | | |
| Xylene (mixed isomers) | 12.9 (44) | | 784.9 (289) | 1,482.4(496) | | 5.2 (34) | 138.0 (44) | |
| Zinc (fume or dust) | | | 4.1 (47) | 1.8 (57) | | | | 0.8 (2) |

*Table A-11 Continued*

| Chemical | 369 Non-metal products n.e.c. | 371 Iron and steel | 372 Non-ferrous metals | 381 Metal products | 382 Machinery n.e.c. | 383 Electrical machinery | 384 Transport equipment | 385 Professional goods | 390 Other industries |
|---|---|---|---|---|---|---|---|---|---|
| Acetone | | 19.2 (1) | 1.5(101) | | 86.5 (42) | 4.6(185) | 639.0(273) | | |
| Acrylamide | | | | | | | | | |
| Acrylonitrile | | | | | | | | | |
| Aluminum (fume or dust) | 155.5(167) | 5,213.9 (37) | 1,006.6(114) | | | | | | |
| Aluminum oxide | | | 859.8(261) | | | 2.9 (47) | 10.0 (27) | | |
| Ammonia | | 105.6 (4) | 21.6(208) | | | 87.4(102) | 63.6 (67) | | 80.1 (25) |
| Ammonium nitrate (soln) | | | | | | | 50.9 (55) | | |
| Ammonium sulphate (soln) | | | | | | | | | 140.5 (2) |
| Aniline | | | | | | | | | |
| Antimony | | 2 (1) | 18.0 (31) | | | | | | |
| Arsenic | | 1.2 (1) | | | | | | | |
| Asbestos (friable) | 2,040.6 (6) | 379.4 (5) | | | | | 130.0 (27) | | |
| Barium | 1.4 (15) | 346.3 (7) | | | | | | | |
| Benzene | | 774.1 (19) | | | | | | | |
| Biphenyl | | 1.5 (2) | | | | | | | |
| Bromomethane (methyl bromide) | | | | | | | | | |
| 1,3-Butadiene | | | | | | | | | |
| Butyl acrylate | | | | | | | | | |
| n-Butyl alcohol | | 66.3 (91) | 72.0(209) | | | | | | |
| 1,2 Butylene oxide | | | 11.8 (10) | | | | | | |
| Cadmium | | 12.9 (4) | | | | | | | |
| Carbon tetrachloride | | | | | | | | | |
| Chlorine | | 1,040.9 (22) | 20.0(208) | | | | | | |
| Chlorine dioxide | | | | | | | | | |

| | | | | | | | |
|---|---|---|---|---|---|---|---|
| Chlorobenzene | | | | | | | |
| Chloroethane (ethyl chloride) | | | | | | | |
| Chloroform | | | | | | | |
| Chloromethane (methyl chloride) | | | | | | | |
| Chlorothalnil(1,3-benzedecarbo-nitrile, 2,4,5,6-tetrachloro-) | | | | | | | |
| Chromium | 11,642.0(119) | 46.6(221) | | 6.4(78) | | 63.0(67) | 3.0(10) |
| Cobalt | 72.2(11) | 524.0(38) | | | | | |
| Copper | 628.3(54) | 1,341.7(554) | 8.8(23) | 5,427.8(83) | 80.4(219) | 3.8(85) | |
| Cumene | 10.6(1) | | | | | | |
| Cumene hydroperoxide | 1.4(2) | | | | | | |
| Cyclohexane | | | | | | | |
| 2, 4-D (acetic acid, 2, 4-dichlorophenoxy-) | | | | | | | |
| Decarbromodiphenyl oxide | | | | | | | |
| Di-(2-ethylhexyl) phthalate (DEHP) | | | | | | | |
| Dibutyl phthalate | 0.5(2) | | | | | | |
| Dichlorobenzene (mixed isomers) | | | | | | | |
| 1,2-Dichloroethane (ethylene dichloride) | | | | | | | |
| Dichloromethane (methylene chloride) | 425.7(12) | 209.2(121) | 13.0(13) | 29.4(63) | 406.5(144) | 218.6(165) | 95.6(32) |
| Diethanolamine | 3.5(1) | | | 12.9(24) | | | |
| Diethyl phthalate | | | | | | | |
| Dimethyl sulphate | | | | | | | |
| n-Dioctyl phthalate | | | | | | | |
| Ethyl acrylate | 3.3(5) | | | | | | |
| Ethylbenzene | 26.3(5) | | | | | | |
| Ethylene | | | | | | | |
| Ethylene glycol | 2,845.4(38) | 77.5(97) | | 1.6(38) | | | 191.0(18) |
| Ethylene oxide | | | | | | | 381.6(37) |

*Table A-11 Continued*

| Chemical | 369 Non-metal products n.e.c. | 371 Iron and steel | 372 Non-ferrous metals | 381 Metal products | 382 Machinery n.e.c. | 383 Electrical machinery | 384 Transport equipment | 385 Professional goods | 390 Other industries |
|---|---|---|---|---|---|---|---|---|---|
| Formaldehyde | | 509.5 (19) | | | | | | | |
| Freon 113 | | 216.5 (6) | | | 205.1(121) | 587.0(381) | 256.9 (21) | 242.0(123) | 31.7 (23) |
| Hydrochloric acid | | 45,191.0 (92) | 1,743.0 (776) | 257.2 (23) | | 8.7(336) | 21.0(142) | | |
| Hydrogen cyanide | | 14.0 (1) | | | | | | | |
| Hydrogen fluoride | | 22,015.4 (35) | 228.4 (128) | | | 8.2 (87) | 150.0 (34) | | |
| Isopropyl alcohol | | 136.8 (5) | 11.0 (50) | | | 17.7 (56) | | | 14.5 (13) |
| Lead | 24.1 (4) | 10,338.5 (58) | 1,573.3 (227) | | | | | | |
| Manganese | 2.8 (32) | 20,978.7(113) | | | | | | | |
| Mercury | | | | | 1.0 (48) | | | | |
| Methanol | | 303.0 (8) | | | 64.0 (80) | 2.2(102) | | | 37.7 (13) |
| Methyl acrylate | | | | | | | | | |
| Methyl ethyl ketone | | 400.9 (7) | 883.0 (308) | 25.0 (24) | 1.7 (66) | 472.9 (98) | 284.2(239) | 24.9 (32) | 63.8 (54) |
| Methyl isobutyl ketone | | 8.9 (1) | 92.0 (111) | | 0.4 (20) | 0.9 (17) | 1.8 (69) | | 7.8 (14) |
| Methyl methacrylate | | | | | | | | | |
| Methylenebis (phyeylisocyante) (MBI) | | 107.9 (11) | | | | | | | |
| Methylene bromide | | | | | | | | | |
| Molybdenum trioxide | | 97.5 (10) | | | | | | | |
| 2-Methoxyethanol | | | 16.5 (3) | | | | | | |
| Naphthalene | | | | | | 19.4 (4) | | | |
| Nickel | | 8,496.0 (96) | 2,978.6 (287) | | 83.8 (57) | 22.1 (43) | | | 49.0 (12) |
| Nitric acid | | 24,585.8 (44) | 428.6 (550) | | | 520.3(216) | 344.0(157) | | 69.0 (24) |
| 2-Nitropropane | | | | | | | | | |
| Phenol | | 3,688.5 (68) | | | | | | | |
| P-Phenylenediamine | | 279.2 (3) | | | | | | | |

| Chemical | Col 1 | Col 2 | Col 3 | Col 4 | Col 5 | Col 6 | Col 7 | Col 8 | Col 9 |
|---|---|---|---|---|---|---|---|---|---|
| Phosphoric acid | 56.3 (32) | | | 666.0 (259) | | 5.7(136) | | | 77.7 (8) |
| Phosphorus (yellow or white) | 1,571.3 (2) | | | | | | | | |
| Phthalic anhydride | 941.0 (10) | | | | | | | | |
| Polychlorinated biphenyls (BCPs) | | | | | | | | | |
| Propylene (propane) | 0.5 (2) | | | | | | | | |
| Propylene oxide | | | | | | | | | |
| Sodium hydroxide (soln) | 7,733.1 (93) | | 3,069.3(1,248) | | 552.4(187) | 1,148.0(593) | 158.0(307) | 16.5 (82) | |
| Sodium sulphate (soln) | | | 119.9 (167) | | | 420.2(244) | | | |
| Styrene | | | | | | | | 8.4(129) | |
| Sulphuric acid | 139.0 (29) | 85,449.3(150) | 3,235.2(1,102) | | 38.5(170) | 544.6(607) | 86.0(280) | | 164.3 (45) |
| Tetrachloroethylene (perchloroethylene) | 333.7 (7) | | | | 174.3 (32) | 245.9 (83) | 363.0 (72) | | 69.3 (14) |
| Trade secret | | | 175.2 (129) | | | 17.7 (8) | | | |
| 1,1,1-Trichloroethane (methyl chloroform) | 21.4 (32) | 5,417.2 (54) | 1,115.5 (572) | 13.0 (75) | | 800.6(463) | 568.6(334) | | 374.3 (82) |
| 1,1,2-Trichloroethane | | 148.2 (2) | | 7.5 (4) | | | | | |
| 1,2,4-Trichlorobenzene | | 1,288.3 (17) | | | | | 7.2 (5) | 11.2 (5) | |
| Trichloroethylene | 7.7 (3) | | 492.2 (286) | | 257.0 (91) | 106.1(130) | 465.9 (75) | | 28.1 (35) |
| 1,2,4-Trimethylbenzene | | 576.4 (28) | 787.1 (276) | | | | | | |
| Toluene | 200.0 (36) | | 58.2 (1) | | 43.0(123) | 38.8(120) | 99.0(244) | 25.6 (32) | 43.0 (74) |
| Toluene-2, 4-diisocyanate | | | | | | | | | |
| o-Toluidine | | | | | | | | | |
| Vinyl acetate | | | | | | | | | |
| m-Xylene | | 5.9 (3) | | | | 22.4 (1) | | | |
| Xylene (mixed isomers) | 831.1 (24) | | 447.3 (365) | 34.4 (43) | 56.9(168) | 70.5(201) | 117.0(242) | 16.6 (24) | |
| Zinc (fume or dust) | 42,274.6 (56) | | 1,083.4 (23) | | | | | | |

*Notes:*
Figures in parentheses are number of firms reporting.
soln = solution

*Source:* EPA (1989)

Table A-12   Amount of all categories of chemical releases and transfers by type of industry in the United States, 1987

| ISIC code | Industry | Total releases/ transfers ('000 lb) | Percent distribution | | | | | | Transfers off-site | Total releases/ transfers (rank) |
| | | | Air | Water | Public sewage | On-site land | Underground injection | | | |
|---|---|---|---|---|---|---|---|---|---|---|
| 311/2/3 | Food products | 287,012 | 6.04 | 10.65 | 71.71 | 8.02 | 0.07 | 3.51 | 10 |
| 314 | Tobacco | 10,462 | 72.32 | 1.27 | 21.93 | 0.10 | 0.00 | 4.38 | 21 |
| 321 | Textiles | 349,911 | 10.95 | 52.12 | 34.16 | 0.18 | 0.00 | 2.89 | 6 |
| 322 | Wearing apparel | 4,770 | 48.11 | 0.90 | 48.99 | 0.03 | 0.00 | 1.98 | 22 |
| 331 | Wood and wood products | 35,961 | 74.75 | 2.78 | 4.30 | 7.30 | 0.00 | 10.87 | 20 |
| 332 | Furniture and fixtures | 59,715 | 85.28 | 0.08 | 1.43 | 0.05 | 0.00 | 13.16 | 17 |
| 341 | Paper and paper products | 2,807,409 | 8.29 | 77.78 | 6.59 | 2.76 | 0.00 | 4.60 | 2 |
| 342 | Printing and publishing | 62,936 | 85.99 | 0.01 | 5.47 | 0.00 | 0.00 | 8.52 | 16 |
| 351 | Industrial chemicals | 12,088,830 | 7.83 | 48.27 | 6.49 | 7.45 | 24.01 | 5.96 | 1 |
| 353/4 | Petroleum refining | 762,361 | 10.38 | 48.02 | 6.63 | 5.21 | 2.78 | 26.99 | 5 |
| 355/6 | Rubber and plastic products | 277,096 | 51.88 | 19.52 | 17.40 | 0.29 | 0.02 | 10.89 | 11 |
| 323 | Leather and fur products | 52,087 | 27.07 | 3.76 | 61.41 | 0.32 | 0.00 | 7.45 | 18 |

| SIC | | | | | | | | | |
|---|---|---|---|---|---|---|---|---|---|
| 361/2 | Pottery, china and earthen-ware and glass products | 116,987 | 23.11 | 1.13 | 6.11 | 21.42 | 5.41 | 42.82 | 13 |
| 371/2 | Primary metals (iron and steel and non-ferrous) | 2,593,238 | 9.03 | 4.09 | 6.96 | 39.39 | 3.49 | 37.04 | 3 |
| 381 | Metal products (fabricated metals) | 306,289 | 35.89 | 2.96 | 25.00 | 1.62 | 0.47 | 34.05 | 8 |
| 382 | Non-electrical machinery | 99,091 | 50.15 | 4.48 | 10.63 | 0.67 | 0.00 | 34.07 | 14 |
| 383 | Electrical machinery | 297,117 | 37.14 | 4.40 | 28.82 | 2.46 | 0.82 | 26.35 | 9 |
| 384 | Transport equipment | 332,397 | 64.25 | 1.17 | 5.48 | 1.62 | 0.01 | 27.47 | 7 |
| 385 | Professional and scientific equipment | 81,141 | 57.10 | 3.89 | 12.04 | 0.20 | 0.00 | 26.76 | 15 |
| 390 | Other manufacturing industries | 36,324 | 68.45 | 0.73 | 5.79 | 0.68 | 0.00 | 24.34 | 19 |
| | Multiple SIC codes in 20–39 | 1,709,984 | 12.36 | 46.73 | 5.87 | 14.59 | 12.74 | 7.71 | 4 |
| | No SIC codes in 20–39 | 147,939 | 9.96 | 13.68 | 6.09 | 62.42 | 0.21 | 7.64 | 14 |
| | Total | 22,519,044 | 11.79 | 42.70 | 8.60 | 10.89 | 14.40 | 11.63 | — |

*Note:* 1 lb = 0.4536 kg

*Source:* EPA (1989, pp. 14–15)

Table A-13  Pollution-abatement capital expenditures on end-of-line and changes-in-production process techniques in the United States 1985[a] ($ millions)

| ISIC code | Industry | Total expenditures | Air | | | Water | | |
|---|---|---|---|---|---|---|---|---|
| | | | Total | By pollution-abatement technique | | Total | By pollution-abatement technique | |
| | | | | End-of-line | Changes in production processes | | End-of-line | Changes in production processes |
| 3 | All industries[b] | 2,809.7 | 1,292.3 | 909.0 (70) | 383.3 (30) | 1,017.9 | 892.4 (88) | 125.5 (12) |
| 311/2/3 | Food products and beverages | 155.1 (5.52) | 66.0 | 52.9 (80) | 13.1 (20) | 77.4 | 71.5 (92) | 5.9 (8) |
| 321 | Textiles[c] | 24.7 (0.88) | 12.2 | 11.0 (90) | 1.3 (10) | 10.3 | 7.9 (76) | 2.5 (24) |
| 331 | Wood and wood products | 34.5 (1.23) | 15.2 | 14.3 (94) | 0.8 (6) | 6.3 | 4.4 (69) | 2.0 (31) |
| 332 | Furniture and fixtures | 14.7 (0.52) | 9.2 | 7.6 (83) | 1.5 (17) | 1.8 | —[d] | —[d] |
| 341 | Paper and paper products | 332.4 (11.83) | 190.9 | 132.9 (70) | 58.0 (30) | 106.0 | 90.9 (86) | 15.2 (14) |
| 342 | Printing and publishing | 39.5 (1.41) | 29.4 | 27.7 (94) | 1.6 (6) | 5.1 | 2.8 (54) | 2.4 (46) |
| 351/2 | Industrial chemicals and other chemical products | 738.1 (26.26) | 194.0 | 148.8 (77) | 45.2 (23) | 271.5 | 233.4 (86) | 38.2 (14) |

| Code | Industry | | | | | | |
|---|---|---|---|---|---|---|---|
| 353/4 | Petroleum refining and miscellaneous petroleum and coal products | 290.4(10.33) | 175.0 | 105.0 (60) | 70.0 (40) | 88.4 | 66.7 (75) | 21.7 (25) |
| 355/6 | Rubber and plastic products | 29.7 (1.05) | 21.3 | 16.6 (78) | 4.7 (22) | 3.2 | 2.3 (72) | 0.9 (28) |
| 323 | Leather and fur products | 1.1 (0.04) | —d | —d | —d | 0.8 | 0.6 (75) | 0.1 (25) |
| 361/2 | Pottery, china and earthenware and glass products | 61.9 (2.20) | 44.4 | 39.1 (88) | 5.4 (12) | 9.9 | 6.9 (70) | 3.0 (30) |
| 371/2 | Primary metals (iron and steel and non-ferrous) | 252.9 (9.00) | 142.9 | 128.6 (90) | 14.3 (12) | 84.3 | 79.4 (94) | 4.9 (6) |
| 381 | Metal products (fabricated metals) | 116.9 (4.16) | 40.4 | 16.1 (40) | 24.3 (60) | 59.7 | 52.2 (87) | 7.5 (13) |
| 382 | Non-electrical machinery | 69.0(24.46) | 21.2 | 17.9(39.9) | 3.3 (16) | 35.1 | 33.0 (94) | 2.2 (6) |
| 383 | Electrical machinery | 137.7 (4.90) | 45.4 | 39.9 (88) | 5.5 (12) | 74.1 | 66.9 (90) | 7.2 (10) |
| 384 | Transport equipment | 456.5(16.25) | 254.5 | 123.7 (49) | 130.8 (51) | 165.1 | 154.9 (94) | 10.2 (6) |
| 385 | Professional and scientific equipment | 24.8 (0.88) | 13.8 | 11.5 (83) | 2.3 (17) | 7.8 | 6.6 (85) | 1.2 (15) |

Notes:
Figures in parentheses are percentage shares.
a.  Statistics in table cover manufacturing establishments with 20 employees or more.
b.  Totals may not agree with detail because of independent rounding.
c.  Excluding major group 23, apparel and other textiles.
d.  Statistical data withheld to avoid disclosing operations of individual companies.

Source:  US Bureau of the Census (1987)

Table A-14  MVA shares and average annual growth rates of MVA, 1970–88

| ISIC code | Industry | Average annual (percentage) growth rates, 1970–88 | | | Ratio of developing countries to developed countries | Share of developing countries in world MVA | |
|---|---|---|---|---|---|---|---|
| | | World | Developed countries | Developing countries | | 1970 | 1988 |
| 3 | Manufacturing | 2.61 | 2.31 | 5.61 | 2.48 | 6.88 | 11.56 |
| 311/312 | Food products | 2.70 | 2.52 | 4.09 | 1.62 | 10.26 | 13.08 |
| 313 | Beverages | 1.48 | 0.96 | 4.24 | 4.42 | 12.51 | 20.26 |
| 314 | Tobacco | 2.40 | 1.89 | 3.83 | 2.03 | 23.15 | 29.73 |
| 321 | Textiles | 1.09 | 0.51 | 4.06 | 7.96 | 12.60 | 21.20 |
| 322 | Wearing apparel | 1.31 | 0.87 | 5.33 | 6.13 | 6.98 | 14.07 |
| 323 | Leather and products | 1.22 | 0.34 | 5.41 | 15.91 | 11.93 | 24.71 |
| 324 | Footwear | 0.63 | 0.20 | 2.81 | 14.05 | 13.46 | 19.83 |
| 331 | Wood products | 1.43 | 1.19 | 3.93 | 3.30 | 6.99 | 10.82 |
| 332 | Furniture, fixtures | 2.68 | 2.60 | 3.82 | 1.47 | 6.23 | 7.59 |
| 341 | Paper and products | 2.56 | 2.31 | 5.93 | 2.57 | 5.23 | 3.35 |

| Code | Industry | | | | | | |
|------|----------|------|------|------|------|------|------|
| 342 | Printing, publishing | 3.37 | 3.29 | 4.76 | 1.45 | 4.50 | 5.73 |
| 351 | Industrial chemicals | 2.87 | 2.53 | 7.38 | 2.92 | 4.71 | 10.21 |
| 352 | Other chemical products | 2.78 | 2.32 | 6.54 | 2.82 | 7.78 | 14.85 |
| 353 | Petroluem refineries | 3.01 | 1.87 | 5.74 | 3.07 | 23.23 | 37.20 |
| 354 | Petroleum, coal products | 3.10 | 2.47 | 9.50 | 3.85 | 5.07 | 14.99 |
| 355 | Rubber products | 1.85 | 1.36 | 5.62 | 4.13 | 8.27 | 15.92 |
| 356 | Plastics products, n.e.c. | 5.62 | 5.37 | 7.90 | 1.47 | 8.39 | 12.33 |
| 361 | Pottery, china, etc. | 2.33 | 2.02 | 4.48 | 2.22 | 10.44 | 15.17 |
| 362 | Glass products | 1.94 | 1.62 | 5.41 | 3.34 | 6.31 | 11.53 |
| 369 | Non-metal products, n.e.c. | 2.31 | 1.83 | 5.85 | 3.20 | 8.83 | 16.33 |
| 371 | Iron and steel | 0.18 | 0.48 | 6.70 | 13.96 | 4.75 | 15.46 |
| 372 | Non-ferrous metals | 1.75 | 0.81 | 4.69 | 5.79 | 6.85 | 12.66 |
| 381 | Metal products | 1.79 | 1.51 | 5.80 | 3.84 | 4.66 | 9.34 |
| 382 | Machinery, n.e.c. | 3.50 | 3.37 | 7.42 | 2.20 | 2.07 | 4.26 |
| 383 | Electrical machinery | 3.54 | 3.22 | 8.47 | 2.71 | 3.66 | 8.84 |
| 384 | Transport equipment | 3.13 | 2.98 | 5.66 | 1.90 | 4.60 | 7.12 |
| 385 | Professional goods | 3.52 | 3.37 | 11.33 | 3.38 | 0.97 | 3.61 |
| 390 | Other industries | 3.21 | 2.73 | 8.01 | 2.93 | 5.97 | 13.54 |

*Source:* UNIDO (1990)

177

# References

Afsah, S., B. Laplante and D. Wheeler (1996), *Controlling Industrial Pollution: A New Paradigm*, Working Paper no. 1672, Washington, DC: World Bank.

Azad, M.S. (ed.) (1976), *Industrial Wastewater Management Handbook*, New York: McGraw Hill.

Barnett, H.J. and C. Morse (1963), *Scarcity and Growth*, Baltimore: Johns Hopkins University Press.

Bringer, R.P. and S. Zoss (1984), *An Environmental Program that Works*, St Paul, Minn.: 3M.

*Business Week* (1990), 'Big cleanup', March 12–18.

Carmichael, J.B. and K.M. Strezepek (1987), *Industrial Water Use and Treatment Practices*, London: Cassell Tycooly.

Campbell, R.P. and W.M. Glenn (1982), *Profit from Pollution Prevention*, Toronto: Pollution Probe Foundation.

Castleman, Barry I. (1974), 'The export of hazardous factories to developing nations,' *International Journal of Health Services*, 9 (4), 37–42.

Chadwick, M.J. (ed.) (1987), *Environmental Impacts of Coal Mining and Utilization*, Oxford: Pergamon Press.

Chazelon, J.C. (1982), *Les Techniques Propres Dans L'industrie Française*, Paris: La Société Objective.

Christiansen, G. and R. Haveman (1981), 'Public regulations and the slowdown in productivity growth,' *American Economic Review*, 71 (2), 100–18.

Council on Environmental Quality (1975), *Environmental Quality*, Washington, DC: US Government Printing Office.

Dasgupta, P.S. and G. Heal (1974), 'The optimal depletion of exhaustible resources,' *Review of Economic Studies*, Symposium issue 3–28.

Data Resources Incorporated (1979), *The Macro-economic Impact of Federal Pollution Control Programs: 1978 Assessment, DRI*, report to the United States Environmental Protection Agency, Washington, DC: US Government Printing Office.

Easter, K.W. (1986), *Irrigation, Investment, Technology, and Management Strategies for Development*, Boulder, Col.: Westview Press.

Economic Comission for Europe (ECE) (1975), *The Demand for Water: Procedures and Methodologies for Projecting Water Demands in the Context of Regional and National Planning*, Natural Resources/Water Series no. 3 (ST/ESA/38), Geneva: ECE.

Economic Commission for Europe (ECE) (1982), *Compendium on Low and Non-waste Technology*, Geneva: ECE.

Economic Commission for Europe (ECE) (1985), *Compendium on Low and Non-waste Technology: Rotalyt-Alutop* (ENV/WP.2/5/Add.24), Geneva: ECE.

Economic Commission for Europe (ECE) (1990a), *Compendium on Low and Non-waste Technology*, 5 (ECE/ENV/36), Geneva: ECE.

Economic Commission for Europe (ECE) (1990b), *Preparation of Molding Sands Containing Recycled Sands* (ENV/WP.215/add.15), Geneva: ECE.

Economic Commission for Europe (ECE) (1990c), *Recovery and Purification Process for Pyridine from Effluent from the Production of Semi-synthetic Antibiotics from Penicillin* (ENV/WP.215/add.131), Geneva: ECE.

Economopoulos, A.P. (1982), 'Rapid wastewater inventories and their use in environ-mental planning,' in D. Stuckey and A. Hamza (eds), *Management of Industrial Wastewater in Developing Countries*, Oxford: Pergamon Press.

Egger, A.J. (1989), 'Hazardous solid waste disposal in geological environment,' in S.P. Maltezou, A.K. Biswas and H. Sutter (eds), *Hazardous Waste Management*, London: Cassell Tycooly.

Ehrlich, P.R., A.H. Ehrlich and J.P. Holdren (1977), *Ecoscience: Population, Resources and Environment*, San Francisco: W.H. Freeman.

Energy Information Administration (EIA) (1985), *Manufacturing Energy Consump-tion Survey: Consumption of Energy, 1985*, Washington, DC: US Government Print-ing Office.

Energy Information Administration (EIA) (1988), Preliminary estimates of energy inputs by industry group and related industries, Washington, DC, Mimeographed.

Energy Information Administration (EIA) (1994a), *Annual Energy Review 1994*, Washington, DC: US Department of Energy.

Energy Information Administration (EIA) (1994b), *Manufacturing Energy Consump-tion Survey: Changes in Energy Efficiency, 1980–1994*, Washington, DC: US Gov-ernment Printing Office.

Environmental Protection Agency (EPA) (1989), *The Toxic Release Inventory, 1987*, Washington, DC: US Government Printing Office.

Environmental Protection Agency (EPA) (1992), *National Air Quality and Emissions Trends Report*, Washington, DC: US Government Printing Office.

Environmental Protection Agency (EPA) (1996), *The Toxic Release Inventory, 1995*, Washington, DC: US Government Printing Office.

Freeman, Myrick A. (1979), *Benefits of Air and Water Pollution Control: A Review and Syntheses of Recent Estimates*, report prepared for the United States Council on Environmental Quality, Washington, DC: US Government Printing Office.

Foeke, T.L. (1988), 'Waste minimization in the electronics production industries,' *Waste Management*, 38 (3), 74–81.

Gardner, L.C. and D. Huisingh (1987), 'Waste reduction through material and process substitution,' *Hazardous Waste and Hazardous Materials*, 4 (2), 67–73.

Gladwin, Thomas N. and Ingo Walter (1980), *Multinationals under Fire: Lessons in the Management of Conflict*, New York: John Wiley.

Golding, I. and L.A. Winters (eds) (1996), *The Economics of Sustainable Develop-ment*, Cambridge: Cambridge University Press.

Golding, I. and D. Roland-Holst (1995), 'Economic policies for sustainable resource use in Morocco', in I. Golding and L.A. Winters (eds), *The Economics of Sustain-able Development*, Cambridge: Cambridge University Press.

Government of Belgium (1966), *White Paper of the Ministry of Foreign Affairs*, Brussels: National Institute of Statistics.

Grossman, G.M. (1995), 'Pollution and growth: what do we know?', in I. Golding and L.A. Winters (eds), *The Economics of Sustainable Development*, Cambridge: Cam-bridge University Press.

Grossman, G.M. and A.B. Krueger (1993), 'Environmental impacts of a North Ameri-can Free Trade Agreement,' in P. Garber (ed.), *The US–Mexico Free Trade Agree-ment*, Cambridge, Mass.: MIT Press.

Hamza, A. and J. Gallup (1982), 'Assessment of environmental pollution in Egypt: case-study of Alexandria Metropolitan Area', *Water Quality Bulletin* 7(2), 11–18.

Hartmen, R.S., D. Wheeler and M. Singh (1994), *The Cost of Air Pollution Abatement*, Working Paper no. 1398, Washington, DC: World Bank.

Henstock, M.E. (1996), *The Recycling of Non-ferrous Metals*, Ottawa: International Council on Metals and the Environment.

Hettige, H., P. Martin, M. Singh and D. Wheeler (1994), *The Industrial Pollution Pro-jection System*, PRWP 1431, Washington, DC: World Bank.

Highley, D.E. (1984), 'Non-metallic resources,' in *Indigenous Raw Materials for Industry*, London: Metals Society.

Hotelling, H. (1931), 'The economics of exhaustible resources', *Journal of Political Economy*, 34, 137–75.

Holtz-Eakin, D. and T.M. Selden (1992), *Stocking the Fires? $CO_2$ Emissions and Economic Growth*, NBER Working Paper no. 4248, Cambridge, Mass.: National Bureau of Economic Research.

Huisingh, D. (1989), 'Cleaner technologies through process modifications, material substitutions and ecologically based ethical values,' in *UNEP Industry and Environment*, January-March, Narobi: UNEP, 98–104.

Huisingh, D. and V. Bailey (1986), *Proven Profits from Pollution Prevention*, Washington, DC: Institute for Local Self Reliance.

*Human Activity and the Environment* (1986), Ottawa: Statistics Canada.

James, D.E., H.M.A. Jansen and J.B. Opschoor (1978), *Economic Approaches to Environmental Problems: Techniques and Results of Empirical Analysis*, Amsterdam: Elsevier Scientific.

Johnnie, Susan T. (1987), 'Waste reduction in Hewlett-Packard, Colorado Springs printed circuit board manufacturing shop,' *Hazardous Waste and Hazardous Materials*, 4 (1), 130–42.

Joint Economic Committee (JEC) (1978), *Special Study on Economic Change*, part 2, JEC Hearings, Washington, DC: US Government Printing Office.

Kapala, J. and H. Herman (1987), 'Air pollution in the Katowice Province: sources and hazards,' *Environmental Protection Engineering*, 13 (3–4), 116–27.

Kneese, A.V. and J.L. Sweeny (eds) (1985), *Handbook of Natural Resource and Energy Economics*, Amsterdam: North-Holland, vols. I–III.

Koopmans, T.C (1973), 'Some observations on optimal economic growth and exhaustible resources', in H.C. Bos (ed.), *Economic Structure and Development*, Amsterdam: North-Holland.

Kosponti, S.H (1986), *State and the Protection of the Environment*, Budapest: Government Statistical Office.

Kucharski, R. and E. Marchwinska (1990), *Exposure of edible and pasture plants and consumers in the Katowice District*, Katowice: Institute of Environmental Protection.

Labys, Walter and L. Waddel (1988), 'Transmaterialization: technology and material demand cycles,' *Materials and Society*, 12(1), 59–86.

Labys, Walter and L.M Waddel (1989), 'Commodity life-cycle in US materials demand,' *Resources Policy*, 15, 238–52.

Lederman, P.B. (1976), 'Management of solid waste' in J.R. Pfafflin and E.N. Ziegler (eds), *Encyclopedia of Environmental Science and Engineering*, vol. 1, New York: Gordon and Breach Publishers, 169–99.

Leiper, C. and U.E. Simonis (1988), 'Environmental damage – environmental expenditures: statistical evidence on the Federal Republic of Germany', *International Journal of Social Economics*, 15, 37–49.

Lovei, M. and B.S. Levy (1996), *Lead Exposure and Health in Central and Eastern Europe: Environmental Action Programs for Central Europe*, Washington, DC: World Bank.

Mann, A.W. (1977), 'Resources', in J.O.M. Brokris (ed.), *Environmental Chemistry*, New York: Plenum Press, 121–78.

Marchwinska, E. (1983), 'Problems of toxic waste accumulation in the Polish industrial sector', *Roczn*, 35 (2), 3–29.

*Minerals Handbook, 1990–1991* (1990), New York: Stockton Press.

Mohanrao, V. and K. Subrahmanyam (1970), *Water Use in India*, New Delhi: Department of Sanitation.

Muelschlegel, J. (1979), *Drinking and Industrial Water Demands in the Netherlands*, Laxenburg, Austria: International Institute for Applied Systems Analysis.

Murgatroyd (1980), 'Industrial energy consumption and potential for conservation,' in Robert Mabro (ed.), *World Energy Issues and Policies*, Oxford: Oxford University Press, 113–26.

Nelson, R. (1985), 'Environmental management for oil refineries,' *Industry and Environment*, April–June, 1–19.

Nemerow, N.L (1987), *Industrial Water Pollution: Origins, Characteristics, and Treatment*, Reading, Mass.: Addison-Wesley.

Nunno, T. (1988), *Toxic Waste Minimization in the Printed Circuit Board Industry*, Park Ridge, New Jersey: Noyes Data Corporation.

OECD (1977), *Emission Control Costs in the Iron and Steel Industry*, Paris: OECD.

OECD (1980), *Control of Chemicals in Importing Countries: Proceedings of the Seminar on the Control of Chemicals in Importing Countries*, Paris: OECD.

OECD (1981), *Emission Control Costs in the Textile Industry*, Paris: OECD.

OECD (1982), *Macro-economic Evaluation of Environmental Programmes*, Paris: OECD.

OECD (1984), *Energy Balances of OECD Countries, 1970–1983*, Paris: OECD.

OECD (1985a), *The State of the Environment 1985*, Paris: OECD.

OECD (1985b), *Environmental Policy and Technological Change*, Paris: OECD.

OECD (1985c), *The Macro-economic Impact of Environmental Expenditure*, Paris: OECD.

OECD (1989), *Environmental Data Compendium, 1989*, Paris: OECD.

OECD (1993), *Environmental Data Compendium, 1993*, Paris: OECD.

OECD (1995), *Environmental Data Compendium, 1995*, Paris: OECD.

Pearce, D.W. and J. Rose (1975), *The Economics of Natural Resource Depletion*, London: MacMillan.

Pearce, D., A. Markyanda and E. Barbier (1989), *Blueprint for a Green Economy*, London: Earthscan Publications.

Piaseck. B. and J. Gravander (1985), 'The missing links: restructuring hazardous waste controls in America,' *Technical Review*, October, 340–49.

Reynolds, B. (1986), *'Wastes from the High-tech Industry,'* in *Industrial Wastes: Proceedings of 33rd Ontario Industrial Waste Conference*, 15–18 June, Ontario: Ministry of the Environment.

Ripley, E.A., R.E. Redmann and A.A. Crowder (1996), *Environmental Effects of Mining*, Delroy: St Lucie Press

Royston, M. (1979), *Pollution Prevention Pays*, Elmsford, NY: Pergamon Press.

Schaefer, D. and C. Stahmer (1989), Input–output model for the analysis of environmental protection activities,' *Economic Systems Research*, 1(2), 189–201.

Sell, Nancy (1981), *Industrial Pollution Control: Issues and Techniques*, New York: Reinhold.

Smith, F.A (1972), 'Waste material recovery and reuse,' in *Population, Resources, and the Environment, 3*, Research reports of the Commission on Population Growth and the American Future, Washington, DC: US Government Printing Office.

Smith, V.K. (ed.) (1979), *Scarcity and Growth Reconsidered*, Baltimore: Johns Hopkins University Press.

Stiglitz, J. (1974), 'Growth with exhaustible resources', *Review of Economic Studies*, Symposium, 123–38.

Street, A. and J.E. Zorn (1983), 'Toward controlling the international movement of hazardous products', *The Corporate Examiner*, 7, 11–15.

Tates, D.M. and P.J. Reynold (1981), 'The regional context of industrial water demand forecasting in Canada', *International Symposium on Water Resources Management in Industrial Areas, 1*, Lisbon: Laboratorio National de Engenharia Civil.

Tietenberg, T. (1992), *Environmental and Natural Resource Economics*, New York: Harper Collins.

United Nations (1976), *The Demand for Water*, New York: United Nations.

United Nations Environment Program (UNEP) (1982), *The World Environment, 1972–1982*, Dublin: Tycooly.

United Nations Environment Program (UNEP) (1988), *Safeguarding the World's Water*, UNEP Environmental Brief no. 6, Nairobi: UNEP.

United Nations Environment Program (UNEP) (1989), *Hazardous Chemicals*, UNEP

Environmental Brief No.4, Nairobi: UNEP.

United Nations Environment Program (UNEP) and Federal Republic of Germany, Ministry for Research and Technology (1985), *Internatiomnal Symposium on Clean Technologies*, Bonn, 7–18 October, Final Proceedings.

United Nations Economic and Social Council (UNESCO) (1985), *Compendium on Low and Non-waste Technology*, (ENV/WP.215/Add. 124), 6 May, Paris: UNESCO.

United Nations Industrial Development Program (UNIDO) (1987), *Industrial Statistics Yearbook 1986*, New York: United Nations.

United Nations Industrial Development Program (UNIDO) (1990), *Industry and Development: Global Report 1990/91*, Vienna: UNIDO.

UNCTAD (1993), *Commodity Yearbook, 1993*, New York: United Nations.

US Bureau of the Census (1987), *Pollution Abatement Costs and Expenditures, 1985*, Washington, DC: US Government Printing Office.

US Bureau of the Census (1989), *Statistical Abstract of the United States 1987*, Washington, DC: US Government Printing Office.

US Bureau of the Census (1994), *Preliminary Report Summary Series*, Washington, DC: US Government Printing Office.

US Bureau of the Census (1996), *Statistical Abstract of the United States 1996*, Washington, DC: US Government Printing Office.

US Department of Commerce (1991), *Survey of Current Business*, Washington, DC: US Government Printing Office.

US Department of Commerce (1993), *Pollution Abatement Costs and Expenditures, 1993*, Washington, DC: US Government Printing Office.

US Department of Commerce (1994), *Survey of Current Business*, Washington, DC: US Government Printing Office.

Uriarte Jr., F.A. (1989), 'Hazardous waste managemnt in ASEAN with emphasis on small and medium industries,' in S.P. Maltezou, A.K. Biswas and H. Sutter (eds), *Hazardous Waste Management*, London: Cassell Tycooly.

Vatakuri, V.S. and R.V. Lama (1986), *Environmental Engineering in Mines*, Cambridge: Cambridge University Press.

Walter, Ingo (1975), *International Economics of Pollution*, London: Macmillan.

Walter, Ingo (1976), *Studies in International Environmental Economics*, New York: Wiley-Interscience.

Wheeler, D. (1993), *Promoting Cleaner Industrial Development*, Outreach no. 12, Policy Views from the Country Economics Department, Washington, DC: World Bank.

Wojewozki, Urzad (ed.) (1981), *Report on the State of Environment for the Katowice Province*, Katowice: Institute for the Environment.

World Bank (1989), *The Safe Disposal of Hazardous Wastes, 1*, Washington, DC: World Bank.

World Health Organization (WHO) (1982), *Hazardous Waste Management Policy Guidelines and Practices*, Copenhagen: WHO.

World Health Organization (WHO) (1983), *Compendium of Environmental Guidelines and Standards for Industrial Discharge*, Geneva: WHO.

*World Resources 1986–1987* (1987), New York: Basic Books.

*World Resources 1988–1989* (1989), New York: Basic Books.

*World Resources 1994–1995* (1995), New York: Basic Books.

# Subject Index